Britain, America, and the Special Relationship since 1941

Britain, America, and the Special Relationship since 1941 examines the Anglo-American strategic and military relationship that developed during the Second World War and continued until recent years. Forged on a common ground of social, cultural, and ideological values as well as political expediency, this partnership formed the basis of the western alliance throughout the Cold War, playing an essential part in bringing stability to the post-1945 international order.

Clearly written and chronologically organised, the book begins by discussing the origins of the 'Special Relationship' and its progression from uneasy coexistence in the eighteenth century to collaboration at the start of the Second World War. McKercher explores the continued evolution of this partnership during the conflicts that followed, such as the Suez Crisis, the Vietnam War, and the Falklands War. The book concludes by looking at the developments in British and American politics during the past two decades and analysing the changing dynamics of this alliance over the course of its existence.

Illustrated with maps and photographs and supplemented by a chronology of events and list of key figures, this is an essential introductory resource for students of the political history and foreign policies of Britain and the United States in the twentieth century.

B.J.C. McKercher is Professor of International History at the University of Victoria, Canada. He is the editor of the journal *Diplomacy and Statecraft* and is general editor of *The Praeger Series on Foreign Policy in the Interwar Period* (with K. E. Neilson) and *The Praeger Series on Diplomacy and Strategic Thought*. His recent publications include *The Handbook of Diplomacy and Statecraft* (2011, edited), *War in the Twentieth Century* (2003, edited with M. A. Hennessy) and *Power and Stability: British Foreign Policy, 1865–1965* (2003, edited with E. Goldstein).

Introduction to the series

History is the narrative constructed by historians from traces left by the past. Historical enquiry is often driven by contemporary issues and, in consequence, historical narratives are constantly reconsidered, reconstructed and reshaped. The fact that different historians have different perspectives on issues means that there is often controversy and no universally agreed version of past events. *Seminar Studies* was designed to bridge the gap between current research and debate, and the broad, popular general surveys that often date rapidly.

The volumes in the series are written by historians who are not only familiar with the latest research and current debates concerning their topic, but who have themselves contributed to our understanding of the subject. The books are intended to provide the reader with a clear introduction to a major topic in history. They provide both a narrative of events and a critical analysis of contemporary interpretations. They include the kinds of tools generally omitted from specialist monographs: a chronology of events, a glossary of terms and brief biographies of 'who's who'. They also include bibliographical essays in order to guide students to the literature on various aspects of the subject. Students and teachers alike will find that the selection of documents will stimulate the discussion and offer insight into the raw materials used by historians in their attempt to understand the past.

Clive Emsley and Gordon Martel
Series Editors

Britain, America, and the Special Relationship since 1941

B.J.C. McKercher

LONDON AND NEW YORK

First published 2017
by Routledge
4 Park Square, Milton Park, Abingdon, Oxon OX14 4RN

and by Routledge
605 Third Avenue, New York, NY 10017

Routledge is an imprint of the Taylor & Francis Group, an informa business

© 2017 B.J.C. McKercher

The right of B.J.C. McKercher to be identified as author of this
work has been asserted by him in accordance with sections 77 and
78 of the Copyright, Designs and Patents Act 1988.

All rights reserved. No part of this book may be reprinted or
reproduced or utilised in any form or by any electronic, mechanical,
or other means, now known or hereafter invented, including
photocopying and recording, or in any information storage or
retrieval system, without permission in writing from the publishers.

Trademark notice: Product or corporate names may be trademarks
or registered trademarks, and are used only for identification and
explanation without intent to infringe.

British Library Cataloguing-in-Publication Data
A catalogue record for this book is available from the British Library

Library of Congress Cataloging-in-Publication Data
A catalog record for this book has been requested

ISBN: 978-1-138-80000-7 (hbk)
ISBN: 978-1-138-80001-4 (pbk)
ISBN: 978-1-315-19952-8 (ebk)

Typeset in Sabon
by Apex CoVantage, LLC

Contents

List of figures	x
Chronology	xi
Who's who	xxiii
Acknowledgements	xxxiii
Abbreviations	xxxiv
Maps	xxxvi

PART I
Prologue 1

1 The Anglo-American 'Special Relationship' 3

PART II
Britain, America, and the origins of the 'Special Relationship' 11

2 The Anglo-American relationship before 1939 13
The uneasy relationship, 1782–1900 13
*Britain, America, and stability in international politics,
    1900–1914 14*
*The drift to co-operation in the First World War,
    1914–1918 15*
*The Paris Peace Conference and the American return
    to isolationism, 1919–1920 17*
Anglo-American economic competition, 1919–1939 18
Arms limitation and international security, 1919–1939 19

3 The Second World War and the advent of the 'Special
    Relationship' 23
*The immediate origins of the Relationship, September
    1939–December 1941 23*

vi   *Contents*

Churchill and Roosevelt: war and diplomacy,
    December 1941–November 1943 29
Britain, America, and the advent of a new world order,
    November 1943–May 1945 33

PART III
Cold War, limited war, and the 'Special Relationship',
1945–2015   39

4   **The 'Special Relationship' and the early Cold War,**
    May 1945–July 1954   41
    The genesis of the Cold War, May 1945–June 1948 41
    The German question and the rise of NATO, June
        1948–May 1954 48
    Britain, America, and decolonisation in East Asia, May
        1945–July 1954 51

5   **From Cold War to détente, 1954–1968**   57
    British decolonisation and the road to Suez,
        1954–1956 57
    Britain, America, and the problem of the Middle East,
        November 1956–November 1968 65
    European defence and the German question,
        1954–1968 70

6   **From détente to renewed Cold War, 1965–1979**   75
    Britain and American involvement in Vietnam,
        January 1965–April 1973 76
    Britain, America, and European economic integration,
        January 1969–December 1979 83
    Soviet Russian expansionism and the Anglo-American
        response, May 1975–December 1979 87

7   **Margaret Thatcher, Ronald Reagan, and the 'Special**
    Relationship', December 1979–December 1988   92
    Carter, Reagan, and Thatcher: to euromissile deployment
        in Europe, 1981–1985 93
    The Falklands War and the strength of the 'Special
        Relationship', 1982–1983 97
    Thatcher, Reagan, and Mikhail Gorbachev: the weakening
        of Soviet Russia, 1983–1988 100

Contents vii

8 **The Special Relationship and the new international order, 1989–2015** 108

George H. W. Bush, Margaret Thatcher, and the end of the Cold War, 1989–1990 108
The 'Special Relationship' and the Gulf War, 1990–1992 112
Britain, America, and the Balkans, 1992–1998 115
George Bush, Jr., Tony Blair, the war against terrorism, and changing international politics, 2001–2007 118
Barack Obama, Gordon Brown, and David Cameron: challenges old and new after 2007 121

PART IV
Epilogue 127

9 **The Anglo-American 'Special Relationship' and international politics since 1941: an appraisal** 129

PART V
Documents 137

1 Churchill, 'The lights are going out' [Broadcast to the United States from London], 16 October 1938 139
2 'Atlantic Charter, August 1941': Avalon Project 139
3 Casablanca Conference: unconditional surrender. Roosevelt radio address, 12 February 1943 140
4 Roosevelt and Churchill to Stalin on Allied strategy, 21 August 1943 141
5 Roosevelt avoids commitment of American forces in post-war Europe: 'Radio Address at a dinner of the Foreign Policy Association', 21 October 1944 141
6 The United States commits to ensuring the peace settlement after the Second World War: 'The Berlin (Potsdam) Conference, July 17–August 2, 1945' 142
7 Truman's secretary of state shows ambivalence about Iran: 'Report by Secretary Byrnes, December 30, 1945, on Moscow Meeting' 142
8 'President Harry S. Truman's address before a Joint Session of Congress, March 12, 1947' 143
9 Kennan proposes the strategy of containment: 'Telegram, George Kennan to George Marshall ["Long Telegram"], February 22, 1946' 143

viii   *Contents*

10 Churchill's 'Iron Curtain Speech'   144
11 Eisenhower outlines the 'Domino Theory': 'The
     President's News Conference of April 7, 1954'   145
12 Eisenhower worries the British might double-cross the
     United States over Suez: 'Memorandum of a conference
     with the president', 29 October 1956   145
13 The Nixon Doctrine   146
14 Europe's NATO members' 'Declaration on Atlantic
     Relations', 19 June 1974   147
15 Kissinger discusses CSCE with Ford: 'Memorandum of a
     conversation', 15 August 1974   147
16 Thatcher, 'Speech at Kensington Town Hall ("Britain
     Awake")', 19 January 1976   148
17 Reagan, 'A vision for America', 3 November 1980   149
18 Reagan to Thatcher, n.d. [but March 1982]   149
19 NSC Meeting, 30 April 1982   150
20 'Falklands: Reagan phone call to Thatcher (urges
     ceasefire)', 31 May 1982   150
21 Reagan's 'Evil Empire' speech: 'Remarks at the Annual
     Convention of the National Association of Evangelicals
     in Orlando, Florida', 8 March 1983   151
22 'Grenada: Reagan phone call to Thatcher', 26 October 1983   151
23 Thatcher and Reagan discuss (i) Gorbachev and (ii) European
     nuclear deterrence, 'Cold War: Thatcher-Reagan Meeting
     at Camp David', 22 December 1984   152
24 Outlining the Reagan Doctrine: Reagan, 'Address before
     a Joint Session of the Congress on the State of the Union',
     6 February 1985   153
25 Thatcher confronts Gorbachev over the nature of Russian
     foreign policy: 'Record of conversation between Mikhail
     Gorbachev and Margaret Thatcher, March 30, 1987, Moscow'   154
26 On Britain, Europe, and the Atlantic alliance: Thatcher,
     'Speech to the College of Europe', 20 September 1988   154
27 George H.W. Bush on support for Poland and liberalisation
     in Eastern Europe: 'Remarks to Citizens in Hamtramck,
     Michigan', 17 April 1989   155
28 George H.W. Bush outlines the new international order:
     'Address before a Joint Session of the Congress on the State
     of the Union', 29 January 1991   156
29 Clinton deprecates the 'Special Relationship': B.M. Seener,
     'Report and Retort: The Special Relationship is not flat',
     8 August 2007   156

30	Major's foreign secretary characterises the fallaciousness of the New World Order: 'Hurd warning over "slide into disorder": Foreign Secretary backs imperial UN and defends Britain's global role to justify permanent Security Council seat', 28 January 1993	157
31	Blair, 'Doctrine of the International Community', 22 April 1999, Chicago Economic Club	158
32	George W. Bush inaugurates the war on terror, 21 September 2001	158
33	George W. Bush declares that the United States will undermine the international 'Axis of Evil': State of the Union Address, 29 January 2002	159
34	Obama and Cameron, 'The U.S. and Britain still enjoy special relationship', 12 March 2012	160
	Further reading	161
	References	170
	Index	194

Figures

3.1	Winston Churchill and Franklin Roosevelt, Yalta, February 1945	29
4.1	Harry Truman and Clement Attlee, Washington, DC, February 1946	43
5.1	Dwight Eisenhower and Anthony Eden, Washington, DC, 1956	64
5.2	Harold Macmillan and John F. Kennedy, Nassau, December 1962	67
6.1	Lyndon Johnson and Harold Wilson, July 1966	80
6.2	Richard Nixon and Edward Heath, London, October 1970	86
7.1	Ronald Reagan and Margaret Thatcher, Washington, DC, February 1981	95
8.1	John Major, George H.W. Bush, and Bill Clinton, March 2008	116

Chronology

1939

3 September — Second World War begins: Anglo-French declaration of war on Germany.

11 September — Franklin Roosevelt writes to Neville Chamberlain and Winston Churchill enquiring about British naval and strategic policy. Beginning of Churchill-Roosevelt correspondence.

2 November — Cash-and-carry bill.

1940

10 June — Italy declares war on Britain and France.

22 June — Fall of France.

2 September — Destroyers-for-bases deal.

1941

8 March — Lend-Lease Bill.

22 June — Nazi Germany attacks Soviet Russia.

14 August — Atlantic Charter.

7 December — Japan attacks Pearl Harbor and the British and Dutch empires in East Asia.

23 December–14 January 1942 — Arcadia Conference; creation of the Combined Chiefs of Staff.

1943

14–24 January — At Casablanca Conference, Churchill and Roosevelt announce that they seek Germany's unconditional surrender.

9–10 July — Invasion of Sicily.

17–24 August — Churchill-Roosevelt First Quebec Conference.

28 November–1 December — Churchill-Roosevelt-Stalin Tehran Conference.

xii *Chronology*

1944

6 June	D-Day: Allied cross-Channel invasion of Normandy.
August	Russians begin to establish pro-Soviet regimes in Eastern Europe.
12–16 September	Churchill-Roosevelt Second Quebec Conference.

1945

4–11 February	Yalta Conference.
12 April	Roosevelt dies; Harry Truman becomes president.
8 May	Germany surrenders.
16 July	America detonates first atomic bomb.
17 July–2 August	Potsdam Conference.
26 July	Attlee and the Labour Party defeat Churchill and Conservatives in general election.
6 and 9 August	Atomic bombs dropped on Hiroshima and Nagasaki.
15 August	Japan surrenders.
2 September	Formal Japanese surrender; Second World War ends.

1946

22 February	George Kennan's 'Long Telegram' articulating 'containment' strategy.
March–May	Iran crisis.
19 December	Indochina War breaks out.

1947

January	Bizonia created.
February	Britain cannot afford to support Greek anti-communist forces.
12 March	Truman Doctrine announced.
5 June	Marshall Plan announced.
July	'X' article published.
14 August	India's independence.

1948

March	Trizonia created.
17 March	Brussels Treaty.
April	Russian blockade of West Berlin begins.
14 May	Israel's independence.
15 May	Arab-Israeli War begins.
16 June	Malayan Emergency begins.
25 June	Berlin Airlift begins.

Chronology xiii

1949

4 April	NATO Treaty.
May	Russian blockade of West Berlin ends.
23 May	Federal Republic of Germany founded.
20 July	Arab-Israeli War ends.
1 August	Allies end the Berlin Airlift.
29 August	Russia successfully tests atomic bomb.
1 October	Communists proclaim the People's Republic of China; Kuomintang party retains control of Taiwan.
7 October	German Democratic Republic founded.

1950

9 January	Colombo Conference.
14 April	NSC-68.
25 June	Korean War breaks out.
10–19 September	UN forces invade South Korea.
25 October	People's Republic of China enters Korean War.

1951

18 April	European Coal and Steel Community treaty signed.
30 August	Philippine-American Mutual Defence Treaty.
1 September	ANZUS Pact.
8 September	Japanese peace treaty.
26 October	Churchill and Conservatives return to office.

1952

27 May	European Defence Community treaty.
3 October	Britain successfully tests atomic bomb.

1953

20 January	Dwight Eisenhower becomes president.
8 March	Joseph Stalin dies.
15–19 August	Anglo-American intervention in Iran.

1954

March–May	Battle of Dien Bien Phu.
7 April	Eisenhower outlines domino theory.
26 April–20 July	Geneva Conference.
30 August	French National Assembly rejects EDC Treaty.
8 September	SEATO created.
23 October	Germany and Italy join the Brussels Pact.

xiv   *Chronology*

1955

4 February	Baghdad Pact.
24 February	CENTO created.
6 April	Churchill resigns as prime minister; succeeded by Eden.
9 May	Germany joins NATO.
14 May	Warsaw Pact.
18 July	Geneva Summit – Britain, France, Russia, United States.
26 October	Ngo Dien Diem becomes president of South Vietnam.

1956

25 February	Nikita Khrushchev's 'de-Stalinisation' speech.
26 July	Gamal Abdel Nasser nationalises Suez Canal.
23 October–14 November	Hungarian Uprising.
24 October	Anglo-French-Israeli Sèvres Protocol.
29 October	Israel attacks Egypt.
31 October–6 November	Failed Anglo-French military intervention in Egypt.

1957

5 January	Eisenhower Doctrine announced.
10 January	Anthony Eden resigns; succeeded by Harold Macmillan.
21–23 March	Macmillan-Eisenhower Nassau Summit.
26 March 1957	Treaty of Rome.

1958

15 July–25 October	Lebanon crisis.
17 July	Britain sends troops to Jordan.
10 November	Khrushchev demands Western withdrawal from Berlin in six months.

1959

February	Macmillan holds talks in Moscow, Paris, and Bonn.
May	North Vietnam through the Vietcong begin guerrilla war to destabilise South Vietnam.

1960

29 March	Macmillan-Eisenhower Camp David Summit.
14 May	Great Power Summit at Paris cancelled.
12 July	Malayan Emergency ends.

Chronology   xv

1961

20 January	John Kennedy becomes president.
20 January–22 November 1963	America supports South Vietnam economically and despatches 15,000 military advisors.
4 June	Khrushchev-Kennedy Vienna Summit.
13 August	Berlin Wall built.

1962

23 July	Geneva Conference on Laos begins.
22 December	Macmillan-Kennedy Nassau Summit.

1963

14 January	Charles De Gaulle vetoes British EEC application.
24 April	Kennedy articulates domino theory.
June	Kennedy and Khrushchev speeches in Berlin.
19 October	Macmillan resigns; succeeded by Alexander Douglas-Home.
1–2 November	Diem assassinated; new regime in Saigon.
22 November	Kennedy assassinated; succeeded by Lyndon Johnson.
10 December	Britain commits troops to Yemen.

1964

16 October	Harold Wilson and Labour Party win general election.

1965

January	Johnson escalates war in Vietnam.
June	Wilson pursues a peace initiative over Vietnam.
11 November	Apartheid Southern Rhodesia declares unilateral independence.

1966

7 March	De Gaulle pulls France out of NATO's integrated command.

1967

February	Through Aleksey Kosygin, the Soviet premier, Wilson pursues a peace initiative over Vietnam.
5–10 June	'Six Day' Arab-Israeli War.
18 July	Britain ends military commitments east of Suez.
October	Richard Nixon publishes 'Asia After Vietnam'.
18 November	Anglo-American sterling and gold crisis begins.
27 November	De Gaulle vetoes second British EEC application.

xvi *Chronology*

1968

31 January	Tet Offensive begins.
18 March	Anglo-American sterling and gold crisis ends.
31 March	Johnson announces he will not seek or accept another term as president.
May	Healy-Schröder NATO strategy report.
20 August	The countries of the Warsaw Pact invade Czechoslovakia.
13 November	Brezhnev Doctrine promulgated.

1969

20 January	Nixon becomes president.
17 November	United States and Russia begin Strategic Arms Limitation Talks.

1970

19 June	Edward Heath and Conservatives win general election.
Summer–March 1974	Douglas-Home fosters bimonthly Cabinet–State Department meetings.

1972

21–28 February	Nixon visits PRC.
26 May	Nixon and Leonid Brezhnev sign SALT I Treaty.
18–29 December	American bombing offensive to get the North Vietnamese to the bargaining table.

1973

1973	Kissinger's 'Year of Europe'.
1 January	Britain joins the EEC.
6–25 October	Yom Kippur War.
14 December 1973	EEC endorses 'Declaration on European Identity'.

1974

4 March	Harold Wilson becomes prime minister again.
April	Portuguese empire in Africa collapses.
19 June	NATO endorses 'Declaration on Atlantic Relations'.

1975

1975	Soviet Bloc begins support of revolutionary Mozambique and Abyssinia.
30 July–1 August	Conference on Security and Co-operation in Europe (CSCE).
November	Cuban forces support MPLA in Angola.

Chronology xvii

1976

19 January	Margaret Thatcher's 'Britain Awake' speech.
6 April	Wilson resigns; succeeded by James Callaghan.
September	Britain forced to secure IMF loans.

1977

20 January	Jimmy Carter becomes president.
7 September	Carter agrees to transfer Panama Canal to Panama.

1978

Winter 1978–1979	Britain's 'winter of discontent'.

1979

February	Carter ends military support to the Somoza regime in Nicaragua.
1 April	Iranian revolution topples the shah.
4 May	Thatcher becomes prime minister.
18 June	Carter and Brezhnev sign the SALT II treaty.
September– December	Britain achieves power-sharing arrangement for Southern Rhodesia, renamed as Zimbabwe.
4 November	Mob invades US embassy in Tehran.
12 December	NATO adopts 'dual-track' policy.
24 December	Russia invades Afghanistan.

1980

1980	America enforces economic embargo on Russia and announces Olympic boycott.
3 January	Carter pulls SALT II out of the Senate.
10 January	Joint Intelligence Committee chaired by Thatcher about British response to Russian invasion of Afghanistan.
23 January	Carter Doctrine announced.
June	Thatcher works to get European support for basing euromissiles.
17 June	Thatcher and Pakistani foreign minister discuss British military assistance.
6 October	Thatcher–Mohammed Zia-ul-Haq meeting.

1981

20 January	Ronald Reagan becomes president.
8 October	Thatcher visits Pakistan.
December	Polish communist government declares martial law.

xviii *Chronology*

1982

1 March	Britain acquires American-developed British-controlled Trident strategic missiles.
2 April	Argentina invades the Falkland Islands.
2 April	Thatcher's Cabinet approves a task force to retake the Falkland Islands.
April	Alexander Haig attempts shuttle diplomacy to resolve Falklands crisis.
May	Reagan proposes START talks.
2 May	Argentinian light cruiser *General Belgrano* sunk.
4 May	Argentinian fighter disables HMS *Sheffield*.
5 May	Thatcher tells Reagan that Britain will carry on the Falklands War.
14 June	Britain defeats Argentina and retakes the Falkland Islands.

1983

26 October	America invades Grenada.

1984

November	Reagan proposes resuming START talks to Chernenko.
16 December	Thatcher meets Gorbachev in London.
19 December	Anglo-PRC agreement about Hong Kong.
22 December	Thatcher-Reagan Camp David meeting.

1985

6 February	Reagan Doctrine announced.
11 March	Mikhail Gorbachev becomes Russian premier.
July	Gorbachev suspends Russian nuclear testing.
November	Reagan-Gorbachev Geneva talks.

1986

January	Gorbachev proposes nuclear disarmament over 15 years; Reagan rejects it.
30 April	WEU emphasises importance of independent British and French nuclear forces.
May	Reagan renounces American commitment to SALT I and II on strategic offensive weapons.
11–12 October	Reagan-Gorbachev Reykjavik Summit.

Chronology xix

1987

20 March	Thatcher tells Gorbachev that Western Powers will resist communists in Yemen, Abyssinia, Mozambique, Angola, Nicaragua, and other countries.
20 July	Russians announces withdrawal from Afghanistan.
26 August	West Germany says it will remove euromissiles if United States and Russia reciprocate.
December	Gorbachev announces Red Army reductions in Eastern Europe.
8 December	INF agreement signed at Washington.

1988

3 November	Thatcher in Warsaw.
4 November	Thatcher in Gdansk.

1989

20 January	George H.W. Bush becomes president.
January–December	Bush 'pause' respecting Russia.
15 February	Last Soviet troops depart Afghanistan.
6 April	Thatcher tells Gorbachev not to worry about 'pause'.
7 May	Electoral fraud favouring East German communists.
31 May	Bush tells German audience, 'We seek self-determination for all of Germany and all of Eastern Europe'.
3–4 June	PRC security forces crack down on dissidents.
August	Elections end Poland's single-party rule.
23 September	Thatcher tells Gorbachev of Britain's opposition to a united Germany.
7 October	Gorbachev indicates that Erich Honecker should retire.
18 October	Honecker resigns.
9 November	Berlin Wall falls.
December	America invades Panama.
2–3 December	Bush-Gorbachev Malta Summit; end of Cold War announced.

1990

2 August	Iraq invades Kuwait.
28 November	Thatcher resigns, succeeded by John Major.
December	Yugoslavia begins breaking up.

xx   *Chronology*

1991

17 January	Coalition forces bomb Iraqi military targets.
29 January	Bush says 'new world order' is emerging.
24–28 February	Coalition drives Iraqi forces out of Kuwait; Bush allows weak Iraq to exist to balance against Iran.
August	Attempted coup against Gorbachev.
26 December	Russian Federation emerges.

1992

3 March	Bosnia declares independence.

1993

20 January	Bill Clinton becomes president.
28 January	Britain criticises American ideas about a 'new world order'.
15 November	NATO begins air support for UNPROFOR.

1995

11–13 July	Serbian genocide of Bosnian Moslems at Srebrenica.
July–October	NATO air operations against Serbian forces.
1–21 November	Dayton Peace Conference.
21 November	Dayton Peace Agreement.

1996

8–15 March	The PRC tests missiles near Taiwan.
8 March	Clinton despatches carrier battle group to waters adjacent to Taiwan.

1997

2 May	Tony Blair becomes prime minister.
1 July	Britain transfers control of Hong Kong to PRC.

1999

March–June	NATO bombings of Serbia in support of Kosovo.
22 April	Blair outlines 'Doctrine of the International Community'.

2000

May–September 2000	Britain intervenes in Sierra Leone.
December 2000	PRC GDP more than doubles since 1990.

Chronology   xxi

2001

20 January	George W. Bush becomes president.
11 September	Al Qaeda attacks World Trade Center in New York and Pentagon in Washington.
21 September	Bush announces 'war on terrorism'.
7 October	America, supported by Britain and other allies, invades Afghanistan.
November	Taliban regime in Afghanistan collapses; Taliban and Al Qaeda begin guerrilla operations against the Western Powers.
22 December	Provisional pro-Western government installed in Afghanistan.

2002

29 January	Bush 'Axis of Evil' speech.

2003

16 February	Monster anti-Iraq intervention rally in London; demonstrations in Glasgow and Belfast.
19 March	Britain and America invade Iraq.
9 April	United States and its allies take Baghdad; Saddam flees.
1 May	Bush announces war in Iraq over. (American forces will continue to fight in Iraq until December 2011.)

2004

1 January	Bush-created President's Emergency Plan for AIDS Relief begins.
7 December	Pro-Western Afghan government takes office after reasonably free elections.

2006

23 December	UN imposes economic sanctions against Iran.

2007

27 June	Blair resigns as prime minister; succeeded by Gordon Brown.

2008

September	International economic crisis rivalling that of the 1930s begins.
29 October	Britain acknowledges Tibet as an integral part of the PRC.

xxii *Chronology*

2009

20 January	Barack Obama becomes president.
April	British forces leave Iraq.

2010

11 May	David Cameron becomes prime minister.
18 December	Revolution in Tunisia precipitates revolutions in other Moslem North African and Middle Eastern states.

2011

19 March	Multinational forces support Libyan insurgents.
24 May	Obama and Cameron publish 'Not just special, but an essential relationship'.
July	Civil war breaks out in Syria.
21 August	Obama warns Syrian government not to cross 'red line'.
23 August	Libyan dictator Muammar Gaddafi killed by insurgents.

2012

12 March	Cameron and Obama: 'The U.S. and Britain still enjoy a special relationship'.
14 May	Cameron meets with Dalai Lama.

2013

21 August	One of many times the Syrian government crosses the 'red line' by using chemical weapons against Syrian rebels.
October	George Osborne, British chancellor of the Exchequer, travels to Beijing.

2014

18 March	Russia annexes the Crimea, a part of Ukraine.
March–April	Russia supports pro-Russian separatists in eastern Ukraine.
June	ISIS launches major offensive to create caliphate.
August	Western coalition created to support Iraq by aerial bombing of ISIS.
October	British forces leave Afghanistan.

Who's who

United States

American presidents, 1940–present

Roosevelt, Franklin D. (1882–1945). In office 4 March 1933–12 April 1945. After September 1939, Roosevelt established a partnership with Winston Churchill, Britain's prime minister (1940–1945) during the Second World War, which produced the Anglo-American 'Special Relationship'. Building on joint strategy and recognition of common goals except economic rivalry and decolonisation, he helped give the Relationship a strategic permanence that lasted for 50 years.

Truman, Harry S. (1884–1972). In office 12 April 1945–20 January 1953. Truman led America in the early Cold War and committed it to the defence of Europe through the strategy of containing Russian power: economically via the Truman Doctrine (March 1947) and Marshall Plan (June 1947) and militarily with NATO (April 1949). Containment also found expression in East Asia by American support of France in Indochina (after 1946), opposing North Korea and the PRC (after 1950).

Eisenhower, Dwight D. (1890–1969). In office 20 January 1953–20 January 1961. A former army general in the Second World War and NATO commander, Eisenhower continued a policy of containment in Europe and East Asia and, after the Suez Crisis (1956) which heavily damaged the Relationship, worked to rebuild Anglo-American relations. His Administration began arrogating for the United States a leading position in the Middle East after early 1957.

Kennedy, John F. (1917–1963). In office 20 January 1961–22 November 1963. Desirous of limiting communist expansion, Kennedy supported containment in Europe and East Asia. In Europe, this policy led to Russo-American rapprochement over Germany following the Berlin Wall crisis (1961–1962); in East Asia, it saw a gradual increase of American support for South Vietnam. Kennedy also believed strongly in the Relationship, conceding to Britain having an independent nuclear deterrent.

xxiv *Who's who*

Johnson, Lyndon B. (1908–1973). In office 22 November 1963–20 January 1969. As *détente* emerged and pre-occupied with Vietnam after 1963 and the Middle East after 1967, Johnson looked for allied support. Britain had different Middle Eastern interests but did everything short of military deployment to assist its ally. Whilst Johnson remained critical of Britain's Labour government, his advisors believed British support was as effective as possible.

Nixon, Richard (1913–1994). In office 20 January 1969–9 August 1974. Nixon looked to exploit *détente* to reduce Russo-American rivalry, especially in nuclear arms limitation which led to SALT I. He also ended the Vietnam War in April 1973. His Administration looked for American allies to bear a heavier defence burden for containment; Britain became crucial to this end in Europe as both a NATO member and, after 1973, a leading EEC Power.

Ford, Gerald (1913–2006). In office 9 August 1974–20 January 1977. Rising to power after political scandal forced Nixon's resignation, Ford amounted to a stopgap president. His Administration participated in the Conference on Security and Co-operation in Europe (CSCE), where Britain and other European NATO-EEC Powers led, and it continued SALT II negotiations with the Russians. It did little to confront Russian adventurism in Angola, Mozambique, and Abyssinia because of domestic constraints.

Carter, Jimmy (1924–present). In office, 20 January 1977–20 January 1981. Taking office after the Nixon political scandals, Nixon's illiberal foreign policy that overthrew a democratically elected Marxist government in Chile, and the Vietnam War, Carter pursued a moralistic foreign policy. Abandoning control of the Panama Canal and allowing the Sandinista regime to emerge in Nicaragua, he negotiated SALT II and engineered an Egyptian-Israeli peace treaty. He also worked with Britain to end apartheid in southern Africa. Carter failed to curb Russian adventurism in Africa and, after the pro-American Iranian regime fell, in meeting Russia's invasion of Afghanistan.

Reagan, Ronald (1911–2004). In office 20 January 1981–20 January 1989. Campaigning against Carter's supposedly weak foreign policy, Reagan undertook a diplomacy designed to weaken Russia by heavy conventional and nuclear rearmament – centred on SDI – and meet perceived Russian aggression in the developing world, especially Afghanistan. He found a ready ally in Margaret Thatcher with regard to Europe and South Asia. Together over obstacles such as the Falklands War, Grenada, and Europe's INF, they restored the Relationship to its Second World War high.

Bush, George H.W. (1924–present). In office 20 January 1989–20 January 1993. Continuing Reagan's foreign policy with more subtlety and thought – wanting international balance – Bush led America as Russia's empire collapsed in Europe and abroad after 1989. He talked about a 'new world order' emerging by 1991, and Thatcher continued as America's principal ally, surrendering Britain's INF but keeping its strategic nuclear deterrent. Although London worried about German reunification, a high point of Anglo-American co-operation came in 1990 and 1991 with joint-action against the Iraqi invasion of Kuwait.

Clinton, Bill (1946–present). In office 20 January 1993–20 January 2001. Taking office after the Cold War, bereft of the Russian threat, Clinton began following a more unilateral foreign policy, especially in the Balkans and East Asia. He privately disparaged the Relationship, and, in 1993, his Administration questioned Britain's possession of a permanent UN Security Council seat. Britain's government responded, 'Once-fashionable talk of a "New World Order" dawning was utopian folly'. The Relationship weakened during Clinton's eight-year presidency.

Bush, George W. (1946–present). In office 20 January 2001–20 January 2009. Bush and his neoconservative Administration became increasingly unilateralist, especially in East Asia. However, Islamist terror attacks on New York and Washington led to the invasion of Afghanistan (2001) and Iraq (2003). Britain's 'New Labour' government supported America to influence Washington. It was unsuccessful. As Bush advisors manipulated intelligence about WMD to justify the war in Iraq, British public opinion turned against America. The Relationship unravelled.

Obama, Barack (1961–present). In office 20 January 2009–20 January 2017. An African American from Hawaii, Obama followed what now was America's foreign policy norm: unilateralism. As new centres of international power developed after the early 1990s, the PRC, renewed Russia, and international organisations such as the EU competed with America in the wider world economically and strategically. Except against the PRC, Obama's America provided reluctant leadership if at all against Russia in Europe and in the Middle East after 2011, especially in Syria and Libya. Britain pursued its own policies.

Notable secretaries of state, 1940–present

Hull, Cordell (1871–1955). In office 4 March 1933–30 November 1944. A former congressman and senator, Hull was the longest-serving American secretary of state. A proponent after 1933 of liberalising trade to reduce international tensions, he pursued American foreign policy along the strategic lines set by Roosevelt. During the war, although supporting the decolonisation of the European empires, he helped smooth Anglo-American relations. He played a prominent part in the creation of the UN.

Byrnes, James F. (1882–1972). In office 3 July 1945–21 January 1947. A former congressman, senator, and Supreme Court justice, during the

xxvi *Who's who*

war Byrnes worked on domestic economic policy. As secretary of state, he played an important role at the Potsdam Conference and within the CFM. However, he appeared to conduct foreign policy independently of Truman and the State Department, his ambivalence over Iran at the December 1945 CFM annoying Truman. Although he hardened his stance against the Russians thereafter, he resigned in January 1947.

Marshall, George C. (1880–1959). In office 21 January 1947–20 January 1949. During the war, Marshall was Army chief and chairman of the Joint Chiefs of Staff and, although critical of the Europe-first strategy and the war in the Mediterranean, was essential to the success of the CCS and the Anglo-American strategic relationship. After the war, retired from the Army, he spent 1946 in China trying unsuccessfully to build a CCP-KMT coalition government. As secretary of state, he was a key architect of containment: enforcing the Truman Doctrine, announcing the Marshall Plan, and working towards NATO. From 1950 to 1951, he was secretary of defence.

Acheson, Dean (1893–1971). In office 21 January 1949–20 January 1953. In the war and after, Acheson served as a senior State Department official, playing a central role in Lend-Lease policies concerning Britain and, following the Tehran Conference, in creating the IMF, World Bank, and GATT. After 1945, supportive of the Relationship, he became a staunch advocate of containment, helping to shape the Truman Doctrine and Marshall Plan and, once becoming secretary of state, creating NATO. Republicans subsequently held him responsible for the threat to the American position in East Asia, especially the outbreak of the Korean War and the 'loss of China' to the CCP.

Dulles, John Foster (1888–1959). In office 21 January 1953–22 April 1959. A senior Republican foreign policy spokesman after 1940, Dulles initially thought it possible to compromise with Russia. But by the time he became secretary of state, he emerged as a steadfast supporter of containment. He mistrusted the British, especially at the 1954 Geneva Conference and over the Suez Crisis (1956). Whilst 'rolling back' communism in Hungary in 1956 proved impossible, he nonetheless advocated the strongest of strong lines against Russia, backed by American nuclear weapons.

Kissinger, Henry (1923–present). In office 22 September 1973–20 January 1977. A Harvard foreign policy scholar, German-born Kissinger served as Nixon's national security advisor from 1969 to 1973. An admirer of Otto von Bismarck, he was an effective advocate of *realpolitik*, helping to end American involvement in Vietnam, negotiating SALT I, and, as in Chile in 1973, ensuring pro-American regimes remained in power. He saw the Relationship as a tool for American policy but when perceiving that American interests had to be protected, as in the Middle East after the 1973 Yom Kippur War, he ensured that American foreign policy promoted those interests above all else.

Who's who xxvii

Vance, Cyrus (1917–2002). In office 23 January 1977–28 April 1980. Vance supported the moral thrust of Carter's foreign policy, especially over the Panama Canal, Nicaragua, ending apartheid, and SALT II. He resigned after breaking with Carter and his national security advisor, Zbigniew Brzezinski, over Iran and the attempted rescue of the captured Americans in the US embassy. In 1993, he worked with former British foreign secretary David Owen in formulating a peace plan for Bosnia.

Haig, Alexander (1924–2010). In office 22 January 1981–5 July 1982. A former army general who served in the Nixon and Ford White Houses and as NATO supreme commander (1974–1979), Haig's efforts as secretary of state to mediate between Britain and Argentina during the Falklands War proved barren. Never a strong supporter on the Relationship, he proposed giving Argentina eventual control of the Falklands. After disputes with others in Reagan's Administration, especially the strongly pro-Britain defence secretary, Caspar Weinberger, and after the Falklands War ended, he resigned.

Baker, James (1930–present). In office 25 January 1989–23 August 1992. A leading Republican politico, Baker held a number of senior positions in government, including Reagan's secretary of the treasury (1985–1988). As secretary of state and not necessarily supportive of the Relationship, he worked with George H.W. Bush to facilitate the peaceful demise of Soviet Russia and the Eastern Bloc. He also played a major role on Middle East policies, especially during the Kuwait crisis (1990–1991). From 1992 to 1993, he served as White House chief of staff.

Other notable Americans since 1940

Stimson, Henry (1867–1950). Roosevelt and Truman's secretary of war, 10 July 1940–21 September 1945. A Republican politico, strong anglophile, and former secretary of state (1929–1933), Stimson came into Roosevelt's Cabinet to provide administrative competence and bipartisan support for American foreign and defence policy. After America entered the war in 1941, he was a key strategic advisor to Roosevelt; in summer 1945, he was adamant that the atomic bomb should be used against Japan to limit American casualties and end the war as quickly as possible.

McNamara, Robert, S. (1916–2009). Kennedy and Johnson's secretary of defence, 21 January 1961–29 February 1968. Previously a Ford Motor Company executive, McNamara brought a new statistical and systems analysis approach to defence planning and policy. Under Kennedy, he promoted the MAD nuclear deterrent strategy. After Kennedy's assassination, he had the leading role in escalating American involvement in Vietnam. He resigned as defence secretary in February 1968 (at the time of the Tet Offensive) and served as president of the World Bank from 1968 to 1981.

xxviii *Who's who*

Zbigniew Brzezinski (1928–present). Carter's national security advisor, 20 January 1977–20 January 1981. A Columbia University scholar of the Eastern Bloc and Soviet Russian foreign policy, the Polish-born Brzezinski brought the element of *realpolitik* to American foreign policy. His vision ran counter to that of the moralistic Cyrus Vance. Brzezinski sought to work with the Eastern Bloc to weaken Russia's hold – for instance, in the CSCE – and he saw SALT II as joined with the Helsinki 'Accords' to promote liberalisation within the Eastern Bloc. In response to the Russian invasion of Afghanistan, he had a central role in the formulation of the Carter Doctrine.

Weinberger, Caspar (1917–2006). Ronald Reagan's secretary of defence, 21 January 1981–23 November 1987. Weinberger was instrumental in American conventional and nuclear modernisation and build-up – especially SDI – to weaken Russia, and he had deep suspicions of Gorbachev's domestic and diplomatic initiatives. He was a convinced anglophile, giving unvarnished support to the Thatcher government during the Falklands War. He resigned amidst criminal charges devolving from Iran-Contra but was pardoned by President George H.W. Bush.

Rumsfeld, Donald (1932–present). George W. Bush's secretary of defence, 20 January 2001–18 December 2006. Serving as Ford's secretary of defence (1975–1977) and in other Republican administrations, Rumsfeld was a convinced neoconservative by 2001. He promoted unilateralism in American foreign policy in 2001 – turning against Europe-first with East Asia as a strategic concern – but helped create the coalitions that fought in Afghanistan and Iraq after 2001. However, his war leadership was questioned by senior American officers and, as public opinion became critical of the Bush Administration, Republican politicians saw him as electoral poison. He resigned after the November 2006 midterm elections.

Cheney, Richard B. (1941–present). George W. Bush's vice-president, 20 January 2001–20 January 2009. With wide experience in past Republican administrations, including as George H.W. Bush's secretary of defence (1989–1993), Cheney's neoconservatism informed his advice to George W. Bush – unusually, he was a vice-president with decided authority in domestic and foreign policy. He propagandised the WMD issue before and during the 2003 Iraq war and publicly disparaged the Relationship by attacking the notion that Margaret Thatcher had had influence with George H.W. Bush during the Kuwait crisis (1990–1991).

Great Britain

British prime ministers, 1940–present

Churchill, Winston S. (1874–1965). In office 10 May 1940–26 July 1945; 26 October 1951–6 April 1955. During the Second World War, Churchill

Who's who   xxix

established a working partnership with Franklin Roosevelt, America's president (1933–1945), that produced the Anglo-American 'Special Relationship'. Building on joint strategy and recognition of common goals except economic rivalry and decolonisation, he helped give the Relationship a strategic permanence that lasted for 50 years. Churchill continued to work for strong Anglo-American relations in his second government, especially an effort to thaw the Cold War after Stalin's death.

Atlee, Clement (1893–1967). In office 26 July 1945–26 October 1951. Attlee took power during the Potsdam Conference, endeavouring to work with the Truman Administration on European and German reconstruction. His Labour government supported the Truman Doctrine, the Marshall Plan, and the creation of NATO as tangible expressions of containment. Embarking on extensive social and economic reforms, he and his ministers began the process of decolonisation by giving India independence in 1947 and shedding the Palestine Mandate in 1948. In doing so, they protected British economic and other interests.

Eden, Anthony (1897–1977). In office 6 April 1955–10 January 1957. A politician with long experience in foreign policy – he was foreign secretary three times (1935–1938, 1940–1945, 1951–1955) – Eden led a brief Conservative government from 1955 to 1957. Although having some success as foreign secretary in meeting decolonisation by shaping the 1954 'Geneva Accords' and in spearheading German rearmament in 1955, Eden mishandled the Suez Crisis (1956) and brought the Relationship to the lowest point in its history.

Macmillan, Harold (1894–1986). In office 10 January 1957–19 October 1963. A Conservative, Macmillan rebuilt Anglo-American relations after Suez by working with Eisenhower over British acquisition of the Skybolt missile, intervention in Jordan, and defence co-ordination; and with Kennedy in procuring an independent British-controlled missile deterrent – Polaris – and supporting American policy in Europe and over the Berlin question. He was also willing to support America militarily in Laos, although nothing came of it. The Macmillan-Kennedy years have been characterised as the 'Golden Days' of the Relationship.

Douglas-Home, Alexander (1903–1995). In office 19 October 1963–16 October 1964. After Macmillan resigned in October 1963, Douglas-Home led a short-lived Conservative government. A staunch pro-American, he continued Macmillan's policies of protecting the Relationship. See 'Foreign secretaries', below.

Wilson, Harold (1916–1995). In office 6 October 1964–19 June 1970; 4 March 1974–6 April 1976. Despite the Labour Party's strong anti-American wing, Wilson provided effective leadership in supporting American involvement in Vietnam short of a military commitment. Facing perpetual

xxx   *Who's who*

economic and financial crises by 1967, however, he and his Cabinet ended Britain's military commitment 'East of Suez'. Nevertheless, with initiatives like NATO's 1969 Schröder-Healey report, his government supported limiting nuclear escalation and improving intra-allied consultation with nuclear weapons reinforcing alliance objectives. He was in office during the CSCE and, although Britain joined the EEC in 1973, the economic crisis after 1974 diverted his attention to domestic affairs. By 1974, Anglo-American strategic relations had gone into suspended animation.

Heath, Edward (1916–2005). In office 19 June 1970–4 March 1974. Less enamoured of the Americans than his predecessors, Heath called the Relationship 'natural' rather than 'special'. His focus centred on British entry into the EEC – which was successful in 1973 – and a more Europe-focussed foreign policy. This concentration saw an active British role in NATO and the EPC, created by the EEC in 1970 to foster intra-community political co-operation with new members. His government had a central role in preparing for the CSCE. Despite Heath's proclivities, his foreign secretary, Douglas-Home, had senior Cabinet bureaucrats consult bimonthly with the State Department 'to keep US-UK relations on an unchanged basis'.

Callaghan, James (1912–2005). In office, 6 April 1976–4 May 1979. Holding several portfolios under Harold Wilson, including foreign secretary (1974–1976), and strongly pro-American, Callaghan took office at a difficult moment in 1976. Poor economic policies and Labour's fealty to the trade unions saw Callaghan's government seek American-supported IMF loans to keep the economy afloat. Apart from working with Jimmy Carter in pressing the southern African apartheid regimes to liberalise, Anglo-American relations continued in suspended animation.

Thatcher, Margaret (1925–2013). In office 4 May 1979–28 November 1990. As opposition leader after 1975, Thatcher, a Conservative, argued for a better-armed Britain to oppose Russia and re-engage more fully with America. Coming to power just before the Russian invasion of Afghanistan, she turned rhetoric into practical foreign policy, working to strengthen Britain militarily, pursue NATO cohesion, and, by endorsing euromissiles, reinforce the Relationship. Ronald Reagan proved a willing ally. Despite obstacles such as the Falklands War, Grenada, and Europe's INF, they restored the Relationship to its Second World War high. Thatcher worked with George H.W. Bush over the liquidation of the Soviet Russia and the Eastern Bloc – not always easy with American support of reunited Germany – and in the first months of the Kuwait crisis (1990–1991).

Major, John (1943–present). In office 28 November 1990–2 May 1997. Major confronted growing American unilateralism with the Clinton Administration's approach to the break-up of Yugoslavia – Washington saw it initially as Europe's problem. Always cautious, Major looked to use the Relationship to bolster British foreign policy but found post–Cold War America increasingly unwilling to co-operate. When Clinton's Administration questioned Britain's continued place as a permanent member of the UN Security Council, Major's government responded, 'Once-fashionable talk of a "New World Order" dawning was utopian folly'.

Blair, Tony (1953–present). In office 2 May 1997–27 June 2007. Blair thought a robust foreign policy crucial in the post–Cold War order to ensure Britain a leading place. Despite growing American unilateralism, he also looked to revitalise the Relationship, a crucial element being his espousal of a 'Doctrine of the International Community' – 'We cannot turn our backs on conflicts and the violation of human rights within other countries if we want still to be secure'. Reckoning that weak Powers could influence strong ones through engagement, his policy foundered on his government's support of coalition actions in Afghanistan and Iraq. The British public's antipathy to George W. Bush's America severely damaged what was left of the Relationship.

Brown, Gordon (1951–present). In office 27 June 2007–11 May 2010. With new centres of power emerging in the post–Cold War international order, Brown sought to bolster Britain's economic position in the wider world, especially within the EU and with the PRC and other Powers. Under Brown, Britain continued the military commitment to Afghanistan and Iraq, and it was willing to allow British integration with the American missile system. However, protecting Britain's economy as an international financial crisis began in 2008 diverted Labour's energies from foreign policy.

Cameron, David (1966–present). In office 11 May 2010–13 July 2016. The Conservative David Cameron took office with the Relationship having disappeared. The American president since 2009, Barack Obama, was concerned more with East Asia and the Pacific than Europe and the Middle East. Although Cameron joined with Obama in March 2012 to publish an article in the *Washington Post* – 'Not just special, but an essential relationship'; it constituted platitudes rather than practical politics. Britain and America had few strategic interests in common.

Notable British foreign secretaries since 1940

Halifax, Viscount (1881–1959). In office 21 February 1938–22 December 1940. Halifax proved important in the development of the Churchill-Roosevelt partnership in the Second World War when he agreed that Churchill should correspond privately with the American president over strategic and other questions beginning in September 1939. After Neville Chamberlain fell from power in May 1940, Halifax continued serving under Winston Churchill, helping over the destroyers-for-bases agreement and other initiatives. He served subsequently as ambassador to Washington from 1940 to 1946.

xxxii *Who's who*

Eden, Anthony (1897–1977). In office 22 December 1940–26 July 1945; 28 October 1951–7 April 1955. Although Neville Chamberlain's foreign secretary from 1935 to 1938, Eden was a strong supporter of close Anglo-American ties when the Second World War began. As Churchill's wartime foreign secretary, he contributed to the inter-Allied conferences and the EAC, although he chafed at American power. After 1951, he played a major role in shaping the 1954 'Geneva Accords' – which annoyed the Americans – and, the next year, bringing about the remilitarisation of Germany – which gratified them.

Bevin, Ernest (1881–1951). In office 27 July 1945–9 March 1951. As a British trade union leader, Bevin had worked against communist influence in the British trade union movement before the Second World War. As foreign secretary, he supported strongly the Relationship from the moment he met American leaders at the Potsdam Conference. Over the next six years, he helped promote Anglo-American strategic interests in Europe, especially in Germany, and he had an important role in the creation of Bizonia-Trizonia, the establishment of the OEEC, Western European defence via the Brussels Treaty and WUDO, and the construction of NATO.

Selwyn Lloyd, John (1904–1978). In office 26 December 1955–27 July 1960. As foreign secretary under both Anthony Eden and Harold Macmillan, he essentially followed on a foreign policy course established by the two premiers. Thus, he bore some responsibility for the disaster of the Suez Crisis – he and the American secretary of state, John Foster Dulles, were not close – and, as Macmillan then revived the Relationship, for improving Anglo-American relations.

Brown, George (1914–1975). In office 11 August 1966–15 March 1968. As foreign secretary, Brown was an ardent supporter of British membership in the EEC, playing an influential role within the Labour Party for Britain's second failed application to join in 1967. He also was the government's spokesman after the Arab-Israeli War in 1967, demanding that Israel return territories won in the war. Whilst Britain looked to improve its relations with the Arab states, America turned towards Israel.

Douglas-Home, Alexander (1903–1995). In office 20 June 1968–28 February 1974. A former foreign secretary (1960–1963) and prime minister (1963–1964), Douglas-Home believed strongly in the utility of the Relationship. Although Prime Minister Edward Heath's orientation was towards Europe, leading to Britain's EEC membership in 1973, and he talked about the Relationship as 'natural' rather than 'special', Douglas-Home kept lines of co-operation open with Washington. He had senior Cabinet bureaucrats consult bimonthly with the State Department 'to keep US–UK relations on an unchanged basis'.

Acknowledgements

Over the years that I have studied modern Anglo-American relations, a number of scholars have shared their insights with me about Britain, America, and the hard world of international politics. I would thus like to acknowledge Larry Aronsen, Chris Bell, Kenneth Bourne, Kathleen Burk, Antoine Capet, Francis Carroll, Michael Dockrill, Saki Dockrill, John Ferris, David French, Erik Goldstein, David Haglund, Michael Handel, Michael Hogan, John Maurer, Gordon Martel, Asa McKercher, Ian Nish, and Zara Steiner. Although we have met only a few times, David Reynold has produced work that has been especially helpful. In addition, the conference on 'The "Special Relationship" 1945–1990', held at the Université de Rouen in November 2002, brought together a range of leading scholars in the field who, from different perspectives, examined the complexities of the transatlantic nexus. The volume it produced –*The 'Special Relationship'/La "relations spéciale" entre le Royaume-Uni et les États-Unis*, edited by A. Capet and A. Sy-Wonyu (Rouen, 2003) – has been decidedly influential in putting the Relationship into both national and international perspectives. And above all else, although we disagreed profoundly on the nature of the twentieth-century relationship, I owe a tremendous debt to Donald Cameron Watt – first, as my doctoral supervisor and, then, as a friend and colleague.

I would also like to thank the staffs of the British Library of Political and Economic Science at the London School of Economics, the Massey Library at the Royal Military College of Canada, the Sterling Library at Yale University, and the University of Victoria Libraries.

On a personal level, my grandchildren, Maria, Mya, and Ayden, have brought tremendous happiness to me the past few years. My wife, Cathie, of course, has always been supportive and the anchor of my life.

Abbreviations

ABM	anti-ballistic missile
ACC	Allied Control Commission
AHR	*American Historical Review*
AIOC	Anglo-Iranian Oil Company
ANZUS	Australia, New Zealand, United States Security Treaty
ASEAN	Association of Southeast Asian Nations
BJIS	*British Journal of International Studies*
BP	British Petroleum
CCP	Chinese Communist Party
CCS	Combined Chiefs of Staff
CENTO	Central Treaty Organisation
CFM	Council of Foreign Ministers
CIA	Central Intelligence Agency
CJH	*Canadian Journal of History*
CSCE	Conference on Security and Co-operation in Europe
CWH	*Cold War History*
CWIHP	Cold War International History Project
DH	*Diplomatic History*
DMZ	demilitarised zone
DS	*Diplomacy & Statecraft*
ECSC	European Coal and Steel Community
EDC	European Defence Community
EEC	European Economic Community
EHR	*English Historical Review*
EPC	European Political Co-operation
EU	European Union
FA	*Foreign Affairs*
FO	Foreign Office
FRUS	*Foreign Relations of the United States*
GDP	gross domestic product
HJ	*Historical Journal*
IA	*International Affairs*
ICBM	intercontinental ballistic missile

IMF	International Monetary Fund
INF	intermediate-range nuclear forces
ICC	International Control Commission
IRA	Irish Republican Army
ISIS	Islamic State of Iraq and al-Sham
JAH	*Journal of American History*
JCH	*Journal of Contemporary History*
JEH	*Journal of Economic History*
JSS	*Journal of Strategic Studies*
KMT	Kuomintang (Chinese Nationalist Party)
MAD	mutually assured destruction
MIRV	Multiple Independently Targetable Re-entry Vehicle
MLF	multilateral force
MPLA	Movimento Popular de Libertação de Angola
MPDRE	Marxist People's Democratic Republic of Ethiopia
NATO	North Atlantic Treaty Organisation
NSA	National Security Archive
OEEC	Organisation for European Economic Co-operation
PLA	People's Liberation Army
PLO	Palestine Liberation Organisation
PRC	People's Republic of China
PSQ	*Presidential Studies Quarterly*
RAF	Royal Air Force
RN	Royal Navy
SCAP	Supreme Commander for the Allied Powers
SDI	Strategic Defence Initiative
SEATO	Southeast Asia Treaty Organisation
SS	surface-to-surface
START	Strategic Arms Reduction Treaty
UAR	United Arab Republic
UN	United Nations
UP	University Press
USN	United States Navy
WUDO	Western Union Defence Organisation

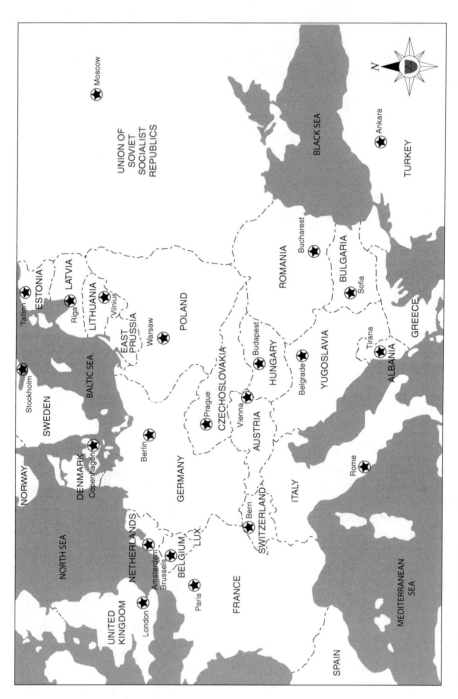

Map 1 Europe, 1937–1939

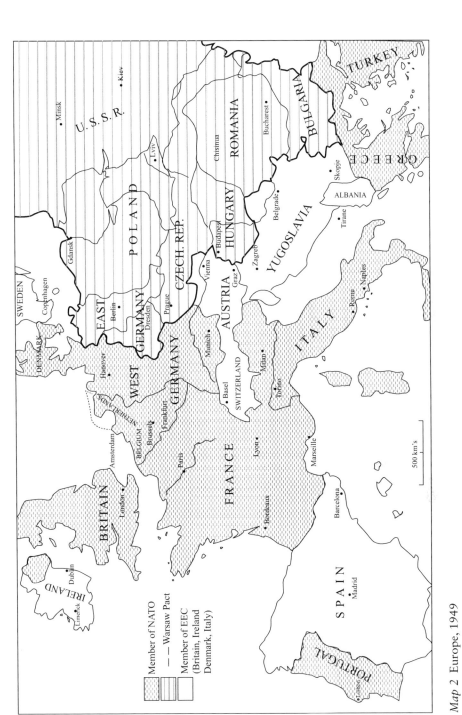

Map 2 Europe, 1949

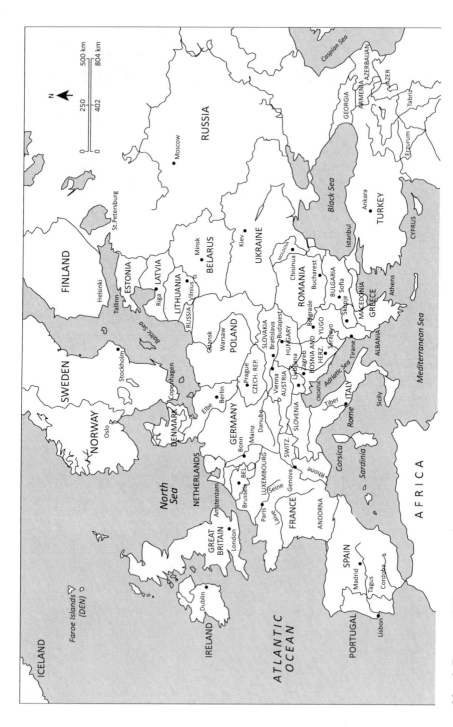

Map 3 Europe, 1998

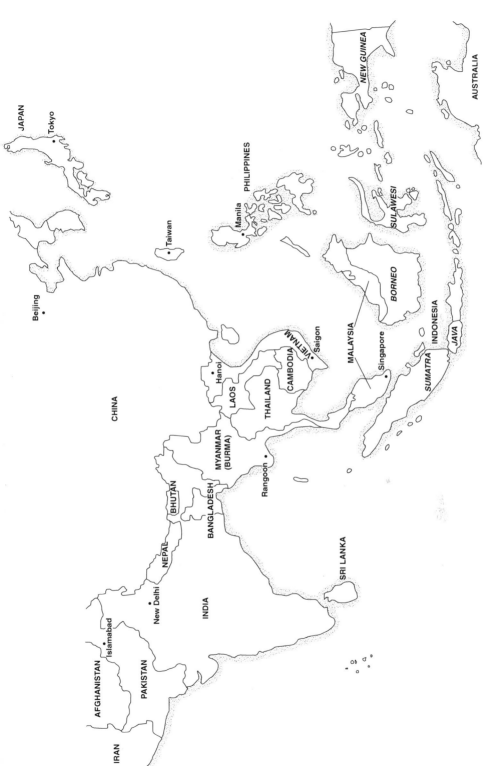

Map 4 East and South Asia, 1965

Part I
Prologue

1 The Anglo-American 'Special Relationship'

The political and military relationship between Great Britain and the United States – the 'Special Relationship' – that developed during the Second World War was a strategic partnership. As the basis of the Western alliance during that struggle and the Cold War, it played an essential part in bringing stability to the evolving post-1945 international order. None of this suggests that social, cultural, and even philosophical ties linking the two English-speaking peoples were unimportant – or remain. They possess a common language, a conviction that ordered society finds basis on common law, a belief that capitalism provides the greatest good for the greatest number, and a confidence in liberal democratic governance and religious freedom. Tied to emotion and sentiment, these links underpinned the diplomatic and military relationship. Nor does it mean that the relationship was always smooth or its 'special' character universally accepted in each country. The perceived national interests of the two Powers did not always converge after 1941 – sometimes they collided spectacularly. Nonetheless, guided and used by British and American leaders for purely pragmatic reasons, the 'special' diplomatic and military relationship developed after September 1939 in a wartime context of expediency and *realpolitik* shorn of emotion and sentiment. After 1945, recognising its diplomatic and military utility, the foreign-policy-making elites in both states sustained it. Quite simply, working together offered the best means to protect and extend their perceived national interests and, thereby, better ensure international stability.

As indicated above, the 'Special Relationship' was unique because of British and American social, cultural, and philosophical bonds. Despite the American Revolution of 1775–1782 and the subsequent almost century of diplomatic unease between London and Washington, Anglo-American relations improved markedly between the end of the American Civil War and the outbreak of the First World War. Transatlantic travel by the upper middle and upper classes of both countries provided appreciation of the traditions, achievements, and ways of life of the other. Marriage between the daughters of wealthy American entrepreneurs and the impecunious sons of the British upper classes became common (Anonymous, 1890) – indeed, Winston Churchill, the British prime minister from 1940 to 1945

4 Prologue

and joint-architect of the Relationship, came from such a marriage. Beyond these social ties, a range of artists, musicians, and writers also crossed the Atlantic to learn, paint, sketch, and draw inspiration from a different geography and a slightly dissimilar society with its own attainments and foibles. The works of William Shakespeare naturally underlay literature, drama, and some history in each country. American writers such as Mark Twain, who lived briefly in London and received an honorary Oxford doctorate in 1907, had a wide British audience (Baetzhold, 1970). From the other side of the Atlantic, Oscar Wilde visited the United States in 1882, where he saw a land of opportunity (Wilde, 1956).

Before 1914, increasing numbers of influential British and American politicians, academics, and others appreciated the obvious cultural, economic, and political connexions between the two countries. The Oxford Regis Professor of Civil Law (1873–1890) and Liberal cabinet minister (1892–1895), James Bryce, wrote cogently on America's political system before being appointed ambassador to Washington (1907–1913) (Bryce, 1888). Maurice Low, long *The Times*' Washington correspondent, sought to explain American 'exceptionalism' to both the British and American publics (Low, 1909–1911). And Esme Howard, who served under Bryce as counsellor and returned to Washington as ambassador in 1924, recorded:

> The fact of the matter is that, unless our two countries should produce some remarkably stupid statesmen, the people inhabiting them are bound and obliged by the force of circumstances to learn that anything approaching serious conflict between them would be not only the most criminal and fratricidal proceeding, but also of such a nature that whatever the outcome, it could only result in such economic and financial loss as could never be compensated by the fruit of victory.
>
> (McKercher 1989: 350–51)

Presidents Theodore Roosevelt, a Republican (president 1901–1909), and Woodrow Wilson, a Democrat (president 1913–1921), personified American anglophilia – although each sought to protect American national interests, which sometimes meant resisting what they saw as British inroads (Tilchin and Neu, 2006). Roosevelt believed strongly in pan-Anglo-Saxonism: that America and Britain had to work in tandem to ensure international security in their various spheres of influence. As he wrote a British friend when Germany threatened to build a blue-water navy: 'I think I have become almost as anxious as you are to have the British fleet kept up to the highest point of efficiency' and in its 'present position of relative power. . . . It is a great guaranty for the peace of the world' (Morison and Blum, 1952: 1159). Like Bryce, a leading academic before entering politics, Wilson was enamoured of law as the basis for effective and enlightened governance. In his work, he placed British common law and its impact on the evolution of liberal democratic values as crucial and, seeing inefficiencies in American governance, thought that a parliamentary system in the United States based on Britain's parliamentary model would have greater value than the American congressional system. In an insightful analysis, he remarked: 'The leaders of English public life have something besides weight of character, prestige of personal service and experience, and authority of individual opinion to exalt them above the anonymous Press. They have definite authority and power in the actual control of government' (Wilson, 1885: 322).

Augmented by the Americans joining the Entente Powers during the First World War to fight Wilhelmine Germany and its allies, and despite America retreating into political isolationism after 1920, this transnationalism became stronger by the late 1930s. Admittedly, the 1920s and 1930s saw ambivalent political and economic relations between the two Powers, moving from disputes (over economic issues and the naval question) in the 1920s to co-operation (over economic issues and the naval question) in the 1930s (Cohrs, 2006). Nonetheless, James Ramsay MacDonald, the Labour and National Government prime minister (1924, 1929–1931, 1931–1935), stood as an unabashed 'Atlanticist' seeking to build on Anglo-American commonalities to better ensure international peace and security (MacDonald to Borah, 1929). Similarly, after resigning as foreign secretary in February 1938, the Conservative Anthony Eden looked on America as a means of underpinning Britain's ability to confront the challenge mounted by both Nazi Germany and fascist Italy (Eden to Baldwin, 1938). Although not as pro-American in the interwar period as he later made out, Churchill waxed eloquent on the unity of the British and Americans as 'English-speaking peoples' by the late 1930s and after re-entering the Cabinet in September 1939 [Document 1]. In the United States, the secretary of state from 1929 to 1933, Henry Stimson, saw Anglo-American co-operation over arms limitation and economic diplomacy as decidedly important in ensuring international stability (Stimson diary 1930). His attitudes were shared by a range of equally influential and well-travelled American statesmen including amongst others Norman Davis, a senior arms negotiator after 1933 and president of the Council on Foreign Relations from 1936 to 1944; Thomas Lamont, a leading Wall Street banker with ties to both the Republican and Democratic parties; and Allen Dulles, a diplomat, international lawyer, and secretary of the Council on Foreign Relations from 1933 to 1944. Not every British and American leader shared these sentiments. Many, such as Neville Chamberlain, the British premier from 1937 to 1940, and William Borah, the powerful Republican chairman of the Senate Foreign Relations Committee from 1925 to 1923, dissented (Kennedy, 2002). But by the late 1930s, leaders on both sides of the Atlantic seemed increasingly willing to co-operate with one another given the changing situation in Europe and the Far East fostered by Axis and Japanese aggressiveness.

Between 1919 and 1939, transnational links augmented the connectedness of the Relationship. Transatlantic travel resumed in 1919, and Britons and Americans visited each other's countries in ever larger numbers.

6 Prologue

Educational and goodwill exchanges and organisations such as the Rhodes Trust, the Pilgrims Society, and the Council on Foreign Relations and its British sister, the Royal Institute of International Affairs, enhanced this process. Thus, throughout the 1920s and 1930s, important Britons and Americans experienced each other's countries – Stimson, for instance, regularly spent time in Britain – and discussed and wrote about foreign policy, the international economy, and other issues of mutual concern, although not necessarily of shared national interest.

Along with popular writers lionised in the other's country – for instance, Sinclair Lewis, Ernest Hemingway, George Bernard Shaw, and Virginia Woolf (Hutner, 2009) – the notion of a transnational culture came to the fore in the most popular medium, cinema, with the usual entertainments of comedy and drama. For instance, there was the American *Thin Man* series (beginning in 1934), comedies of manners centred on an upper class New York couple who solved murder mysteries, and the British *Invitation to the Waltz* (1935), a musical about British espionage and a love triangle during the Napoleonic Wars. But deeper and more complex motion pictures also crossed the Atlantic – such as the 1937 British *Big Fella*, starring the African American singer Paul Robeson, showing the nobility and integrity of Black workers. Two years later came *Four Just Men*, which explored some Great War veterans working against the enemies of the country. In the United States, by the late 1930s, Warner Brothers Studios produced a series of popular films starring Errol Flynn that showed the inherent sensibilities and strength of 'England' against dictatorial adversaries: *The Adventures of Robin Hood* (1938), *The Charge of the Light Brigade* (1936), and *The Private Lives of Elizabeth and Essex* (1939). Perhaps the zenith came with the 1939 American film *Gone with the Wind*, which had a star-studded Anglo-American cast: especially Leslie Howard and Vivien Leigh from Britain and Clark Gable and Olivia de Havilland from the United States.

The basis for a 'special relationship' – 'the *tendency*, the *inclination*, and the *desire* to work together' – existed by 1939 (Kimball, 2003: 213). The Second World War provided the catalyst, through the conscious efforts of Churchill and President Franklin Roosevelt. Even before America entered the war in December 1941, working with Churchill, Roosevelt moved the neutral United States into Britain's orbit. After December 1941, the two leaders and their governments worked closely to combine strategy, determine war aims, and, militarily, collaborate with Soviet Russia and their other allies to attain victory. As Churchill remarked in March 1946, six months after final Allied success:

> Neither the sure prevention of war, nor the continuous rise of world organisation will be gained without what I have called the fraternal association of the English-speaking peoples. This means a special relationship between the British Commonwealth and Empire and the United States.
>
> [Document 10]

To a degree, Churchill overstated the strength of the relationship that arose from the war and its continuing ability to ensure international peace and security – or, at least, peace and security as defined in London and Washington. The two Powers were then competing for advantage in a number of areas of the world – particularly the Middle East, over oil (Ashton, 2014). Moreover, a principal American war aim articulated by Roosevelt and his advisors after 1941 had been to decolonise the great European empires, create new regimes, and build a new international order based on more liberal trade – in which, of course, America would acquire significant advantage (Louis, 1977; Thorne, 1978). In early 1946, as South and East Asian nationalist movements sprang forth, Britain was restructuring its empire: moving to give India independence and maintain order in Palestine. The United States under Roosevelt's successor, Harry Truman, was making only limited efforts to preserve stability in Central Europe and Iran; how much it would do beyond these initiatives remained moot (Fawcett, 1992). Although the Special Relationship existed, its wartime basis – achieving Axis defeat – had disappeared by 1945. Would it continue?

Of course, it did so and strengthened. The reason lay in the deepening Cold War between America and its chief ally, Britain, on one side, and Soviet Russia on the other (Reynolds, 2013: Chapter 3; Woolner, 2013). As divided Germany became the main Cold War battlefield and East-West tensions arose in the next 15 years in China, Korea, the Middle East, Southeast Asia, Africa, and the Caribbean, Britain and America moved closer to meet perceived communist aggression. In this process, some American leaders forgot a lesson that their British *confrères* had grasped since at least the late eighteenth century, when Britain moved toward global Power status: pre-eminence does not mean an omnipotence (Brinkley, 1990). As Washington in Democratic or Republican guise came to understand, however, even superpowers needed allies; and for Cold War America – despite continuing Anglo-American rivalry over trade and international investment – the British stood as their chief and most trusted confederates. The wartime experience provided for continued strategic co-operation in Europe and the wider world; and although crises occasionally threatened the foundation of Anglo-American relations – the 1956 Suez Crisis, particularly (Nichols, 2011) – London and Washington shared a range of strategic interests that sustained the Relationship.

Even after the Cold War's first phase ended in 1963, the Relationship proved essential to the two Powers. When the United States became mired in Vietnam (1963–1973), Britain proved helpful to the Relationship and its own interests in both Europe and the developing world (Ellis, 2004). Tied to the British musical invasion of the United States in 1964 with the Beatles and their brethren the Rolling Stones, The Who, and The Dave Clark Five, who followed the 1950s popularity in Britain of Elvis Presley and other American rock-and-rollers, a new era in Anglo-American transnationalism seemed to have begun (Harry, 2004). Despite Britain's decision to withdraw

8 Prologue

militarily east of Suez in the late 1960s and turn to the EEC in the early 1970s, London and Washington found common ground to work together for agreed strategic ends. In all of these issues, whilst the United States remained the leading Power in the relationship, Britain retained its position as the chief American ally.

When the Cold War returned with a vengeance in the latter half of the 1970s with Russian adventurism in Africa and Afghanistan, the Relationship responded. In the 1980s, it revived to levels not enjoyed since the Churchill-Roosevelt partnership. Margaret Thatcher in Britain (1979–1990) and Ronald Reagan in America (1981–1989) produced an unambiguous transatlantic nexus looking to achieve a strategic victory over Soviet Russia and its empire – through economic means and a military build-up the Russians could not equal (Cooper, 2012). And when Reagan and Thatcher departed the political scene at the end of the 1980s, their successors, John Major (1990–1997) and George H.W. Bush (1989–1993), continued the process that by 1991 saw the end of Soviet Russia (Craddock, 1997; Maynard, 2008).

By the mid-1990s, as crises erupted in the Balkans and as former Soviet satellite states in Eastern Europe re-established themselves as sovereign political and economic entities, a different generation of Anglo-American leaders were confronting a new international order that had arrived in significant part by Anglo-American efforts. However, whilst Major and his Labour successor Tony Blair (1997–2007) still saw the Relationship as a core element of British foreign policy, President Bill Clinton (1993–2001) and his successors George W. Bush (2001–2009) and Barack Obama (2009–2017), did not view America in the same light. With a restructured Balkans, a united Germany, and an expanded NATO, Europe received a new life. Other regions of instability appeared, however – primarily the Middle East and South Asia (Riedel, 2010). China, a revived Russia, and other Powers emerged as America's political and economic rivals. America would meet these problems on its own; the Relationship unravelled.

George W. Bush's election as president in 2000 proved crucial to the Relationship. Embracing American 'exceptionalism', he populated his Administration with neoconservatives who never learnt the lesson that pre-eminence does not mean omnipotence; like those in the previous administration, they began their tenure determined to go their own way in foreign and defence policy and pursue alone what they perceived as American strategic interests (Daalder and Lindsay, 2003). Less than a year later, however, America suffered terrorist attacks on New York and Washington. Finding allies became a priority once again, and America found support from Britain for wars in both Iraq and Afghanistan (Auerswald and Saideman, 2014; Nau, 2008). This Anglo-American co-operation in the Middle East and South Asia frayed the Relationship, however. The British public turned against both Bush and the Iraq intervention because the *casus belli* – Baghdad's 'weapons of mass destruction' – never existed; Washington had manipulated the evidence. The

The Anglo-American 'Special Relationship' 9

transatlantic nexus in international security issues touching both Powers diminished. After 2009, as Obama's foreign policy focus moved away from Europe, and a succession of British governments – led by Gordon Brown (2007–2010) and David Cameron (2010–2016) – were forced to concentrate on domestic policy, the Relationship evaporated.

Nonetheless, for almost 50 years, the Anglo-American relationship was integral to the Western alliance that arose during the Second World War and served the interests of both Powers during the Cold War. Social, cultural, and philosophical links between the two English-speaking peoples remained important and strengthened the Relationship's diplomatic and military dimensions. Guided and used by British and American leaders for purely pragmatic reasons, the 'special' diplomatic and military relationship emerged in a wartime context of expediency and *realpolitik*. After 1945, recognition of its diplomatic and military utility by leaders in both states sustained it. Quite simply, working together offered the best means to protect and extend their perceived national interests and, thereby, better ensure international stability.

Part II

Britain, America, and the origins of the 'Special Relationship'

2 The Anglo-American relationship before 1939

> While I should look with horror upon anything in the nature of a fratricidal strife, I should look forward with pleasure to the possibility of the Stars and Stripes and the Union Jack floating together in defence of a common cause sanctioned by humanity and by justice.
>
> Joseph Chamberlain, British Colonial Secretary,
> January 1896 ('Episodes of the Month', 1896: 739)

The uneasy relationship, 1782–1900

The Special Relationship was not inevitable. What became the United States of America was originally the thirteen southernmost colonies of Britain's early North American empire (Black, 2008). It emerged as a sovereign state by 1782, after colonial oligarchs led a successful rebellion. For almost a century afterwards, Anglo-American relations were rarely warm. Indeed, in 1812, after Britain imposed a maritime blockade against Napoleonic France and its European allies, America launched a naval war against Britain in the Atlantic and Great Lakes and attempted to conquer Britain's Canadian colonies (Flavell and Conway, 2004). However, whilst the War of 1812 did little to change North America's balance of power or dint Britain's assertions about wartime blockade, it shaped Anglo-American relations for much of the nineteenth century (Bourne, 1967; Burk, 2008). Looking benignly on America, the British maintained their formal empire in the Western Hemisphere and expanded their informal one based on trade and investment; they treated the United States as a lesser Power – like Brazil – when protecting and extending their regional economic and strategic interests. For their part, the Americans accepted the British Empire's existence in the Americas – in Canada, the Caribbean, and Central and South America; they avoided confrontation with Britain, relying instead on diplomatic initiative to settle territorial and other questions. Possessing limited sea power after enunciating the Monroe Doctrine in 1823, American leaders understood grudgingly that the Royal Navy protected their burgeoning North and South American interests – as it did those of Britain – from aggrandising European Great Powers (Colucci, 2012).

14 *The origins of the 'Special Relationship'*

During the nineteenth century, the Western Hemispheric balance of power transformed. Given increasing demands amongst British electors that government expenditure, including Imperial defence, remain in check, British leaders came to see that formal empire – acquiring new colonies, with costs for administration and garrisoning defence forces – was burdensome. The only exception occurred if territories remained crucial to Imperial and trade defence; the best example was Britain's occupation of Egypt in 1882 to protect the Suez Canal. Respecting North America, Whitehall understood by the early 1860s that it would be impossible to defend Canada from an increasingly powerful United States – something helped by failed Canadian rebellions in 1837 and 1838, the advent of responsible government in the Canadian colonies, and English- and French-Canadian desires for independence (Martin, 1995). In July 1867, Canada received its independence. Thus, politically, whilst the North American balance changed with an independent Canada, Britain reserved its strategic position by retaining naval bases at Halifax and Esquimalt; economically and financially, nothing changed, as the British maintained significant levels of investment in their former colonies. As the century progressed, what remained true in North America mirrored Britain's interests in the Caribbean and South and Central America. Existing colonies such as Jamaica and Tobago retained strategic importance and were sites for investment and trade, and Britain developed and expanded markets in independent states such as Chile and Argentina.

Within the Royal Navy's security cocoon and recognising benefits from a less confrontational Anglo-American relationship tied to economic and political stability, the small United States expanded its territory to the south and west in wars of conquest against Mexico and aboriginal tribes. Underwriting this expansion with far-seeing policies encouraging massive European immigration into conquered and older territories, Washington encouraged the untrammelled development of agriculture and industry. By 1895, the republic stretched across North America, from the Atlantic to the Pacific. After this expansion and consolidation, with a growing population and vitalising sinews of vigorous economics and finance, the United States emerged as the leading regional Power in the Americas. The process had not been easy: between 1861 and 1865, a bloody civil war between breakaway southern states and northern ones supporting the federal government had almost sundered the country. Fought over state legislative independence – the focus was slavery, the southern states' economies, and growing nationalism – the North's victory forced American political unity, strengthened the legislative power of the national Congress, and entrenched presidential authority, especially over foreign and military policy (Foreman, 2012).

Britain, America, and stability in international politics, 1900–1914

In a largely separate development in North America after 1782, the two Powers gradually came to see each other as non-threatening. Of course, issues

Anglo-American relations before 1939 15

of contention still existed. Three were of particular importance towards the end of the nineteenth century: a Venezuela–British Guiana frontier dispute that, for Washington, touched the Monroe Doctrine; a simmering quarrel after 1898 over the Alaska-Canada boundary caused by gold strikes in the Klondike; and Newfoundland-American disagreement over fishing rights (Gibb, 2005). However, after 1899, the Boer War placed Britain in a difficult position vis-à-vis its European Great Power rivals – especially Germany. The Germans looked to build a blue-water navy, and their foreign policy had the potential to disrupt the European balance – stability crucial to British national security. British governments, led by the Third Marquess of Salisbury (1895–1902) and Arthur Balfour (1902–1905) essentially conceded over Venezuela, Alaska, and Newfoundland. Improving relations allowed for concentrating British diplomatic and military resources in other places. Moreover, reversing the earlier trend, American ability to enforce the Monroe Doctrine now maintained the hemispheric status quo, integral to which were British colonies, trade, and investment. Although other issues dogged Canadian-American relations into the first decade of the twentieth century – for instance, reciprocal mining rights – London increasingly let Ottawa resolve these problems (Adams, 2005). In 1905, when Britain withdrew strategically from the Americas to concentrate more on national security and Imperial defence, Anglo-American relations entered a quiescent phase until the outbreak of the Great War in 1914.

During this period, the United States solidified its dominance in the Western Hemisphere. War against Spain in 1898 saw America acquire Cuba, Puerto Rico, the Philippine Islands, and Guam (Hendrickson, 2003). Tied to this process was American naval expansion. In the 1890s, Alfred Thayer Mahan, an American naval historian, connected Britain's sea power with its success since the seventeenth century in both its formal and informal empire; his writings proved a catalyst amongst a range of American leaders seeking to expand American economic interests and create an American presence amongst the Great Powers (Mahan, 1894). President Theodore Roosevelt pushed to expand the USN; when he left office, America possessed a growing fleet (Hendrix, 2009). Yet, Roosevelt saw the British and Americans as 'Anglo-Saxon' cousins. Under Roosevelt, in its limited participation in Great Power politics – for instance, at the 1907 Algeciras Conference, which resolved the First Moroccan Crisis in favour of Britain and its French Entente partner against Germany – Washington sided with London. By 1914, Anglo-American relations were experiencing a 'great rapprochement' (Perkins, 1968).

The drift to co-operation in the First World War, 1914–1918

The outbreak of the Great War in 1914 saw Britain and its Entente partners, France and tsarist Russia, fight Germany, Austria-Hungary, and their allies in Europe and on its south-eastern periphery (Strachan, 2001). Other theatres of operation emerged in Africa, East Asia, and the Pacific Ocean.

16 The origins of the 'Special Relationship'

Although the heaviest fighting occurred on land, both alliances used naval power to strangle each other economically. Germany mounted a submarine campaign to sink ships carrying food and raw materials to Britain and France – and industrialised and trade goods to overseas markets – while the Royal Navy (RN) applied a blockade to starve German industry of raw materials, interdict trade, and reduce the ingress of foodstuffs (Osborne, 2004). In this process, America had a pivotal position. Under Woodrow Wilson, America proclaimed neutrality. Arguing that neutral Powers possessed the right to unimpeded trade – 'freedom of the seas' dating to the War of 1812 – Washington opposed both Germany's submarine campaign and Britain's blockade (Coogan, 1981).

In May 1915, after the Germans sank a British liner, *Lusitania*, carrying American passengers, American diplomatic pressure saw Berlin announce a policy of restricted submarine warfare that translated into leaving passenger liners and neutral shipping alone. But where Germany caved to American pressures, Britain did not. With a legal system underpinning the blockade, the British continued intercepting neutral merchantmen and determining whether cargoes were contraband. Given American championship of the freedom of the seas and the electoral strength of anti-British Irish- and German-American voters, Anglo-American relations experienced unquestionable strain in 1915 and 1916. The net result was that, concurrent with the November 1916 American presidential elections, Congress passed legislation to build 'a navy second to none'.

Wilson won re-election partly by promising to keep America out of the war. In early 1917, however, desperate to weaken the Allies, Germany embarked on unrestricted submarine warfare. Worried that America might join the war, Germany sought to entice Mexico to declare war on America. The Mexicans did not bite. Still, unrestricted submarine warfare seriously threatened American national interests and, when the British leaked intercepted secret telegraphic correspondence between Berlin and Mexico City on 1 March, anti-German war fever broke out in America (Boghardt, 2012). Changing German strategy threatened American security. Notwithstanding his electoral promise, Wilson engineered American entry into the war on the Allied side. The United States declared war on Germany on 6 April 1917 and, conforming to its tradition of avoiding entangling alliances, joined the Allies as an Associated Power.

Almost immediately, Britain began raising Allied war loans on America's money market (Horn, 2002). As America commenced building an army for deployment in Europe, the United States Navy (USN) immediately reinforced the blockade (Besch, 2002). American ground forces joined the fighting on the Western Front in early 1918 – Britain's Russian ally had collapsed in November 1917 – and although some have questioned the American army's contribution to Allied victory, American troops augmented the Allies' fighting capacity (Trask, 1993). With its vast agricultural, industrial, and financial strength, America emerged from the war as a recognised Great Power (Kennedy,

Anglo-American relations before 1939   17

1987). Moreover, after April 1917, Wilson endeavoured to frame the eventual peace settlement with American-inspired ideals. On 8 January 1918, he outlined publicly 'Fourteen Points' as the basis of any peace settlement (Ambrosius, 1991). Amongst other objectives, he advocated ending secret diplomacy, creating a League of Nations to maintain international peace and security, recognising national self-determination in constructing post-war frontiers, and ensuring the freedom of the seas. Although Britain's prime minister, David Lloyd George (1916–1922), announced British war aims three days earlier – including an international organisation to settle international disputes and national self-determination, but not freedom of the seas – Wilson's 'Fourteen Points' had a wider appeal (Woodward, 1971). When Germany surrendered on 11 November 1918 – its allies had already collapsed – it did so based on Wilson's peace formula.

The Paris Peace Conference and the American return to isolationism, 1919–1920

Sitting in Paris from January 1918 to August 1920, representatives of the victorious Powers determined the peace treaties amongst themselves – often by difficult debate – and presented them as faits accomplis to Germany and its former allies (Boemeke et al., 2006). In this way, the leaders of the four principal Allied Powers – Britain, America, France, and Italy – made the major decisions. The first treaty, the Treaty of Versailles, dealt with Germany. Germany was disarmed, forced to pay heavy reparations to the European Allies, and made to surrender territory to France and Belgium in the West and the 'successor' states of Poland and Czechoslovakia in Central Europe. The other treaties followed Versailles's model: Austria, Hungary, Bulgaria, and Ottoman Turkey retained limited armed forces, had to pay reparations, and lost territory to their enemies and 'successor' states that arose from their former lands (Hobeck, 1999).

In this process, British and American interests diverged. Lloyd George's government resisted including the freedom of the seas in the peace settlement, warranted that 'national self-determination' did not apply to the British Empire, and opposed hobbling British foreign policy unnecessarily by the new League of Nations. Wanting the League above all else, Wilson retreated on naval issues to win British support. He also pushed his vision of national self-determination, even when it countered his allies' interests – for instance, Italy's Balkan ambitions. Wilson looked to 'new diplomacy' that eschewed secret agreements, large militaries, and balances of power – 'old diplomacy' – that he and other critics held had precipitated war in 1914. To protect France against a revived Germany and soften French Army demands to enfeeble Germany further, he and Lloyd George agreed on a post-war Anglo-American guarantee of French security.

After returning to Washington, Wilson failed spectacularly to win congressional support for Versailles and the League. One reason stemmed from

18 *The origins of the 'Special Relationship'*

ill health – he suffered a stroke in autumn 1919; another involved political miscalculation: America's Peace Conference delegation included no Republicans, thus impeding bipartisan political support for his diplomacy. Congress refused to ratify Versailles and American League membership. The Anglo-American guarantee also died. With America outside the League, Europe alone had to provide security for France and those Powers that profited from Germany's defeat, stymie German revanchism, meet revolutionary threats posed by Bolshevik Russia, and stabilise open and bitter competition amongst the Eastern-Central European 'successor' states.

Anglo-American economic competition, 1919–1939

In November 1920, the Republicans won control of the White House and Congress largely by arguing for a return to isolationism. Three Republican presidents held office until 1933: Warren Harding (1921–1923), Calvin Coolidge (1923–1929), and Herbert Hoover (1929–1933). Importantly, whilst each interpreted isolation as detachment from international political affairs, none included isolation from the international economy. Supported by Washington, American financiers, industrialists, unions, and farm organisations pursued aggressive economic diplomacy to enrich themselves and strengthen the United States. Britain stood as America's principal economic adversary. United States' industrial production, of course, surpassed that of every Power after 1918. Nevertheless, whilst its industrial prowess weakened by 1918, Britain remained economically strong. Never coming solely from industrial production, British wealth devolved more from financial resources and expertise in international banking, commerce, insurance, and investment – and concerning trade, Britain's lifeblood, America only drew even in the 1920s. The Great Depression's arrival in 1929 prevented the United States from overtaking Britain in this important indicator of economic strength (McKercher, 1988).

Commercial competition suffused Anglo-American relations during the 1920s and into the 1930s. In Europe, South America, the Middle East, and East Asia, British and American entrepreneurs competed over cables, air routes, access to raw materials, and investment. The record shows neither unchecked American success nor Britain's unavoidable enervation (Hogan, 1977; cf. Tooze, 2014). First, whilst intense and occasionally vituperative, seeking commercial advantage lacked the sustained emotive quality that marked issues such as naval competition. Second, and more important, the two Powers' central banks – the Bank of England and Federal Reserve Bank of New York – found it more profitable to co-operate (James, 2013). And, when states encouraged foreign development of their commodities after 1919, such as Venezuela's oil, British interests tended to respond first and American ones followed; this pattern laid the basis for Anglo-American competition in oil development both in Venezuela and in the Middle East over the next ten years (Stivers, 1982).

Anglo-American relations before 1939   19

This does not downplay Anglo-American rivalry (Costigliola, 1977). However, outside the Western Hemisphere, Britain withstood American pressures. In China, for instance, the State Department and American business concerns failed to dislodge British influence by the late 1930s, an achievement coming from actions by Whitehall and private British enterprises (Dayer, 1981). In the mid-1920s, Chinese nationalism created instability in China. In response, the British foreign secretary, Austen Chamberlain, issued the 1926 'Christmas memorandum' outlining London's willingness to modify existing agreements with China – such as the unequal treaties stretching back to the nineteenth century – and adjust other outstanding questions (Grayson, 1997). Although China's instability continued through indigenous warlords and the Japanese competing for advantage, British willingness to assuage Chinese nationalism continued. In May 1935, after Chinese complaints about having only low-ranking Western diplomats in their capital, Britain upgraded its Beijing legation to an embassy.

The residue of war finance was also important. By 1918, Britain owed about \$4 billion in war loans to private American lenders, although Britain advanced its former allies more – \$10 billion (Kent, 1989). Before and after April 1917, Americans bought war bonds to finance the Allied war effort. In the mid-1920s, Britain and other Powers negotiated debt agreements with Washington on behalf of American bondholders (Kent, 1989). Each June and December, Britain's Exchequer paid £60 million in gold to the Americans; however, by 1933, the Great Depression made it difficult for most Powers, including Britain, to meet their payments – the problem was not poverty but a lack of cash flow. Franklin Roosevelt's Administration proved willing to accept token biannual British payments of £15 million in silver. Anglophobe American politicians baulked, killing 'token' payments and, pushed by California Senator Hiram Johnson, passing legislation prohibiting future loans to governments that defaulted on their obligations (Dallek, 1995). War debts had proved an emotive issue before this moment, especially when Britain and France sought vainly to link war debts with German reparations payments to the former Allies. However, inter-Allied agreement in 1932 saw the end of the post-war reparations regime, and the finality of the Johnson Act and the Great Depression's grinding impact on all industrialised economies saw war debts disappear as a first-class foreign policy problem by 1935 (McKercher, 1999: Chapters 2 and 5). Indeed, in the late 1930s, although uncertainty exists about their usefulness, tripartite Anglo-Canadian-American trade agreements emerged to mitigate the impact of the international economic crisis.

Arms limitation and international security, 1919–1939

American re-embrace of isolationism in 1920, with no hope of League membership, meant that international security fell largely to the European Great Powers. Ironically, because of the naval question and narrow American

20 The origins of the 'Special Relationship'

trading interests in East Asia, Harding's Administration convened a conference at Washington in 1921 to settle both naval questions resulting from the war and how to maintain stability in revolutionary China (Goldstein and Maurer, 1994). The Washington Conference (12 November 1921–6 February 1922) produced three agreements: a five-Power naval treaty, a four-Power Pacific Pact, and a nine-Power treaty concerning China. The naval treaty created parity in capital ships – battleships, battle cruisers, and aircraft carriers over 10,000 tons – between the British and American navies. In a building ratio of 5:5:3, Britain and the United States received 535,000 tons each; Japan, 315,000 tons. France and Italy, lesser naval Powers, received a proportion of 1.7. Japan accepted a reduced fleet because of the Pacific Pact: Britain, France, Japan, and the United States accepted the status quo in the Pacific, meaning that the British could fortify no bases east of Singapore and the Americans none west of Pearl Harbor. The payoff for the Japanese navy was dominance in the western Pacific and its littoral. Built around a commitment to the 'Open Door' – equal opportunity for the commerce and industry of all foreigners in China – the treaty recognised China as a sovereign Power. Despite lacking enforcement provisions, the Washington treaties brought a system of security to post-war East Asia by early 1922.

A European system proved more problematic; difficulty revolved around French policies to keep Germany weak militarily and economically. Thus, when Germany defaulted on reparations payments in late 1922, French and Belgian troops occupied the Ruhr Valley, Germany's industrial heartland, to siphon off its production (Fischer, 2003). The Ruhr occupation proved a disaster of the first order for France. German resistance saw executions of resisters; extremist German political parties on the left and right, including the Communists and Adolf Hitler's National Socialist Party, won support from disenchanted Germans; and the economic and financial benefits to Paris and Brussels proved non-existent. Most critical, London and Washington, desiring a strong German economy to boost trade and provide European stability, pressured Paris by undermining the franc.

For three years, the British attempted to ease Franco-German tensions and provide a Western security system (Ferris, 1989). Finally, in early 1925, Austen Chamberlain joined with the French and German foreign ministers to negotiate a Rhineland pact. At Locarno, after eight months of deliberation, the British and Italians, led by Benito Mussolini, guaranteed the Versailles-defined Franco-German border. If either Germany or France invaded the other, Britain and Italy would join with the invaded Power. Given the fate of the proposed 1919 Anglo-American guarantee to France, Locarno constituted a bold step by the British. Balancing the Washington system in East Asia and the Pacific, Locarno brought a system of security to Europe. Five months after its conclusion in March 1926, the League established a Preparatory Commission to draft a treaty for an eventual World Disarmament Conference.

In the run-up to this conference, which began in February 1932, Anglo-American relations suffered strain over the naval question. The Washington five-Power treaty had not limited warships below 10,000 tons, chiefly cruisers. By the mid-1920s, the British reckoned that the RN needed a minimum of 70 cruisers to ensure national security and defend sea routes and overseas markets: 45 light cruisers, circa 6,000 tons with six-inch guns; and 25 heavy, 10,000-ton cruisers with eight-inch guns. London justified this fleet with a doctrine of 'absolute need': effective defence required 70 vessels. Countering with a doctrine of 'relative need' – what others built would determine USN cruiser strength – Washington countenanced a maximum fleet of 45 cruisers: 25 heavy and 20 light (McKercher, 1984). When the Preparatory Commission bogged down through disparate demands of land-based Powers led by France and maritime ones guided by Britain and America, in early 1927 Coolidge invited the five Washington treaty naval Powers to a conference limiting warships under 10,000 tons. France and Italy declined. However, it was surmised, if the three major naval Powers found agreement, they could foist it on the World Conference. Held in Geneva in summer 1927, the Coolidge Conference failed because Anglo-American compromise became impossible – Anglo-American relations fell to one of their lowest points in the twentieth century. Coolidge did not contest the 1928 presidential election; but after an ill-timed Anglo-French disarmament compromise in summer 1928 to reconcile ground and naval proposals in the Preparatory Commission, he announced in November that the United States would build the world's largest navy.

Cooler heads prevailed. By early 1929, the British Conservative government led by Stanley Baldwin (1924–1929) agreed that Britain would never surrender belligerent rights – explicit in cruiser equality, since these vessels were the principal defenders of sea routes. However, Baldwin was willing to travel to Washington to discuss the naval question with Coolidge's successor, Hoover. Preparations were underway for this visit when, in June, the Conservatives lost a general election to the Labour Party, led by MacDonald (McKercher, 1999: Chapter 1). MacDonald took over where Baldwin left off; working with the Cabinet and the Foreign Office – but not the Admiralty – he went to America in September 1929. He and Hoover struck a compromise; Anglo-American co-operation proved decisive at the London naval conference of January–April 1930 that renewed the Washington naval treaty for five more years. Anglo-American naval rivalry ended just as the Great Depression began.

Beginning in October 1929, the Depression proved a watershed in European and East Asian international politics as economic and financial disorder, massive unemployment in countries large and small, and its concomitant social and political dislocation saw radical prescriptions such as Nazism emerge to solve the crisis. Between 1931 and 1933, the advent of a military-dominated government in Tokyo fostered Japanese conquest of the Chinese province of Manchuria, its absorption into Japan's empire, and Japanese control of China north of the Great Wall. Undermining the Washington nine-Power treaty, Japan's conquest also threatened the East Asian

22 The origins of the 'Special Relationship'

balance of power. Hitler's appointment as German chancellor in January 1933 portended a shift in Europe's balance, which became clear to the British in October 1933, when Germany left the League and the World Disarmament Conference. In a perceptive analysis, the years 1929–1933 were 'hinge years', when the economic and security achievements of the 1920s were weakened irreparably (Steiner, 2005).

British and American responses to both situations differed. Isolationist America, even after Roosevelt took office in 1933, avoided involvement in meeting the changing patterns of power in Europe and East Asia. Congressional passage of neutrality laws after 1935 reinforced American isolation (Dallek, 1995). British coalition governments led by MacDonald (1931–1935) and Baldwin (1935–1937) supported rearmament and, with the Foreign Office, looked to maintain the European and East Asian balances. Although rearmament continued with increased spending, British strategy changed when Neville Chamberlain succeeded Baldwin in May 1937 (McKercher, 2008). Opting for appeasement, he sought to meet the reasonable demands of the dictator Powers, now including fascist Italy; but when Germany absorbed non-German-speaking Czech lands into the Reich in March 1939, appeasement was abandoned. To deter German aggression, Chamberlain's government guaranteed the sovereignty of Poland (Hitler's apparent next target), introduced peacetime conscription, began joint military planning with the French, and considered an Anglo-Soviet accord. Berlin moved first, negotiating the Nazi-Soviet non-aggression pact by 23 August 1939 and, reckoning that the British and French would do nothing, invaded Poland on 1 September (Steiner, 2011; Watt, 1989). Two days later, as America and the rest of the world watched, Britain and France honoured the Polish guarantee and declared war on Germany.

3 The Second World War and the advent of the 'Special Relationship'

The Relationship's strategic basis arose during the Second World War. It developed partly through a political partnership formed between Churchill and Roosevelt in the two years after Germany attacked Poland. After America became a belligerent in December 1941, Churchill and Roosevelt's collaboration increased. Their friendship mesmerised the popular mind, underscoring Churchill's sentimentalism about 'fraternal association' (Reynolds, 2003: 45). Yet beyond these personal ties – the Relationship long survived the demise of both men – and shared cultural, economic, and political traditions, the Powers acknowledged common strategic interests. Of course, whilst their war aims did not always intersect, they needed one another; and although America emerged by 1945 as the dominant partner, the Relationship with its transnational sentiments developed in a wartime context of expediency and *realpolitik*.

The immediate origins of the Relationship, September 1939–December 1941

The outbreak of war in Europe saw Chamberlain reorganise his government. With appeasement and deterrence proved hollow, the temper of his party and Parliament compelled him to bring his chief foreign policy critic into the War Cabinet. On 3 September, Churchill became first lord of the Admiralty (Neville, 2006). Another detractor, Eden, became dominions secretary. With a new ambassador to Washington, Lord Lothian, a staunch pro-American beginning his duties on 31 August, the political authority of leaders who promoted closer Anglo-American ties became amplified.

On 11 September, writing to Chamberlain and Churchill, Roosevelt suggested high-level Anglo-American contact: above polite insincerities, he wanted to know of British naval and strategic policy (Reynolds, 1981). Importantly, possessing little initial personal regard for Chamberlain or Churchill, Roosevelt wanted to reinforce British opposition to Germany by underlining his concern for Britain's predicament. Chamberlain and Churchill understood the importance of American support, although Churchill, too, had little personal regard for Roosevelt (Ball, 1979). Still,

24   The origins of the 'Special Relationship'

during winter 1939–1940, supported by Chamberlain and his foreign secretary, Lord Halifax, Churchill corresponded with Roosevelt, outwardly about naval developments, but really seeking aid for Britain's war effort by constructing political links with the centre of the American government.

The first seven months of the conflict was a 'Phony War' (Imlay, 2004). Although there were naval skirmishes and economic warfare – German submarines attacked Allied warships and merchant shipping; the RN blockaded Germany – there was no ground war until spring 1940. In this period, America remained in the second rank of British strategic calculations as Chamberlain's government pursued military and foreign policies mirroring Britain's 1914–1918 experience: devising Anglo-French strategy; developing a Supreme War Council; finding European allies; and dividing responsibilities – the French commanded the land war whilst London ran sea and British aerial operations (Gibbs, 1976).

Anglo-French efforts proved inadequate to blunt Germany's spring 1940 offensive. Norway and Denmark fell in April; Holland and Belgium, by 14 May; and, following German victory at Sedan on 15 May, Anglo-French forces in north-eastern France retreated (Jackson, 2003). The Germans moved south towards Paris and north to the Channel. Surrounded at the port of Dunkerque, the British Army with some French and Belgian units withdrew across the Channel by early June. A new French government surrendered on 22 June – Italy had declared war on Britain and France 12 days earlier. Chamberlain proved another of Hitler's victims. A parliamentary rebellion against his war leadership forced him from office on 10 May 1940; Churchill became premier (Self, 2006).

During the Phony War, two considerations shaped Anglo-American relations: Allied acquisition of American materiel and Roosevelt keeping the United States out of the fighting. Crucially, contemporaries did not see the Phony War as a prelude to inevitable German victory (Reynolds, 1981). Many thought the Anglo-French coalition could defeat Hitler. Thus, Chamberlain's government looked to America to augment Allied military strength. Concurrently pursuing Western Hemispheric security through their military and foreign policies, Roosevelt and his advisors sought to assist Britain and France without compromising American neutrality.

On 12 September 1939, Washington proclaimed an arms embargo and restricted American travel on belligerent ships. Lothian pressed Roosevelt and his secretary of state, Cordell Hull, to loosen the neutrality laws concerning Britain (Lothian to Halifax, 1939). Then receiving reports from Lothian, American diplomats in Europe, and others, Roosevelt wanted the embargo cancelled (Dallek, 1995). Following intensive White House lobbying and bipartisan intervention by internationalist Republicans, Congress amended the neutrality law by 2 November. Loans to governments that failed to pay war debts remained forbidden, and belligerents could not use American harbours as supply bases; but belligerents could purchase American goods on a cash-and-carry basis: using gold or dollars and transporting

The advent of the 'Special Relationship' 25

the goods themselves. Cash-and-carry benefitted the Allies because Germany lacked adequate sea power. As a result, Allied purchases increased markedly (Mitchell, 1990). Although London faced new problems – devalued sterling and dwindling dollar-gold holdings – and Allied purchases reduced American grain exports to Britain, a foundation for Anglo-American collaboration was in place by June 1940.

Co-operation also emerged over naval matters. After September 1939, Britain's blockade did not provoke the impassioned American reaction of 1914 to 1917. On 3 September, London explained that British actions would conform 'with the recognised rules applicable to the exercise of maritime belligerent rights' (Medlicott, 1952: 43–62). At Hull's suggestion, a committee of experts from Lothian's Embassy and the State Department established a certificate system mirroring one late in the First World War to reduce American annoyance. On 5 September, Roosevelt declared that American naval and air forces would patrol the Atlantic in a 'security zone' 300 miles from the coast (Baker, 2011: 28).

Roosevelt, several of his chief advisors, assorted politicians, some leading organs of the American media, the Roman Catholic hierarchy, and influential British émigrés supported British efforts during the Phony War. A growing group of prominent Americans saw it as in their country's interest to provide material and moral support to Britain simply because it was better that Britain, rather than the United States, fight Germany (Doenecke, 2000). In February and March 1940, Roosevelt attempted a half-hearted peace mission led by a State Department official, Sumner Welles. Although London approached this mission cautiously, Welles empathised with British reluctance to negotiate with Hitler (Casey, 2001: 13). Reporting that responsibility for the crisis lay in Berlin, he reckoned that supporting Britain could help restrain Hitler. The events of the following months demonstrated that restraint was impossible.

After France surrendered, Roosevelt saw German-dominated Europe as a strategic threat to the Western Hemisphere, a calculus pushing Britain and America closer together. In the next 17 months, until Japan attacked Europe's East Asian empires and the American colonies of Hawaii and the Philippines, their strategic interests merged. Obviously, some dimensions of Anglo-American relations remained problematic. Depleted British gold and dollar reserves endangered Britain's control over its informal empire – for instance, shortly after France fell, Roosevelt told a senior British official to sell Americans some British Argentinian securities (McKercher, 1999: 286). Assistance had a price, particularly in the Western Hemisphere, where American economic diplomacy and national security overlapped.

On 16 May 1940, facing congressional opposition, Roosevelt refused Churchill's request for loaning the RN 50 destroyers. French defeat changed the situation; Roosevelt decided to do everything possible to assist Britain. As general American opinion still opposed American action beyond the Western Hemisphere, he advised Churchill on 14 June, 'while our efforts

26 The origins of the 'Special Relationship'

will be exerted towards making available an ever increasing amount of materials and supplies', it was going to take time (Kimball, 1984: 47–8). He also indicated that the RN must not fall into enemy hands. Churchill then heard nothing for nearly two months.

American tradition limited presidents to two terms in office. Deciding to seek an extraordinary third term, Roosevelt had to prepare the political ground. At the Democratic National Convention in Chicago on 16 July, he won his party's nomination on the first ballot (Dunn, 2013). He appointed strong-willed Republican interventionists to his Cabinet to invigorate policymaking – Henry Stimson became war secretary – and secure bipartisan support for his policies. The War and State departments were to eliminate barriers blocking British access to American materiel. With senior military advisors, especially Army chief of staff General George Marshall, pressed to agree that supporting Britain would not dent hemispheric defence (Haglund, 1980), Roosevelt moved to improve its North American variant. On 17 August 1940, he met the Canadian premier, William Lyon Mackenzie King, to establish a Canadian-American Permanent Joint Board on Defence (Stacey, 1970). A series of its recommendations became operational by late August. Parallel to these efforts – reflecting Stimson's resolve to strengthen American external policy – the Selective Service Act allowed peacetime conscription (Clifford and Spencer, 1986).

Thus, Roosevelt revitalised American military policymaking, began strengthening the armed forces, addressed North American defence, and fortified his domestic political position. His policy reorientation unleashed dormant American diplomatic and military power tied to the country's long-standing economic, financial, and industrial strength. This strategy lacked altruism: America could exploit a weakened Britain. Thus, Roosevelt's first message to Churchill after two months' silence offered to trade 50 older destroyers for leases to build American naval and air bases in Britain's Newfoundland and Caribbean colonies and a commitment that if the RN found itself in an 'untenable' position in European waters, its warships would move to 'other parts of the Empire'. Because Britain stood alone fighting the Axis, Churchill accepted Roosevelt's demands (Reynolds, 1993). Still, Churchill bound neutral America to belligerent Britain. Fracturing isolationism, Roosevelt demonstrated to American voters that they acquired concrete rewards in the destroyers-for-bases deal – Wendell Willkie, the Republican presidential nominee, was exploiting this shift in opinion to back greater support for Britain. Equally significant, Roosevelt aligned with Britain against the Axis and, by obtaining bases at British expense, strengthened American forces strategically for possible struggle against them.

Between the 2 September 1940 signing of the destroyers-for-bases deal and 7 December 1941, when Japan attacked Pearl Harbor, Britain and America drew closer together. Whilst the Churchill-Roosevelt partnership remained vital, more important were converging interests concerning Axis defeat in Europe and, until Pearl Harbor, limiting Japan's East Asian ambitions.

The advent of the 'Special Relationship' 27

London's basic concern during those 15 months resided with obtaining food, raw materials, war materiel, and other supplies to defend the home islands and Britain's Mediterranean position. Roosevelt endeavoured to provide these resources and, concurrently, push American rearmament. His double task became easier after he defeated Willkie on 5 November (Blower, 2014).

Even before the destroyers-for-bases deal, Britain increasingly pressed America for expanded support. During the Battle of Britain, Churchill and Lothian lobbied Roosevelt; finding Washington helpful, the British Purchasing Commission obtained as much American materiel as possible (Kimball, 1984: 71, 74, 78). To demonstrate its commitment, Britain began transferring important and highly secret technical information to the American army and navy (Phelps, 2010). However, London overestimated Roosevelt's commitment to go to war (Bailey, 2013: Chapter 4; Reynolds, 1981). By mid-November, Lothian reported that although American opinion was moving towards greater intervention, full support was yet impossible. On 7 December 1940, the newly re-elected Roosevelt received a 20-page missive from Churchill that concentrated on German submarine attacks and addressed financial and strategic issues, munitions supply, and British war production.

With Roosevelt convinced about increasing aid, Churchill and Lothian's lobbying spurred the White House. Legislation reached Congress to lend or lease American-produced war materiel to any Power that the president calculated could safeguard the United States. Despite isolationist dissent, Congress passed the Lend-Lease Bill on 8 March 1941. Whilst the bill avoided explicit mention of Britain – Roosevelt wanted the liberty to aid other pro-American regimes – Churchill was elated (Churchill, 1949a: 569). Whether American voters grasped these motives, concrete co-operation expanded (Butler, 1957). Secret Anglo-American staff talks occurred in Washington in January 1941 to canvass both a combined global strategy and plans for Atlantic defence. By April, as the US Navy created a security zone running in the Atlantic from the Azores to Greenland, American vessels assisted RN anti-submarine operations by notifying London of German U-boat sightings.

Until the attack on Pearl Harbor, Roosevelt's Administration continued protecting American interests, especially economic ones, as much as assisting Britain. Lothian understood this purpose as early as April 1940 (Lothian despatch to Halifax, 1940). Roosevelt was guided by *realpolitik*. Thus, Washington drove hard bargains over wheat exports, sterling-dollar balances, and merchant shipping, which strengthened America. Whilst American policies galled some British leaders, such as Indian Secretary Leopold Amery, (Barnes and Nicholson, 1988), Churchill showed pragmatism. To safeguard the home islands, fight in the Mediterranean, and retain the empire, Britain needed assistance; Roosevelt's price required payment with British economic, political, and strategic capital.

Lend-Lease came as the war's landscape transformed. By early 1941, Italian armies confronted an effective Greek counteroffensive in the

28 *The origins of the 'Special Relationship'*

Balkans and a British one in North Africa; Hitler responded with German forces in both places (Blau, 1997; Kitchen, 2009). By late May, the Germans controlled the Balkans; reckoning that he could ignore a weakened Britain until his submarine offensive enfeebled it more, Hitler shifted his focus. Believing Germany secure in Western Europe, the Balkans, and North Africa, his armies attacked Russia on 22 June 1941 (Hartmann, 2013). Britain was now no longer alone in fighting the Axis. Although the Germans had initial success, by December cold weather and Red Army resistance halted the Germans on a front stretching from the Crimea in the south to Leningrad and Moscow in the north. Receiving Lend-Lease aid by autumn 1941, Russian forces began regrouping, rearming, and planning a counterstroke in 1942. Their operations rekindled British efforts in the other theatres.

The Far East also changed (Tohmatsu and Willmott, 2004). By mid-1939, Japanese forces controlled Manchuria, China's coast, and the important rivers; however, in other areas of China they confronted armed KMT and CCP opposition. Notwithstanding the Chinese quagmire, Japan retained territorial ambitions in East Asia. It fought Russia fruitlessly in summer 1939 on the Manchurian-Siberian frontier. Thereafter looking southwards, Tokyo consolidated its position in China and profited from White Imperial Power concentration on the mounting European crisis. By August 1939, other matters – primarily Washington ending the Japanese-American trade treaty, London granting China export credits, and conclusion of the Nazi-Soviet non-aggression pact – had seen Japan enter a quiescent period respecting Britain, America, and the other White Imperial Powers.

A core element of British strategy involved despatching a fleet to Singapore to meet a Far Eastern crisis (Callahan, 2002). But following France's defeat and Italy's offensive against Egypt, British forces concentrated on defence of the Mediterranean and the home islands. After Japan occupied French Indochina in July 1940, Churchill remained cautious. Europe and the Mediterranean were more important strategically; and, until 7 December 1941, although many of his advisors disagreed, Churchill reckoned a Japanese offensive unrealistic. He thought the possibility of American armed intervention would deter Japan. Confronting Germany and Italy in the West, Churchill's government relinquished the Far East to the Americans. Britain's regional influence declined; America's increased.

Japanese-American talks had been progressing since March 1941 (Ford, 2012). War in the Pacific seemed avoidable, despite a Russo-Japanese non-aggression pact concluded in April: Roosevelt and his advisors seemed willing to accept Japan's Manchurian conquest and acknowledge its leading position in China if, precluding further expansion, Tokyo withdrew north of the Great Wall. Unwilling to withdraw from French Indochina and southern China, Japan's leadership refused; in pursuit of raw materials, especially oil, it looked to fashion a new East Asian order. Although negotiations continued, Japanese-American compromise proved elusive. Ultimately, Tokyo chose war. On 7 December 1941, whilst striking south into Malaya, the Philippines, and the Dutch East Indies, Japanese forces attacked Pearl Harbor. Four days later, Germany and Italy declared war on America. Churchill's desire for American participation in the European war was now realised. Anglo-American relations would never be the same.

Churchill and Roosevelt: war and diplomacy, December 1941–November 1943

British and American forces fought together in the Atlantic, in the air war against Germany and Italy, in North Africa after November 1942, during the subsequent invasion of Italy and southern France, and, beginning in June 1944, in the cross-Channel Normandy invasion and final offensive against Nazi Germany (Connelly, 2001; Haslop, 2013; Lieb, 2014; O'Hara, 2015). Whilst the Americans fought in the Pacific virtually by themselves – which was what they wanted – the British moved from India to recapture Burma, Malaya, and Singapore from the Japanese (Dunlop, 2009). Little doubt exists that the Russians proved vital in Europe in defeating Germany, whilst the KMT and CCP tied down Japanese forces on mainland China (Liedtke,

Figure 3.1 Winston Churchill and Franklin Roosevelt, Yalta, February 1945
© Everett Collection Historical / Alamy

30   *The origins of the 'Special Relationship'*

2016; Mitter, 2013). Nonetheless, Anglo-American military co-operation strengthened the strategic relationship developing before December 1941. It was sometimes fraught with disagreements and differing perceptions, which affected war-making and spilt historical ink. For instance, Churchill opposed the American proposition to invade southern France in mid-August 1944 because it would divert men and materiel away from the 'soft underbelly of Europe' – Italy and Yugoslavia – and his desired assault on Germany from the south (Gassend, 2014). Given American financial and material support for Britain, the British general Sir Bernard Montgomery rankled American commanders' sensitivities with imperious demands for men and equipment and efforts to dominate western Allied strategy after the cross-Channel invasion – code-named D-Day (Eisenhower, 1986). Nonetheless, overall, British and American forces fought together effectively, overwhelmed Japan and fascist Italy, and helped to defeat Nazi Germany.

As Britain served as the strategic base for Anglo-American European operations, the presence of several hundred thousand American soldiers, sailors, and aviators in the country deepened cultural connexions between the two peoples. Motion pictures stressed the fight against the common enemy, collective values, and shared efforts by Anglo-American leaders and their armed forces. From a huge number of war movies to the 1942 Humphrey Bogart vehicle *Casablanca*, to Gainsborough Studio's *2,000 Women*, all emphasised the jointness for victory. Many cinema actors – for instance, Laurence Olivier, James Cagney, and Greer Garson – became Anglo-American stars (Bennett, 2012). Shared and popular music and dance – especially the jitterbug – with vocalists such as Vera Lynn and Bing Crosby and bandleaders such as Henry Hall and Glenn Miller, became central to a wartime culture (Fauser, 2013: Chapter 3). Perhaps most important, marriage between American servicemen and British women produced 70,000 families with transnational ties (Reynolds, 1995). As the American Transatlantic Brides and Parents Association remarked in 1947: 'Our aims are to foster Anglo-American relationships and continue TBPA as a permanent link with our British heritage' (Virden, 1996: 126).

With social and cultural connexions below and the military confrontation at the fore, beginning in 1941 the Relationship's sinews emerged in bilateral and multilateral diplomacy that set alliance policy and created a series of institutions by which Britain and America co-operated more fully. Churchill and Roosevelt first met face-to-face in mid-August 1941 at Placentia Bay in Newfoundland (Wilson, 1991). Each leader had specific goals for the meeting that went unrealised. Churchill wanted to entice the Americans into the war or at least increase military assistance and have Washington caution Tokyo against further aggression in East Asia. Roosevelt looked to embolden the American public to support entering the war on the Allied side and have Britain end imperial duties established in 1932 as repayment for its Lend-Lease supplies.

The advent of the 'Special Relationship' 31

However, the Atlantic Conference produced a 'Charter' that in effect amounted to Anglo-American goals for after the war. [Document 2]. Britain and America eschewed territorial aggrandisement; territorial changes would respect their populations' wishes; self-government would be restored to those who lost it; freer trade would occur; international co-operation would improve economic and social conditions by tackling fear and want; freedom of the seas would ensue; and after disarming the aggressor Powers – presaging the League's demise – resolving crises by force would be abandoned. Thus, Churchill brought the Americans closer to Britain despite not getting Roosevelt to join the armed struggle. For his part, harkening back to Wilson's Fourteen Points, Roosevelt helped produce a set of internationalist goals that the American public generally could support in addition to pursuing narrow national interests. With the promotion of self-government lay one issue of future contention: decolonising the British Empire.

The attack on Pearl Harbor accelerated Anglo-American co-operation. Before Christmas 1941, Churchill travelled to Washington to confer with Roosevelt in discussions code-named Arcadia (Dallek, 1995; Gilbert, 1986). From 23 December 1941 to 14 January 1942, they agreed on a combined strategy and built a structure to implement effective decision-making. Discussions were sometimes uneasy, a function of pressures on Roosevelt to deal with Japan and, reflecting distrust of Britain amongst some of his key advisors, distaste for using American power to prop up the British Empire. Nevertheless, the crucial decision involved a 'Europe-first' strategy. Two principal motives underlay it: ensure Britain's survival – it would be the base for operations on the continent – and demonstrate to Joseph Stalin, the Soviet dictator, that Russia was not fighting alone – given the Nazi-Soviet pact, a separate Russo-German peace settlement was not beyond the realm of possibility.

Although Moscow pressed for a second front against Germany via a cross-Channel invasion (Watson, 2002), Churchill succeeded in winning Roosevelt's approval for a 'peripheral strategy': whilst clearing the Axis out of North Africa, invading Italy, and moving north to Germany, the British and American air forces would heavily bomb Germany and its allies. The reasoning lay with inadequate numbers of troops and ships to cross the Channel – the British Army was committed in North Africa – and uncertainty whether amphibious landings in northern France would succeed. Accordingly, in 1942 it was decided to fight in North Africa, send American bomber forces to Britain, and, to better confront Japan, strengthen British Far Eastern forces. At Arcadia, Roosevelt overcame the military advisors' arguments against the 'peripheral' strategy, although Anglo-American operations in North Africa would augment Britain's ability to defend its Mediterranean position and, thus, access to its eastern empire. To demonstrate Allied solidarity, a 'Declaration by the United Nations' was drafted affirming the Atlantic Charter and obliging its signatories – Russia and 23 other Powers – not to conclude separate peace agreements with the Axis (Roll, 2013).

32 The origins of the 'Special Relationship'

More important, Churchill and Roosevelt created a Combined Chiefs of Staff (CCS) in Washington to determine strategy, co-ordinate supply, and make all military decisions (Rigby, 2012). Each Power's service chiefs or their deputies would meet in regular session and, should decisions there prove impossible, send issues to Churchill and Roosevelt for resolution. Ultimately, the CCS constituted a large organisation of subordinate experts, a secretariat, and subcommittees advising on matters of supply, shipping, and strategy. It also commanded Allied forces in their various theatres of war; accepting Anglo-American leadership, Allied governments were consulted when necessary. By mid-1942, responsibility for the various theatres had been determined: the Americans would handle the Pacific; the British, the Middle East and Indian Ocean; Europe and the Mediterranean-Atlantic became an Anglo-American responsibility. In China, the KMT would command its forces in collaboration with the Americans.

By late 1942, Anglo-American forces had Germany's *Afrikakorps* on the run and, after stymieing Japan's offensive the previous June, the Americans began advancing slowly towards the Japanese home islands (Henry, 2003; Prange et al., 1982). At the same time, the British and American air forces were bombing Germany, occupied Europe, and Italy (Davis, 2006). In Europe and North Africa, the record proved mixed. The CCS assumed that North Africa would be cleared by December 1942, but it was not so until the next May (Atkinson, 2002). Moreover, the Russians learnt that a cross-Channel invasion was impossible in 1943, underscored by a failed raid at Dieppe to test Germany's Channel coast defences (Zuehlke, 2012).

In this atmosphere, Churchill and Roosevelt were to meet Stalin at Casablanca in January 1943 (Farrell, 1993). With the critical Battle of Stalingrad underway, however, Stalin remained in Moscow to ensure effective leadership at home. American and British civilian officials and senior officers had been divided over a range of issues concerning both Powers' long-term objectives – for instance, administering oil-rich Middle Eastern territory – and many Americans felt the British were more concerned with the European rather than the Pacific war (Stoler, 2000). With some acrimony, the central issue addressed by the two leaders and the CCS involved strategy for 1943. Parroting Marshall's advice, Roosevelt sought a cross-Channel invasion; Churchill – backed by his Army chief, Sir Alan Brooke, and with Dieppe as a lesson – argued for invading Italy once Axis forces were dislodged from North Africa. Roosevelt also criticised the British for not committing fully against Japan. A compromise emerged: the peripheral strategy involving Italy would continue, and Churchill promised increased forces and materiel in Southeast Asia to aid the KMT.

Perhaps most important was Roosevelt's unexpected announcement on the final day of the conference that Britain and America were fighting for Axis 'unconditional' surrender (O'Connor, 1971). It surprised Churchill, who said nothing publicly. Roosevelt did not want to repeat 1918: Hitler

The advent of the 'Special Relationship' 33

had exploited the notion that the German Army had not lost that war but that defeatists had betrayed it at home. Thus, applying 'unconditional' surrender to the enemy regimes, Roosevelt emphasised, 'We mean no harm to the common people of the Axis nations' [Document 3]. His reason for the announcement also concerned letting Stalin know of continuing Anglo-American support for Russia's war effort, which was at a critical juncture because of Stalingrad. The two Western Powers were now committed to complete military victory and no negotiated settlements.

Britain, America, and the advent of a new world order, November 1943–May 1945

By late 1943, Allied successes had begun to mount. Following Mussolini's overthrow in July and conquering Sicily by August, Anglo-American-Canadian forces invaded Italy and slowly advanced up the peninsula. Confronting an increasingly brutal Anglo-American bombing campaign, the Germans were also losing the Battle of the Atlantic through effective Allied anti-submarine warfare and America's mammoth industrial production of warships and merchantmen. In the Pacific and Southeast Asia, British and American forces were slowly forcing the Japanese to retreat; and most important, Russian victory at Stalingrad by February initiated Soviet counteroffensives that decimated the *Wehrmacht* and forced it westwards.

Churchill and Roosevelt met at Quebec City in August – principally agreeing to explore a cross-Channel invasion, augmenting strategic bombing against Germany, increasing Allied forces in Italy, fixing strategy for the continuing offensive against Japan, and co-ordinating Anglo-American-Canadian development of the atomic bomb; with the exception of the atomic decision, Stalin was informed of these conclusions [Document 4]. However, the key intra-Allied conference occurred at Tehran in November: the 'Big Three' – Churchill, Roosevelt, and Stalin – met for the first time.

Beyond further considering strategy, the Tehran Conference signified two things (Mayle, 1987). It saw the first serious discussion of the post-war international order and witnessed clear American dominance over Britain. In discussions with Churchill and Roosevelt, Stalin demanded eastern Polish territory lost in 1920; in return, Poland would acquire German territory east of the Oder-Neisse rivers. Plebiscites in line with the Soviet constitution would determine the Baltic States' fate. Created the previous month, the European Advisory Commission comprising the 'Big Three' foreign secretaries – Eden, Hull, and Vyacheslav Molotov – would examine defeated Germany's division into Allied zones of occupation. And a 'Declaration of the Three Powers Regarding Iran' was agreed. The British and Russians had occupied that country in 1941 to overthrow its pro-Nazi emperor – Britain also controlled southern Iranian oilfields. In essence, the 'Declaration' promised Allied economic assistance during and after the war and the maintenance of Iranian sovereignty and territory.

34   *The origins of the 'Special Relationship'*

The Tehran Conference also established committees to examine creating a new international security organisation, the UN, and to address post-war economic and financial reconstruction.

To Churchill's chagrin and despite the president's public bonhomie, Roosevelt pointedly met privately with Stalin. Red Army success in 1943 gave Stalin decided diplomatic strength and, looking for post-war co-operation with a powerful Russia, Roosevelt sought common ground. He believed that he could balance between the conservative monarchist Churchill and the Bolshevik revolutionary Stalin. As America's contribution in blood and treasure had to produce effective post-war international security, he elaborated to Stalin on the UN, where 'four policemen' – Britain, China, Soviet Russia, and America – would lead. Smaller Powers would be there, but the new organisation had to reflect international realities: Soviet Russia would have a prominent part and an America willing to work with it. Stalin reiterated strongly his long-standing demand for a cross-Channel invasion. The Red Army's 1944 summer offensive, he said, would not happen until such an invasion occurred. Roosevelt agreed to an assault in spring 1944, forcing Churchill to yield to his partners' resolve for a 'second front' in northern France and accept an American supreme military commander, General Dwight Eisenhower (Mayle, 1987). If not clear already, this major strategic decision demonstrated that Britain had become subordinate to America and Soviet Russia. Preparations for the cross-Channel invasion, plus those for the UN and the financial and economic organisations, then ensued.

Britain's weakening political influence within the alliance had not occurred suddenly in November 1943. Much devolved from the parlous state of British finances and massive American economic and material support for the Allied war effort (Hancock and Gowing, 1975; cf. Barnet, 1986). Still worried about a cross-Channel invasion succeeding and transferring troops from southern Europe, Churchill hoped to delay D-Day. In March 1944, he sought a meeting with Roosevelt 'not so much [because] . . . there are new departures in policy to be taken but there is a need after more than 90 days of separation [since Tehran] for checking up and shaking together' (Churchill to Roosevelt, 1944: 3–4). Roosevelt politely declined, citing slight illness. Although Churchill pressed for a get-together, his overtures failed – possibly due to foot-dragging – until after D-Day.

As 1944 progressed, Washington stood as the power centre in Anglo-American relations; Roosevelt wanted the emerging post-war international structures to profit the United States. Eden now represented British disfavour with American policies; 'Anything referred to the U.S.A. is at once blocked by Hull or President who are afraid of anything being done at all except by themselves' (Harvey, 1978: 348). After D-Day, Allied strategy in Western Europe and the Mediterranean divided the CCS: the Americans advocated transferring troops and resources from Italy north, leaving only enough forces to protect the gains made; the British disagreed (Annexes in CCS, 1944). Churchill told Roosevelt on 28 June that 'The deadlock between our

The advent of the 'Special Relationship'   35

Chiefs of Staff raises most serious issues' (Kimball, 1984: 212–13). Broad strategic questions of where post-D-Day Allied forces should fight – and in what strength – needed examination at the highest level. Roosevelt relented, meeting Churchill again at Quebec City in mid-September after Allied armies broke out of northern France towards Germany and the Red Army commenced its summer offensive.

At Quebec, Churchill and Roosevelt examined Allied occupation zones in post-war Germany, German demilitarisation, further lend-lease aid to Britain, and RN deployment against Japan – and Roosevelt promised joint Anglo-American control of atomic weapons (Woolner, 1998). However, by September 1944, Churchill and his advisors were disturbed about Russia's position in post-war Europe; in August, the situation became critical because of Poland, where the Red Army refused to aid the non-communist resistance in a deadly struggle against the Germans in Warsaw and then helped the Polish communists assume power (McKercher, 1998). With a continuing American presence in Europe uncertain after the war, a Soviet Russian–dominated continent would diminish Britain's ability to protect its economic and financial security and political interests. Churchill had to balance between Roosevelt and Stalin. Roosevelt learnt that Churchill and Eden intended to travel to Moscow 'to clinch [Stalin's] coming in against Japan and, secondly, to try to effect a friendly settlement with Poland' (Kimball, 1984: 340–1). Roosevelt held mixed views about this enterprise, frowning on high-level meetings he could not attend – he was then seeking a fourth presidential term. Still, wanting to promote good Soviet-American relations blemished since Tehran over Poland, the UN talks, and other issues, he supported the Churchill-Stalin meetings – but to allow disapproval of any agreement he opposed without any American presence (Dallek, 1995). A Churchill-Stalin trade-off in October established spheres of interest in south-central Europe and the Balkans in a 'percentages' agreement that kept the Russians away from the Mediterranean (Holdich, 1987).

After the conference at Quebec, Churchill remained uncertain about Britain's place in the higher direction of the war. Admittedly, he had made gains. Whilst acquiring a free hand in Poland, the Russians would remain out of the Mediterranean. Britain retained a leading role in the Mediterranean and Southeast Asian campaigns, it helped determine Germany's zonal occupation, its forces in post-war Europe would revert to British command, and there would be Anglo-American collaboration over atomic energy. Yet, Roosevelt's strategic vision to defeat Germany remained unchanged, and Britain would interfere little in America's Pacific strategy in the final offensive against Japan; moreover, Roosevelt had said nothing about the percentages agreement and virtually nothing about Poland. He seemed more concerned about post-war Soviet-American amity and running for a fourth term. Whilst talking about committing to the UN, he avoided mentioning a post-war American presence in Europe [Document 5]. The British had

36 The origins of the 'Special Relationship'

to consider that supported only by liberated France, they might face a militarily potent Russia in post-war Europe without American support.

In February 1945, with German defeat imminent, the 'Big Three' met at Yalta in the Crimea (Harbutt, 2010). Through hard bargaining, they reached several crucial decisions that ultimately shaped the post-war international order. With America's long-term military commitment in Europe uncertain, Churchill wanted a French occupation zone in Germany. Roosevelt and Stalin agreed – the latter as long as it was not carved from the anticipated Soviet zone. To quicken Japan's defeat – the atomic bomb's effectiveness was yet to be seen – Roosevelt sought Russian intervention against Japan; Stalin agreed to comply within three months of German defeat. Churchill and Roosevelt paid his price for the French zone and declaring war against Japan by recognising the legality of the pro-Soviet regimes emerging in Eastern Europe, their elections, and borders – including Poland. Furthermore, the Russians would take some Japanese territories, principally southern Sakhalin and the Kuril Islands, plus a lease for Port Arthur. Affirming unconditional surrender, the three agreed to split post-war Germany and Berlin each into four occupation zones. Germany would be demilitarised and de-Nazified, Nazi war criminals would face trial, and a committee headquartered in Russia would determine reparations. Although the Tehran-inspired economic and financial organisations – the World Bank and IMF – were to come into existence, Roosevelt laid great emphasis on establishing the UN. In prickly talks with Roosevelt, Stalin agreed finally on Soviet membership, the key concession being that three Soviet republics – Russia, Byelorussia, and Ukraine – would become members, to offset the Western Powers and their allies. Wanting to create the organisation as soon as possible to build on wartime Allied solidarity, Roosevelt pushed for a founding conference, which began meeting at San Francisco in late April. The Yalta Conference remains an issue of great historical controversy because Roosevelt and Churchill acceded to Russian dominance of Eastern and Central Europe (Meacham, 2005). However, the situation required difficult decision-making. Churchill and Roosevelt had particular aims, and, with the Red Army entrenched in the region, bargained with Stalin to achieve them. It was a simple matter of *realpolitik*.

Thus, as victory in Europe neared, Anglo-American relations remained firm, although Roosevelt looked to work with Russia. He and his advisors did not downplay Britain in their calculations. Despite American desires for decolonisation, Britain, with its empire, remained a Great Power. The social and philosophical links between the two English-speaking peoples had not diminished; shared cultural and sentimental connexions amplified by fighting the war together had strengthened them. More important, strategically, Britain would constitute America's chief ally in rebuilding the international order in whatever guise the United States cloaked itself. Isolation was unlikely, but the level of American commitment to international security and reconstruction remained unclear. Still, vis-à-vis both America and Soviet Russia, Churchill's government faced difficult decisions. Churchill grasped American economic, financial, and military potency and the importance of America underwriting British efforts to maintain international peace and security. With peace, however, the Relationship would confront different international circumstances. When Roosevelt died suddenly on 12 April 1945, three weeks before German surrender, the personal partnership underpinning the Relationship ended.

Part III

Cold War, limited war, and the 'Special Relationship', 1945–2015

4 The 'Special Relationship' and the early Cold War, May 1945–July 1954

In the half decade after 1945, despite continuing Anglo-American rivalry over trade, investment, and the beginnings of British decolonisation, the 'Special Relationship' was strengthened. Notwithstanding beliefs that Great Power co-operation would ensure international peace through the UN, Western perceptions of Soviet aggression in Europe and the Middle East led America to commit to the economic and military security of those areas of the world where it and its allies had major interests. In this equation, Britain stood as America's principal ally, partly as the legacy of the Second World War and partly because the new leaders in Washington and London realised that their strategic interests intersected.

The result was 'Cold War', with America, Britain, and their allies on one side and Russia on the other. Bernard Baruch, a presidential advisor since Wilson, first used the term in April 1947. With atomic weapons in the background and 'hot' war involving Great Powers unlikely, protecting national interests saw rivalry based on diplomatic confrontation, economic competition, propaganda, threats of intervention, using proxy Powers, and other actions. For realist diplomatists in Washington, the Kremlin, and Whitehall, this situation was unsurprising. Great Powers had existed in an international anarchy since the mid-seventeenth century. Stability rather than peace constituted the new order's leitmotif. However, suffused by ideology – liberal democracy versus Marxism-Leninism – the Cold War created new contours of the Relationship and ensured that its wartime achievements remained the basis of the Western alliance system.

The genesis of the Cold War, May 1945–June 1948

On becoming president, Truman relied on advisors who, unlike Roosevelt, mirrored British mistrust of Stalin's foreign policy. Secretary of War Stimson, US ambassador to Moscow Averell Harriman, and Admiral William Leahy, the presidential chief of staff, looked for a leading American international role once peace returned. They and others tended to perceive the Russians as aggressive and brutal adversaries whom it was dangerous to trust. Truman was a foreign policy neophyte having made his reputation in

42   *Cold War and limited war, 1945–2015*

domestic politics; Roosevelt had confided little to him, especially regarding atomic bomb development. The first inclination that Truman's attitudes differed from those of his predecessor came in late April 1945 when the Soviet foreign minister, Molotov, visited Washington en route to the San Francisco conference: Truman bluntly told Molotov that he felt as though Soviet policy concerning Poland violated the Yalta agreement (Anslover, 2014).

Soviet consolidation in Central and Eastern Europe over the next few months, with growing Anglo-American misgivings about Stalin's objectives, provided the background of another 'Big Three' meeting at Potsdam, outside Berlin, in late July (Feis, 1967). Apart from decisions made at Potsdam, a signal event occurred in Britain during the deliberations. On 26 July, Churchill and the Conservatives lost the British general election – the socialist Labour Party took power under Clement Attlee; different leaders would now guide and exploit the Relationship.

The meeting at Potsdam was to address pressing issues before a final peace settlement – a Council of Foreign Ministers (CFM) of the American, British, and Russian ministers would handle issues arising from Potsdam, including preparing for the peace conference [Document 6]. The most important concerned Germany, where the Big Three sought demilitarisation, de-Nazification, democratisation, decentralisation, and decartelisation. In line with previous discussions, Germany and, now treated separately, Austria – and their two capitals, Berlin and Vienna – would each have four occupation zones. Separate ACCs comprising the Allied military commanders would govern them. Nullifying Hitler's territorial conquests, Germany's eastern border would move west to the Oder-Neisse line, and Germans inhabiting Poland, Czechoslovakia, and Hungary would be expelled. Nazi Party members would be removed from government, industry, and finance, and Nazi war criminals would face prosecution. With Allied political control to prevent the revanchism that had occurred under Hitler, neutering Germany's war-making potential – destroying or controlling all industry with military potential – would produce an economy based on agriculture and light manufacturing. Additionally, surplus industrial capacity determined by the ACCs would become reparations, and potential war-making capacity such as metallurgy, chemicals, and electronics would be limited to rudimentary German requirements. Further blocks entailed Allied control of trade. The Soviets could take reparations from their occupation zone and, within two years, 10 percent of surplus industrial capital investment in the Western ones.

Although the Yalta Conference had dealt with Poland, the 'Big Three' recognised the emerging communist government – the Red Army occupied the country – which for Britain meant formally abandoning the Polish guarantee. Along with the Oder-Neisse frontier – legal recognition would come at the anticipated peace conference – Poland would acquire sections of East Prussia and the port of Danzig.

Respecting the Far East, American planners reckoned fighting would continue into 1946. However, with the atomic bomb's successful test, Truman informed Stalin on 24 July that America now possessed 'a new weapon of unusual destructive force'. The Russian premier, he noted, 'showed no special interest' (Truman, 1955: 416; cf. Churchill, 1949b: 669–70). Stalin had interest – his intelligence services were penetrating the Anglo-American-Canadian bomb project (Andrew and Mitrokhin, 1999) – but he could say little. Always realistic, he accepted that the Americans temporarily had stolen a march on Russia and Washington's diplomacy had added potency. Nonetheless, Japanese defeat in French Indochina meant that non-American troops needed deployment there – the thrust to Japan diverted American forces. The British would occupy the south and the KMT the north until French forces could return – highlighting post-war geopolitical realities interfering with American desires for decolonisation. On 26 July, because of the Soviet-Japanese non-aggression pact, Truman, Churchill, and Chiang Kai-shek, the KMT leader, issued the 'Potsdam declaration' laying out unconditional peace terms – for instance, disarming all Japanese forces – and threatened Japan with 'prompt and utter destruction' if it did not surrender ('Proclamation defining terms . . .', 1945).

At Potsdam, the new Anglo-American leadership – Truman, his secretary of state, James Byrnes, Attlee, and Ernest Bevin, Attlee's foreign secretary – met

Figure 4.1 Harry Truman and Clement Attlee, Washington, DC, February 1946
© Bettmann / Getty

44 *Cold War and limited war, 1945–2015*

for the first time. The British leaders continued Churchill and Eden's policies and, at the highest level, Truman and Attlee developed 'business-like' relations 'without any special personal rapport' (Miscamble, 2007: 204). This fact demonstrated that the Relationship went beyond personal diplomacy, although the strongly anti-communist Bevin, a trade unionist who long opposed Marxist socialists, appeared far more animated in desiring co-operation with the Americans (Bullock, 1983). Truman and Byrnes initially thought Bevin 'graceless and rough' (Bullock, 1983: 205n127), but his staunch support for the Anglo-American relationship overcame such prejudices.

On 6 August 1945, the Americans used the atomic bomb on Japan, at Hiroshima, and, when Tokyo failed to surrender, bombed a second city, Nagasaki, on 9 August (Hasegawa, 2005). Six days later, Japan capitulated, its only caveat that the emperor remain on his throne – despite unconditional surrender, the Americans conceded, to ensure a peaceful American occupation of Japan. In line with the Yalta agreement, Russian forces invaded northern China on 8 August, seizing substantial territory, and with European armed forces returning to their colonies, the Far East was shaping into a region of Great Power rivalry. Some historians see Truman's decision to use the bomb as demonstrating to Stalin a need to tread carefully where American interests were involved – with Japan near surrender, the Americans needlessly killed Japanese civilians and initiated the Cold War (Alperovitz, 1965). Realistic views argue that Truman saved several hundred thousand American lives by using the bomb rather than invading Japan's home islands; that Russia could be instructed in American power remained an important benefit (Miscamble, 2007: Chapter 6). Growing mistrust already existed between the British and Americans, on one side, and the Russians, on the other, over the delayed second front and Soviet actions in Central and Eastern Europe. With Japan's formal surrender on 2 September, the Cold War was underway.

Seeking strategic advantage on Russia's southern reaches before Potsdam, Moscow pressured Turkey over bases on and access to the straits connecting the Black and Mediterranean seas (Mark, 1997). Moreover, seeking strategic advantage for his navy in the Mediterranean, Stalin demanded a share in administering Libya, Italy's former North African colony – the two Western Allies occupied Italy. Anglo-American resistance held firm about Turkish territorial integrity – neutral until March 1945, Turkey had joined the Allied side; the British and, later, the French had jointly occupied Libya after Axis defeat there in 1943. Just as Stalin brooked no interference in Central and Eastern Europe, Britain and America did not intend to do so in areas liberated by their armies. This crisis accentuated Anglo-American perceptions of Soviet expansionism.

More crucial was Iran. In 1942, Britain and Russia agreed to end their occupation of Iran six months after the war. Affirmed at Tehran and CFM meetings in London in September to October 1945, complete troop

The early Cold War, May 1945–July 1954   45

evacuation would occur by 2 March 1946 (Kennedy-Pipe, 1995). The British began evacuating, but the Russians reinforced Red Army units and promoted separatism in Azerbaijan Province, adjacent to their border. Looking to build a buffer and acquire oil rights, Russian action precipitated a crisis that, unexpectedly for Stalin, brought the Americans into play. With Byrnes ambivalent about Iran at the December CFM [Document 7], Stalin believed he would deal with the British, but Truman decided to support Britain, which meant possible American military involvement – with the atomic bomb in the background (Rahman et al., 2013). The president was motivated by supporting Britain to meet Russian regional aggrandisement and growing disfavour in Congress towards Soviet policies. By May, with UN involvement to resolve the situation, Russian forces were withdrawing, Azerbaijani separatism weakened, and an uneasy stability returned to the region.

Concurrent extension of Soviet influence in Eastern and Central Europe added to Western perceptions of Russian aggressiveness. Perhaps the Soviets honestly wanted to build a defensive perimeter there – Russia had suffered invasion from the west in 1812, 1914, and 1941. They might have even tried to reconcile establishing post-war spheres of influence in Europe by co-operation with Britain and America (Roberts, 1999). However, imposing communist regimes subservient to Moscow – plus the brutality with which Soviet-backed security forces imposed totalitarian rule – added to perceptions of the Soviet threat. In a letter supposedly written to Byrnes but then read to him, Truman observed: 'unless Russia is faced with an iron fist and strong language another war is in the making. Only one language do they understand – How many divisions have you' (Ferrell, 1980: 79–80). In London, still unclear about finding a *modus vivendi* with Moscow, some in Bevin's Foreign Office advocated a stronger stand against the Russians (Warner, 1996).

Perhaps the best expression of growing Anglo-American perceptions of the Soviet menace came from Churchill. Now leader of the Opposition, he spoke in March 1946 at Westminster College in Fulton, Missouri – Truman's home state. After receiving an honorary degree, with the president sitting beside him, Churchill delivered his so-called Iron Curtain speech:

> From Stettin in the Baltic to Trieste in the Adriatic an *iron curtain* has descended across the Continent. Behind that line lie all the capitals of the ancient states of Central and Eastern Europe. Warsaw, Berlin, Prague, Vienna, Budapest, Belgrade, Bucharest and Sofia, all these famous cities and the populations around them lie in what I must call the Soviet sphere, and all are subject in one form or another, not only to Soviet influence but to a very high and, in some cases, increasing measure of control from Moscow [Document 10].

Although the Americans had made specific but limited efforts to preserve stability in Turkey and Iran, Churchill outlined the Russian threat in Europe.

46 Cold War and limited war, 1945–2015

In a clarion call for joint Anglo-American action, he asserted, 'Neither the sure prevention of war, nor the continuous rise of world organisation will be gained without what I have called the fraternal association of the English-speaking peoples'. 'This means', he emphasised, 'a special relationship between the British Commonwealth and Empire and the United States'. Whilst the speech's impact on all American policymakers and the public might be overestimated (Hopkins, 2014: 8–26), Churchillian rhetoric reaffirmed the apparent dangers posed by Soviet Russia to the West gestating in the two governments and amongst many voters. Whilst Washington would construct its foreign policy based on the cold calculation of national interest rather than on sentiment, Churchill suggested that Britain and America concert against the Russians because of the ties developed between 1941 and 1945. It meant a new incarnation of the Europe-first strategy.

Accordingly, apart from Germany – discussed below – the Special Relationship cemented further over the next year because of crisis in Greece. During Germany's occupation of Greece, there were two main resistance forces: one communist and one royalist (Iatrides and Wrigley, 1995: especially Chapter 1). After German withdrawal in October 1944, the communist political arm declared a provisional government rejecting the Greek monarch and the royalist government-in-exile. Given their Balkan sphere of influence conceded by Stalin in the percentages agreement and seeking regional stability, the British intervened and forced the creation of a communist-royalist government in Athens. However, when internal problems saw the coalition collapse, communist-royalist civil war broke out early in December 1944. British forces intervened, and, in March 1946, as Churchill spoke at Fulton, a Greek general election produced a royalist government. However, sensing that liberal democratic electoral politics would never produce a Marxist government, Greek communists rose in rebellion that same month. The civil war resumed, Britain backed the royalists, and, although Stalin honoured the percentages agreement, the new communist Balkan Powers of Yugoslavia and Albania supported the rebels. London poured money into the royalist side and looked to improve its army's training but, by February 1947, with other more pressing international and Imperial commitments, the cost became prohibitive. Having acquired American (US$3.75 billion) and Canadian (US$1.2 billion) loans, Attlee's government confronted major difficulties in post-war economic reconstruction, retained wartime regulations to control the economy, and embarked on massive economic and social reform (Addison, 2010).

On 21 February 1947, London informed Washington that it could no longer support Greek royalist forces financially beyond 31 March; with strategic implications in the eastern Mediterranean given Russian pressures on Turkey, it asked the Americans to defend the Western position in Greece (Bullock, 1983). Truman's Administration debated how to respond. Despite some initial suspicion that the British were seeking to inveigle America into a greater commitment to European defence, Marshall, who had just

The early Cold War, May 1945–July 1954   47

been appointed secretary of state; Dean Acheson, his undersecretary; and James Forrestal, the navy secretary, pushed to reorient American foreign policy. Truman needed little convincing. On 12 March, asking Congress for US$400 million for both Athens and Ankara, he wanted American civilian and military advisors and equipment sent to the region.

In a narrow strategic sense, the Truman Doctrine had two dimensions [Document 8]. It first maintained that communist victory in Greece would imperil Turkish security and, thus, Middle Eastern stability. Given that region's significance to American interests – Truman did not mention oil specifically – he pitched his argument ideologically: 'it must be the policy of the United States to support free peoples who are resisting attempted subjugation by armed minorities or by outside pressures'. The United States could no longer sit complacently in North America and permit Russia to challenge sovereign and independent non-communist Powers. Because American – and allied – interests lay outside the Western Hemisphere, America had to look beyond hemispheric security. Accordingly, Truman sought an economic commitment to safeguard those Powers integral to a broader interpretation of American security. In a wider sense, he advocated the formal end of American isolationism; it might have been passing incrementally since 1939; when Congress appropriated immediate funds for Greece and Turkey, America crossed the line.

At this moment, Washington was reassessing its overall strategy vis-à-vis Russia. George Kennan, a senior American diplomat in Russia since 1944, had sent a 'long telegram' to the State Department in February 1946 [Document 9] (Gaddis, 2011). Admitting that Soviet policy might be defensive, he argued that Russian aggressiveness in pursuing it threatened American and allied security: 'World communism is like malignant parasite which feeds only on diseased tissue'. Americans needed education in the realities of the Soviet threat; allied Powers, especially weaker ones recovering from the war, had to re-establish sound economies and mitigate social privations long exploited by communism. His response that America lead in organising resistance to Soviet inroads found a ready audience in the Administration. He returned to Washington to head the State Department's Policy Planning Staff.

Over the next year, confronting the Soviets in Europe, in the Mediterranean, and in Iran, Truman and his senior advisors considered American options. In September 1946, the president received a report from two White House advisors, Clark Clifford and George Elsey: 'American Relations with the Soviet Union'. Clifford and Elsey had consulted the State, War, and Justice departments, the Joint Chiefs of Staff, intelligence officials, and Kennan and another expert on the Soviet Union, Charles Bohlen. They concluded that whilst pursuing good Russo-American relations should not be abandoned, 'the United States should maintain military forces powerful enough to restrain the Soviet Union and confine Soviet influence to its present area'. Then, in July 1947, without Kennan's foreknowledge, his 'long telegram' appeared

48   *Cold War and limited war, 1945–2015*

in modified form in *Foreign Affairs* as an anonymous piece written by 'X' – Forrestal lay behind publication (1947). Advocating 'a long-term, patient but firm and vigilant containment of Russian expansive tendencies', America had to lead in countering 'Soviet pressure against the free institutions of the Western world' by an 'adroit and vigilant application of counter-force at a series of constantly shifting geographical and political points, corresponding to the shifts and maneuvers of Soviet policy'. Counter-force would produce either 'the break-up or the gradual mellowing of Soviet power'. Quickly identified as coming from Kennan, the article demonstrated publicly that America would now seek to contain Soviet power. And the 'X' article added a comment not in the 'long telegram': 'It would be an exaggeration to say that American behavior unassisted and alone could exercise a power of life and death over the Communist movement and bring about the early fall of Soviet power in Russia'. That meant that American allies, most especially Britain, had to assist in containment.

Rather than expanding American forces still deployed in Europe as envisaged by Clifford-Elsey, Truman opted to use economic power to contain Soviet power. His doctrine provided short-term *ad hoc* economic support to meet limited crises. An 'adroit and vigilant application of counter-force' emerged in June 1947, when Marshall proposed a comprehensive European reconstruction programme. Although Russia and its Eastern Bloc allies could join this initiative, Stalin demurred. He seemed frightened of possible American economic domination of Eastern Europe and exposing Soviet strategic weaknesses – the European Powers had to outline faults in their economies in order to qualify for aid to fix them. Nonetheless, with Bevin playing a prominent role, the Western Europeans inaugurated the OEEC in April 1948 to administer Marshall Plan monies (Hogan, 1987). Joined by America and Canada, the OEEC began distributing more than US$12 billion over four years to rebuild Western Europe's economies. Its signal achievements were unprecedented economic growth, political stability, and limiting communist influence in the region, especially from indigenous communist parties. It unsurprisingly benefitted the American economy by providing an expanding market for American goods and investment. Apart from expected propaganda on both sides – including historians (Esposito, 1994) – it proved an effective block to Soviet aggressiveness in Europe.

The German question and the rise of NATO, June 1948–May 1954

With the Marshall Plan's implementation by spring 1948, a defining Cold War crisis erupted. Despite East-West confrontation in Iran, Greece, and Turkey, Germany remained as the main Cold War battlefield (Zubok, 2007). Given Hitler's legacy and growing dissonance between the two sides over post-war Germany's shape, East-West tensions gradually increased. The Kremlin looked to prevent a unified Germany – especially a liberal

The early Cold War, May 1945–July 1954 49

democratic one; London and Washington wanted a demilitarised but economically capitalist state that, given Germany's past strength, would anchor European recovery. Western zone reparations did not move eastwards after December 1947 because promised Soviet delivery of foodstuffs westwards had not occurred – Germany's eastern reaches traditionally served as its breadbasket. Finally, the brutal methods of forced communisation in eastern Germany added to Western ill feelings.

To hasten economic reconstruction in their zones and foster their de-Nazified political development, the British and Americans united them in January 1947 as 'Bizonia' (Lewkowicz, 2010). The German *Länder* within the two zones received limited self-government, and a number of joint bodies emerged – for instance, the Bizonia Economic Council. When communist ministers left France's post-war government that summer, the French melded their zone with Bizonia by March 1948, producing 'Trizonia'. Anglo-French-American agreement the same month to extend the Marshall Plan to Trizonia came with a new currency, to improve the three zones' economic integration. Although designed to curb inflation – the Soviets were printing vast amounts of the *Rentenmark* used in all four zones – and asking the Soviets to accept the new *Deutsche Mark* but under stringent regulation, the British, Americans, and French looked to strengthen western German support for their brand of liberal democracy as a dimension of containment. In June, the three Western Powers joined by the Benelux, agreed to create a separate western German state.

On 20 March 1948, the German ACC met and, under Kremlin orders, the Soviet chair, Marshal Vasily Sokolovsky, unexpectedly adjourned the meeting (Hopf, 2012). Stalin decided to teach the three Western allies about Soviet power (Gaddis, 2005: 33). Having suffered major strategic defeats in Iran, Greece, and Turkey, he wanted a success. In those places, the Red Army had relatively little influence; the opposite was true in Central Europe. Moreover, Stalin seemed unworried about the American atomic bomb, which he judged Washington would never employ in Europe. Beginning on 1 April, the Russians began restricting access to West Berlin, about 160 kilometres inside the Soviet zone. By mid-June, they had blockaded all Western road, rail, and water traffic to and from the city. On 3 July, Sokolovsky laid out conditions for ending the blockade: ignoring the currency question, he demanded the Western Powers abandon the formation of a separate western German government. It was now a matter of maintaining the blockade, starving West Berlin of food and other necessities, and waiting for the Trizonia Powers to concede to Russian demands or leave the capital.

The only Western access to West Berlin was by air. Although an earlier Soviet-Western agreement kept these routes open, the Russians assumed it impossible to use this means of supply. In discussions with his advisors and consulting Attlee and Bevin, Truman determined that there could be no surrender; airlifting supplies to Berlin's Western zones was the only option. As the bulk of Allied air transport was American, it raised important strategic considerations: American airlift from all over the world would concentrate

50   Cold War and limited war, 1945–2015

in Europe; thus, should another crisis flare, say in East Asia, the American position might be exposed.

Nonetheless, Truman gambled and, almost immediately, the Western Powers began the airlift. Starting slowly but increasing weekly, more than 2.3 million tons of supplies reached West Berlin between 25 June 1948 and 1 August 1949 (British Berlin Airlift Association). It proved a signal strategic achievement, including flying in a complete powerhouse and daily coal supplies to run it as the main city powerhouse – cut-off – lay in the Soviet zone. As the leading Cold War scholar has observed: 'The western-allies improvised an airlift for the beleaguered city, thereby winning the emphatic gratitude of Berliners, the respect of most Germans, and a global public relations triumph that made Stalin look both brutal and incompetent' (Gaddis, 2005: 33–4). Denied victory, Stalin lifted the blockade in May 1949. Just as important was behind-the-scenes diplomacy. The Western Powers looked initially to the UN for a resolution, but Soviet obfuscation prevented any settlement. The Russians stretched out private discussions, hoping the blockade would work – Stalin sometimes indicating to visitors that resolution was conceivable; Molotov always then saying one was impossible; they thought until autumn 1948 that time was on Moscow's side. However, as the airlift worked, the Western Allies proved disinclined to bargain. They could out-wait Stalin.

The Berlin Blockade had two outcomes for the Russians that added significantly to their failure. On 23 May 1949, working with western German politicians, America, Britain, and other Western allies acceded to create the Federal Republic of Germany from Trizonia. Given Berlin's parlous strategic position, the Rhineland city of Bonn became the 'provisional' capital. Bolstered by the Marshall Plan and placed under the Western defence umbrella, West Germany emerged as a liberal democratic, capitalist socioeconomic state tied to the West. Although de-Nazification was incomplete and decartelisation stopped, democratised West Germany existed as a stable demilitarised federation. The former mayor of Cologne, Konrad Adenauer, was elected chancellor in September 1949. The creation of West Germany was not a perfect way to strengthen containment in Central Europe – many Germans wanted a united Germany. Stalin countered the move quickly. By October 1949, the Soviet zone had received nominal independence as the German Democratic Republic, had claimed Berlin as its capital, and stood as a leading member of the Soviet bloc.

The second outcome saw the British, Americans, and their Western European allies convinced that economic containment required a military dimension. On 17 March 1948, Britain, France, and the Benelux concluded the mutual defence Brussels Treaty. Bevin played a major role in devising it and, although positing Western European self-defence even against a revived Germany, it anticipated a broader Atlantic agreement. Britain and its allies needed an American military commitment to Western Europe. Bevin looked to 'induce the Americans to treat as quite separate issues the Brussels Treaty and the project for an Atlantic defence system' (Bevin to Inverchapel [British

The early Cold War, May 1945–July 1954 51

ambassador, Washington], 24 March 1948, in Insall and Salmon, 2014: 131). Truman remained unconvinced – the OEEC was about to disburse Marshall Plan funds. In concurrent Anglo-American-Canadian military talks at Washington, the Americans indicated that Truman's support for an agreement beyond Brussels needed Senate approval (Inverchapel to Bevin, 22 March 1948, in Insall and Salmon, 2014: 128–31). Nothing substantive from Washington emerged.

A year later, largely because the blockade fostered harsh anti-communist rhetoric during the November 1948 American elections, which Truman won, the situation changed. Because America had not committed militarily to Europe, in September 1948 Brussels Treaty members established a defence organisation, WUDO. Beginning in autumn 1948, discussions occurred amongst WUDO, America, and Canada. By early spring 1949, they had agreed to a wider alliance founded on European–North American security guarantees and mutual commitments to further contain the Soviets (Kaplan, 2013) – Norway, for instance, faced difficulties along its Russian frontier. Ignoring fascist Spain, the Brussels Treaty Powers thus brought Norway, Denmark, Iceland, Italy, and Portugal into the consultations; convening in Washington, the Powers signed the NATO Treaty on 4 April.

Despite subsequent criticism (Young and Kent, 2004: 130), NATO existed by 1949 as the military expression of containment tied to the Marshall Plan and the Truman Doctrine. Although constituting America's first peacetime military alliance with Europeans, its origins lay heavily with British efforts to have Washington support Western European defence (Baylis, 1992). The Relationship proved important – Acheson, now secretary of state, and Bevin worked well together (Acheson, 1969). NATO also constituted collective security outside the UN. In May 1948, a senior Republican senator, Arthur Vandenburg, argued that Western European security arrangements conform to the UN Charter whilst avoiding reference to the Security Council and possible Soviet veto. His resolution passed; Congressional opposition began to melt. Significantly, NATO collective security applied only to meeting attacks on the signatory Powers in Europe and North America, exempting those concerning European imperial holdings. To meet European demands for American military aid, Truman engineered congressional passage the next October of a Mutual Defense Assistance Program – US$1.4 billion to build Western European defences. As 1950 dawned, divided economically, militarily, and politically, Cold War Europe had emerged; it was not the one conceived at Yalta and Potsdam – no peace treaty ensued. It was nonetheless the new reality, and Anglo-American strategic relations had a prominent part in its creation.

Britain, America, and decolonisation in East Asia, May 1945–July 1954

Just as Cold War Europe developed in ways unexpected at Yalta and Potsdam, so did East Asia. Here 'hot' war broke out and, despite Rooseveltian goals of

52 *Cold War and limited war, 1945–2015*

China as one of the four 'policemen' and the advent of colonies transformed into liberal democratic governments tied to freer trade, the region became as divided economically, militarily, and politically as Europe.

The United States had emerged as a Pacific Power because of Japanese defeat. Unlike Germany, Japan was occupied only by American forces, with small British Commonwealth contingents (Takemae, 2002). The December 1945 CFM established a Japanese ACC, the Far Eastern Advisory Commission, composed of 13 members including Britain, China, America, and Russia. Whilst decisions came from majority vote, the four 'policemen' had veto power. Nonetheless, in reality, the Americans ran the occupation authority, and the American military commander, General Douglas MacArthur, took absolute control and ruled with some advice from Washington. There then followed major reforms under MacArthur, his successor, and a range of American advisors. They provided demilitarised Japan with a liberal democratic government, transformed its war industries into peaceful producers of trade goods – automobiles, electronics, and more – established a capitalist economy, and modernised – but not necessarily westernised – its society. By 1951, with the conclusion of a peace treaty – Moscow refused to sign – Japan stood in the Western bloc as a firm American ally (Price, 2001).

Outside Japan, both Britain and the United States moved after summer 1945 to solidify their positions in the Pacific and East Asia. The American advance towards Japan after June 1942 restored a strong military presence in the Philippines and saw the reinforcement of Guam, Wake Island, and islands off Alaska. With its Pearl Harbor naval base and occupation forces in Japan, America acquired a dominant position in the Pacific – some forces remained after 1951. On 30 August 1951, tied to the Japanese peace treaty, Washington concluded a Mutual Defence Treaty with the Philippines and, two days later, a defence arrangement with Australia and New Zealand – the ANZUS pact. The former allowed for mutual support if either Power faced attack, the latter consultations in moments of crisis. Although each had an element centring on Japanese revanchism, the principal result concerned containing communism in East Asia and the Pacific. ANZUS had added piquancy for London: feeling that Britain had been unhelpful against the Japanese after December 1941, the South Pacific dominions put themselves under America's defence umbrella (Waters, 1995).

For Britain, the return to peace meant re-establishing control over its principal Southeast Asian colonies – Malaya, Singapore, and Burma, although the latter was technically part of British India – as well as island holdings such as Sarawak, Brunei, and North Borneo. As the wartime Southeast Asia Command had been British, this process was relatively straightforward (Lowe, 2009: Chapter 1). It also embodied efforts to re-establish Britain's economic and financial informal empire in China, centred in Hong Kong and Shanghai; but on mainland China, the outbreak of civil war between the KMT and CCP and interventionist American and Russian policies blunted success (Xiang, 1995). Unlike America's position, Britain's in East Asia and

The early Cold War, May 1945–July 1954 53

the Pacific waned after late 1945. Whilst able initially to secure their eastern empire – and that of French Indochina until liberated France could transfer troops and administrators east – the British lacked the military and financial resources to sustain their former presence; the Americans willingly took their place. Yet, as much as American ambitions, nationalism unleashed by Japanese success against the White Powers after 1941 stoked demands by indigenous leaders and their followers for decolonisation. East Asian nationalism – and its South Asian, African, and Middle Eastern variants – began tearing apart the European empires.

Crises in China, Korea, and Southeast Asia created a rigidly divided Cold War East Asia, mirroring Europe. China's civil war proved the most important. Following Japan's defeat, the KMT and CCP resumed fighting to control their country (Bernstein, 2014). In a bloody struggle that produced CCP victory by October 1949 on the mainland – fleeing to the island province of Taiwan, the KMT still declared sovereignty over all of China – CCP forces were more cohesive, better organised, courted important social groups such as the peasantry by promising land reform, and, unlike the KMT, demonstrated a lack of corruption.

Truman's Administration attempted to end the war by forging a KMT-CCP political compromise – before becoming secretary of state, Marshall spent 1946 in China trying to do so (Miller, 1974). Roosevelt's earlier view of KMT China as an American ally proved hard to dispel, even though a range of American journalists and diplomats on the spot thought the CCP offered more to the Chinese and wrote and reported favourably on Mao Zedong, the CCP leader, and his ambitions (Gurman, 2012: Chapter 1). By late 1948, Truman and some of his key advisors had begun turning away from the KMT, with the result that shrill anti-communist American politicians such as Richard Nixon, a Republican, heavily criticised the Democratic Administration. Nonetheless, when the civil war ended, Truman and Acheson began serious consideration of recognising the new regime (Tucker, 1983). In January 1950, Britain did so for purely pragmatic reasons: continued British control of Hong Kong. However, on 25 June 1950, Communist North Korea suddenly attacked the non-communist South. To meet this aggression, Truman's Administration decided to contain communism on the peninsula, ordering USN forces into the straits separating Taiwan from mainland China to protect the KMT, ending the process of recognising the PRC, and preparing to send forces to South Korea.

As in Germany, Allied armies had divided Japan's Korean colony into a communist-dominated north and an anti-communist south at the 38th parallel. By September 1948, two opposing Koreas had emerged and, by 1949, most Russian and American troops had withdrawn from the peninsula. A speech by Acheson in January 1950 implied that South Korea lay beyond America's defensive perimeter, which emboldened the North Korean dictator, Kim Il Sung, to seek Stalin and Mao's assistance in absorbing the South. Stalin approved but would only supply war materiel, not

54   *Cold War and limited war, 1945–2015*

troops (Haruki, 2014). After the surprise attack drove South Korean forces down the peninsula, Truman turned to the UN. Thanks to Soviet boycott of the Security Council to protest the KMT holding China's seat, the Americans and British won UN approval for a 'police' force to repel the invaders and defend the South. The Americans would lead; MacArthur would command.

In a three-year struggle, the war proved nothing militarily. Successful UN amphibious landings in September 1950 produced a North Korean rout. By late October, as American-led forces drove to the Yalu River separating the PRC from North Korea and threatened the CCP revolution, PRC forces had joined the war on North Korea's side. They drove UN forces back to roughly the 38th parallel. Until an armistice in July 1953, a stalemate emerged. In the interim, using the deadlock to their political advantage, the PRC scored several propaganda victories that portrayed UN action as imperialist, damaging the American and British images amongst the emerging states in East Asia and Soviet-dominated Europe (Rawnsley, 2009). Eisenhower won the 1952 American presidential election for the Republicans partly by promising to end the war. The armistice was arranged in mid-1953 to return stability to the region. A peace conference ultimately convened at Geneva beginning in May 1954.

In Southeast Asia, French Indochina added to East-West tensions. Before French forces and administrators returned to the colony, Vietnamese nationalists led by the communist Ho Chi Minh declared the Democratic Republic of Vietnam and sought American backing (Lawrence and Logevall, 2007). Truman's Administration baulked; it did not want to risk losing French military support in Europe by supporting Vietnamese decolonisation. And despite promoting a 'French Union', a semi-federal structure to replace its empire and give its imperial possessions limited local autonomy, Paris did not intend to give its colonies independence. This attitude produced a colonial war – for the Vietnamese, a war of national liberation. This struggle's first phase lasted until the outbreak of the Korean War; French and anti-communist Vietnamese troops fought the communist Vietminh led by General Vo Nguyen Giap in a guerrilla war that produced military stalemate. The other two components of French Indochina, Laos and Cambodia, also faced destabilisation. Then in 1950, concurrent with the Korean crisis, the PRC and Russia recognised Ho's regime, providing it and the Vietminh with material support.

America responded with containment, recognising a French-sponsored anti-communist authoritarian government in Saigon and supplying materiel and financial assistance (Lawrence, 2005). Whilst Washington concentrated on Korea and Europe after 1950, the French had a free hand fighting Ho and the Vietminh. Clear-cut victory proved elusive. Nevertheless, the Korean armistice and impending Geneva peace conference led the French military to draw the Vietminh into a decisive battle at Dien Bien Phu. Victory would enhance Paris's hand diplomatically at Geneva, but the Vietminh triumphed decisively. With French public opinion having turned against seemingly interminable war, Paris indicated that France might leave Indochina.

The early Cold War, May 1945–July 1954 55

The British – Attlee's government and a new Churchill ministry replacing it in October 1951 – supported American policy in Southeast Asia as essential to the Relationship (McKay, 2007). Beginning in June 1948, Malayan communists rose in rebellion, threatening Singapore's security plus the colony's economic reconstruction and British wealth deriving from Malaya's rubber and other production. As early as December 1948, Bevin sought Anglo-American co-operation:

> The French forces in Indo-China are already stretched, and if the Viet Minh were to be strongly re-inforced as a result of a Communist-controlled China, the situation might well become untenable for the French, at any rate in the north. There would be an increased threat to South-East Asia in general through the strengthening of the Communist position in Indo-China.
>
> (Nong, 2010: 32)

Meanwhile, Britain met the Malayan 'Emergency' with a robust military and political response. Building on their Second World War experience in jungle warfare, British forces began protecting strong points, targeting communist food supplies, and forcing the relocation of potential communist sympathisers – as ethnic Chinese fighters largely comprised the guerrillas, this meant ethnic Chinese Malays. This strategy proved far more effective than France's political-military approach in Indochina; by 1952, the British had broken the guerrillas, although the 'Emergency' lasted until after Malay independence in 1957. London's decision to grant both Malaya and Singapore independence whilst ensuring British economic and strategic interests was of signal importance. The peninsula became the Federation of Malaya and Singapore an independent city-state that allowed continued RN use of its naval base. Both new states joined the Commonwealth.

The Geneva conference of April–July 1954 gave form to evolving Cold War East Asia (Cable, 1986). Its ostensible purpose involved settling the Korean War and restoring peace to Indochina. Whilst several smaller Powers attended, the talks were dominated by Britain, America, France, Russia, and the PRC, despite American non-recognition of its existence. Each Power worked for its own advantage and supported the interests of its regional allies: North and South Korea and the emerging Powers in Southeast Asia. A Korean settlement proved barren, because the North and South had irreconcilable demands. For instance, the South wanted UN forces to remain in the peninsula and UN-monitored national elections; the North demanded the exit of all foreign forces and elections under an all-Korea electoral commission. What each Korea really wanted was to eliminate its rival, which produced a divided peninsula, a DMZ separating the competing states, and the larger Powers supporting their clients.

Indochina seemed more hopeful with the negotiation of the 'Geneva Accords'. Along with ceasefire agreements for Laos and Cambodia, a DMZ

56 *Cold War and limited war, 1945–2015*

at the 17th parallel would divide Vietnam temporarily: Ho's Vietminh would govern the North; Bao Dai, the former emperor, would lead the South. Tied to French forces moving to the South and the Vietminh to the North, there would be unimpeded movement as the population could choose between the zones. Neither the North nor the South could join any military alliance or seek military aid. To monitor the ceasefire, the conference created an ICC along Cold War lines: Western Power Canada, Soviet-bloc Poland, and, as chair, neutral India.

At Geneva, however, Anglo-American discord arose. Eden, again Churchill's foreign secretary and the British delegate, sought a negotiated settlement as the basis for regional stability. Eisenhower's secretary of state, John Foster Dulles, wanted to avoid even the breath of another Yalta sell-out to the communist Powers (Kaufman, 2001). With staunch anti-communism infecting American domestic politics – its arch-practitioner, Senator Joseph McCarthy, had reached the zenith of his influence – Dulles departed the conference early and left the delegation to his deputy, Walter Bedell Smith. Having spoken in the 1952 election campaign of 'rolling back' communism, Dulles charged that the British did not support either joint–Western Power action or American policy towards Indochina – that is, weakening the PRC or Ho's regime. When the British got the conference to agree that national elections would occur by July 1956 to create a unified Vietnamese state, Eisenhower's Administration refused to endorse them. Nonetheless, when the conference adjourned in late July, it achieved an East Asian settlement. The fighting had stopped. More important, the Korean and Indochina settlements were provisional and could produce greater stability. That they might become permanent and set the course for renewed Cold War tensions in East Asia was problematic.

5 From Cold War to détente, 1954–1968

Decolonisation strained the Relationship in the mid-1950s. Although both Powers shared responsibility for the rift, recognition of shared strategic interests healed it. After August 1949, Russia's successful atomic bomb test made Cold War rivalry more complex (Holloway, 1994), and it was compounded by 1953, when both America and Russia developed more powerful thermonuclear weapons (the Geneva Conference occurred just after Russia's thermonuclear achievement). As the Western allies and Russians subsequently developed and refined both the new weapons and delivery systems, 'hot' war between them assumed decided danger. Consequently, with an understanding that nuclear weapons would be used only in the direst circumstances, each side pursued traditional diplomacy to maintain their respective interests. An expression of this tradition, the Relationship ultimately provided decided benefits to the Americans and British.

British decolonisation and the road to Suez, 1954–1956

British decolonisation in Asia conformed to the Attlee government's determination to give India independence after 1945. The MacDonald-Baldwin governments had passed the Government of India Act ten years earlier, but Indian nationalists proved lukewarm to this made-in-Britain solution – a federation of British India and the princely states (Muldoon, 2009). Over the next decade, nationalist pressures had mounted; the war intervened and the nationalist movement splintered along religious and political lines: the Hindu Congress and Moslem League. Still, British control diminished. Taking office, Attlee's Cabinet considered the question; after much debate, delay, and opposition from diehard Imperialists such as Churchill, the July 1947 Indian Independence Act partitioned the subcontinent into Hindu India and Moslem Pakistan (Talbot, 2013); Ceylon and Burma had separate instruments for their independence in early 1948. Indian-Pakistani independence was to occur in summer 1948, but sectarian violence, British costs to maintain order, and Hindu-Moslem nationalist pressures saw the date advanced to August 1947. Both India and Pakistan immediately joined the Commonwealth; Ceylon did, too, whilst Burma, adhering to neutralism, did not.

58   Cold War and limited war, 1945–2015

Although American pressures for decolonisation had not abated, Britain's decision came through determining its interests (Moore, 1983). 'Indianisation' of the colony's bureaucracy was underway, pushing the liberation idea forward. In addition, Labour contained a strong anti-Imperial wing and, as costs for a continued Imperial presence was prohibitive for a government confronting post-war economic and financial reconstruction, independence could assist an over-burdened Exchequer. Finally, despite diehard opposition, British public opinion supported ending British rule, believing it increasingly anachronistic in the modern world. However, the British ensured their presence in the Indian and Pakistani economies, if not true informal empire then at least means to acquire wealth without administration and defence costs. Moreover, the legacy of cultural links and new South Asian immigration to Britain saw enduring transnational ties.

Americans long believed that independent India would become an ally (Weigold, 2008). It did not happen. After independence, India and Pakistan fought over the territory of Kashmir given to India. Using the UN, Washington looked to balance between the two states – pleasing neither – even after the conflict ended in stalemate (Schaeffer, 2009). Ultimately, the Truman and Eisenhower Administrations found Pakistan a better ally in meeting the Russian threat in South Asia because of its Moslem leadership's strong anti-communism. From the moment of independence, India's premier, Jawaharlal Nehru, refused to align with either Cold War bloc; America, in his view '"dominated by the dollar", pursued economic imperialism and posed "a serious threat to the development of a higher type of world civilization"' (Brands, 1989: 32). Roosevelt's widow, Eleanor, observed after visiting India in 1953: 'In India, after the departure of the British, the resentment previously felt towards them was in large measure transferred to us' (Roosevelt, 1954: 90; cf. McGarr, 2013: Chapter 1).

Equally challenging for Washington was Palestine, a British mandate tied to the UN. By the late 1930s, large-scale Jewish immigration to Palestine had produced bitter Arab-Jewish tensions that saw London seek a compromise – in 1917, to acquire war funding from Jewish-controlled banks, London had promised a Jewish homeland, its definition vague (Schneer, 2010). Although the Second World War suspended the dispute – Jewish nationalists wanted not to imperil Britain's struggle against Germany – war's end saw renewed Jewish-Arab fighting and operations by Jewish guerrillas against British targets (Chaitani, 2000). For instance, in July 1946, the King David Hotel, a British headquarters, was bombed, killing 91 and injuring 45. Creating two states was now certain, as Attlee's government allowed the UN to resolve the crisis – the cost in blood and treasure remained high and, as with India, British public opinion generally supported withdrawal. In May 1946, the General Assembly approved partitioning the Mandate, acknowledging Arab Trans-Jordan's independence; in November 1947, it agreed to establish a Jewish state. With a provisional government, Israel achieved independence on 14 May 1948.

Cold War to détente, 1954–1968   59

Although inconclusive Anglo-American soundings had occurred (Cmd. 6808, 1946), Washington became involved at this stage. Without consulting Marshall and the State Department, who thought partition would create regional instability, Truman recognised the provisional government and Israel's *de facto* existence (Ottolenghi, 2004). He and his advisors had earlier discussed American strategic goals: find a peaceful solution, avoid using American forces, and deny Russia any advantage. Desirous of achieving these objectives through supporting Israel, Truman moved unilaterally when American decision-making seemed blocked. When Israel's Arab neighbours– Egypt, Syria, Jordan, Iraq, and Lebanon, along with Palestinian fighters – attacked on 15 May, America condemned the invaders but embargoed arms against all belligerents (Brecher, 2013). Seeking advantage, the Russians were also condemnatory; unsurprisingly, the UN was too. Jewish militias had prepared for a confrontation and defended the new state.

The war ended in 1949 through separate UN-brokered armistices between Israel and each Arab Power rather than a peace treaty: Egypt (February), Lebanon (March), Trans-Jordan (April), and Syria (July) (Ben-Dror, 2016). Iraq withdrew its forces, giving its zone to Trans-Jordan. Israel acquired about one-third more territory than the UN partition proposed, including West Jerusalem. Egypt occupied the Gaza Strip; Trans-Jordan occupied the West Bank and East Jerusalem. The UN monitored the ceasefires, oversaw the armistices, and prevented any escalation of troubles. Nonetheless, a ragged peace gave uncertain stability. Losing more territory than the UN offered, the Arabs were revanchist. Additionally, several hundred thousand displaced Palestinians were living in camps, particularly in Jordan – its name changed. Russian meddling remained a possibility. Anglo-American inability to co-operate over competing Middle Eastern interests appeared. British pro-Arab sentiments increased through fighting Jewish nationalists after 1945 and seeking economic advantages with the heavily populated Arab states; they had added weight because Jordanians received British arms and training with a British commanding officer. Wanting to work with Israel but protect their expanding petroleum interests in Saudi Arabia and other Arab states, the Americans again tried to find balance (Painter, 2012). Beginning in 1950 and successfully underway by 1954, the Israelis – through their ambassador in Washington, Abba Eban – embarked on a concerted effort to build an Israeli-American 'special relationship' (Siniver, 2015: 65–83).

Behind these developments, the Americans strengthened their foreign policy to buttress containment – the latter despite Dulles's commitment to 'roll back [communism]'. By early 1950, after the Soviets had acquired the bomb, Paul Nitze had replaced Kennan on the Policy Planning Staff. In April, his group drafted a memorandum, 'United States Objectives and Programs for National Security', advocating a more robust response to Moscow. It went to the National Security Council created in 1947 to advise the president about foreign policy and security. Given the ordinal number NSC-68, this

60 *Cold War and limited war, 1945–2015*

document argued that with Soviet Russia increasingly hostile to American interests, Washington must undertake a massive military build-up: strengthening conventional and atomic forces and tripling the defence budget (May, 1993). Little occurred for two months, as the Administration studied the document's proposals – they threatened Truman's desire to lessen defence spending. However, the Korean War proved the catalyst for NSC-68's implementation. Although criticism exists that Washington's ensuing determination to expand American armed forces deepened the Cold War, the communist record in Turkey, Iran, Greece, and Europe – plus Korea and Southeast Asia – suggests otherwise (Hogan, 1998). Eisenhower followed his predecessor's rearmament policies.

Although NSC-68 sought to augment American power and influence, Britain took part in multilateral efforts to expand containment in the decolonising and developing world. The first was in January 1950 at Colombo, Ceylon: Bevin and Commonwealth foreign ministers moved to strengthen Britain's former South Asian and Pacific colonies: Australia, Canada, India, New Zealand, Pakistan, and Ceylon (Watababe, 2015). They created the Colombo Plan to limit communist influence by social and economic improvement of less developed Commonwealth members through the provision of aid and technical assistance from the developed countries. Within four years, Burma, Indonesia, Japan, Laos, Nepal, the Philippines, Thailand, and the United States joined the effort.

By 1954, economic containment was not enough. In late summer, Churchill and Eden looked to repair damage to Anglo-American relations in East Asia created at Geneva. Eisenhower wanted the same. They established SEATO in September 1954, headquartered at Bangkok (Fenton, 2012: Chapter 1). Joining Australia, France, New Zealand, Pakistan, the Philippines, and Thailand, Britain and America established a defensive perimeter to strengthen the post-Geneva status quo. Unlike NATO, however, SEATO provided more a diplomatic arrangement than an alliance. Each major Power had different reasons for signing. SEATO underlined America's commitment to Southeast Asia – Eisenhower's Administration had already supported anti-communist South Vietnam by putting a pro-Western and Catholic strongman, Ngo Dinh Diem, in power in Buddhist Saigon (Miller, 2013). Churchill and Eden saw it improving the Relationship and, although Washington had not signed the Geneva Accords, underwriting the new regional status quo by other means. French membership gave Paris some postcolonial influence. SEATO, nevertheless, had limitations. Located elsewhere, most members had interests in either the region or the organization: Pakistan, for instance, reckoned membership might help it against India. Many Southeast Asian states did not join: the Accords blocked Vietnamese, Laotian, and Cambodian accession; Burma and Indonesia – the former Dutch East Indies – remained neutral; moving towards independence, Singapore and Malaya wanted to avoid being seen as supporting imperialist Powers. India refused. Most important, as the Americans opposed using their armed forces against regional guerrillas

Cold War to détente, 1954–1968   61

and insurrections – Europe remained their primary commitment – SEATO lacked an automatic response for military action. The treaty called only for consultation, rather than assistance, in a crisis; thus, members would meet threats on their own or, if some chose, collectively. Still, notwithstanding its limitations, SEATO underwrote containment in Southeast Asia and solidified Anglo-American relations.

Possessing strategic bases on Russia's southern frontier, oil reserves, and key communications routes, the Middle East remained vital for Western interests. Despite South and East Asian decolonisation after 1945 and ending the Palestine mandate, Britain remained the dominant Western Power in the region – its strong link with Jordan mirroring one with Iraq, it had bases throughout the region. Between April 1954 and February 1955, recognising shared interests, Churchill's government and Eisenhower's Administration fostered a series of regional diplomatic agreements (Persson, 1998). Turkey joined NATO in February 1952 and, in April 1954, a Turco-Pakistani security agreement emerged. In February 1955, Turkey and Iraq concluded a 'mutual co-operation' treaty to which Iran, Pakistan, and Britain adhered. This was the Baghdad Pact and, with a special Anglo-Iraqi arrangement, a pro-Western political-military bloc appeared in the Middle East. Although not joining the pact, becoming an observer, America reached agreements with each pact member – for instance, an Iraqi-American military assistance programme. Whilst the pact transformed into CENTO, a consultative arrangement like SEATO, it produced regional containment joining that of NATO and SEATO on its flanks.

Admittedly, CENTO had limitations. An Egyptian revolution overthrowing King Farouk saw a pan-Arab nationalist, Gamal Abdel Nasser, come to power in 1954; vying with Iraq's strongman, the pro-British Nuri al-Said, to lead the Arab states, Nasser portrayed the organisation as colonial means to isolate Egypt (Jankowski, 2002). Because of domestic opposition to CENTO, Jordan's king, Hussein, also rejected adherence. And two CENTO regimes appeared fragile. Iran suffered a nationalist revolution in summer 1953, threatening Western petroleum interests – many Iranians thought these interests, led by the British-controlled AIOC, exploitive – and a possible opening by Tehran to Moscow (Bayandor, 2010). When the pro-Western emperor, Shah Reza Pahlavi, fled after botching a coup against the democratically elected nationalist government of Mohamed Mossadegh in August 1953, the CIA – working with British intelligence – intervened, ousted Mossadegh, and put the shah back on his throne. In early 1954, in a reformed petroleum agreement, Britain's BP, a reorganised AIOC, became part of an Iranian consortium composed of American, Dutch, and French multinationals. Still, the shah relied on American military and multinational support to survive. Reflecting this situation, Nuri also faced domestic unrest – partly from CENTO membership – and controlled it by repressive measures (Elliot, 1996). For Baghdad, CENTO membership had as much to do with domestic Iraqi politics as with meeting any Soviet threat.

62 *Cold War and limited war, 1945–2015*

For the Relationship, colonialism and the Cold War combined in 1956. The pan-Arab Nasser retained ambitions to make Egypt the leading Middle Eastern Power; but despite its large population and relative military strength, it lacked a modern industrial economy. After seizing power, Nasser and his advisors embraced a long-considered solution: a dam at Aswan on the Nile River to improve irrigation – thus increasing agricultural production – and provide unlimited industrial hydroelectric power. Nasser found London and Washington, for different reasons, willing partners. Churchill and Eden looked to improve Anglo-Egyptian relations after the Farouk coup. Concurrent with Baghdad Pact negotiations, Britain and Egypt reached agreement in October 1954 on phased evacuation of British troops from the Suez Canal Zone: all troops withdrawn by mid-1956, with Britain holding the right to return for seven years; in return, Egypt abandoned its claims to Sudan (Louis, 1989). Eisenhower believed that Nasser could help galvanise Middle Eastern containment – Farouk's regime was thought to be anti-American – by leading the Arab League. This grouping emerged after 1945 and, by 1955, comprised Egypt, its adversary Iraq, Jordan, Saudi Arabia, Yemen, Lebanon, and Syria.

Working with the World Bank and announced in December 1955, Dulles and Eden, now prime minister, arranged project financing – London would contribute $14 million, Washington $56 million, the World Bank $200 million, and Egypt more in labour and materials (Matthews, 2006). However, reluctant to be beholden solely to the West – and seeking to improve Egypt's position vis-à-vis Iraq – Nasser balanced Anglo-American aid by opening to the Soviet bloc: acquiring Czechoslovak arms and, on 30 May 1956, recognising the PRC. These events rankled the Americans, especially Dulles, who, without consulting Eden, cancelled American–World Bank financing for Aswan on 19 July. A week later – British troops had left the Canal Zone in June – Nasser nationalised the Suez Canal Company; its profits would pay for the dam.

A major crisis erupted. With Anglo-French regional investment and prestige undermined, Nasser's stature grew in the Arab world for standing up to the Imperial Powers. Israelis saw an emboldened Egypt as an immediate danger (Troen, 1990). Although America and Western Europe had concern about Middle Eastern oil supplies, the bulk passing through Suez, Dulles and Eisenhower reckoned that Egypt could be isolated diplomatically and a solution found (Brands, 1986). With presidential elections scheduled for November, the Americans dragged out negotiations with a diplomatic placebo, a proposed Suez Canal Users Association, and the UN to pre-empt military action. Eisenhower explained to Eden on 3 September: 'American public opinion flatly rejects the thought of using force, particularly when it does not seem that every possible peaceful means of protecting our vital interests has been exhausted without result' (Verbeek, 2003: 102). Eden told Eisenhower on 1 October that Nasser was Mussolini-like, implying that appeasement would constitute a disaster (Lucas, 1996: 69). Nonetheless,

Cold War to détente, 1954–1968   63

Eden supported UN efforts, but the organisation's half-hearted approach brought no resolution.

The French and Israelis began conferring in late July – the Israelis worried about their security; the French saw Suez as part of Nasser's effort, along with supporting rebels in French Algeria, to undercut their position in North Africa. They discussed military action to seize the canal and, not coincidentally, debase Nasser's appeal in the Arab world. Eden came reluctantly to support this enterprise. On 24 October 1956, Britain signed a secret protocol with France and Israel at Sèvres; operations would begin a week later with an Israeli offensive portrayed as defensive (Shlaim, 1997). In line with the 1954 Anglo-Egyptian agreement, after diplomatic niceties, Britain and France would invade the Canal Zone to re-acquire Suez. The three Powers papered over some differences. The Israelis mistrusted the British; the French would not move without British support; and because of its strong links with several Arab states, London worried about any connexion with Israel. However, despite American caution, the stakes were too high to do nothing.

On 29 October, Israel struck; Egypt responded. London and Paris despatched an ultimatum to each Power the next day: cease fire and withdraw from the Canal Zone. When Nasser refused, the British and French began bombing Egyptian targets on 31 October (Thomas, 2014). Nasser blocked the canal by sinking ships travelling through it. Anglo-French airborne forces – built up in Cyprus but delayed, to propagandise the sham of no pre-planning – reached Egypt on 5 November. In the week between Israel's assault and the Anglo-French airdrop, the situation got away from London and Paris. Arab leaders, including Nuri, declared the Anglo-French response as colonialism. Amongst Arabs generally, the perception of Nasser as the icon of Arab self-esteem and pride strengthened. Key members of the Commonwealth – India, unsurprisingly, but also Canada – criticised Anglo-French action. Despite crushing an uprising in Hungary – see below – the Russians threatened intervention on Nasser's side. Most important, with presidential elections on 6 November and not wanting to imperil America's image and its regional interests, Eisenhower and Dulles blunted their NATO allies' action (Watry, 2014). Brutally demonstrating their power, the Americans forced a devaluation of sterling and the franc, condemned Anglo-French policies, demanded Anglo-French withdrawal, and looked for a UN settlement.

Apart from personal anger towards Eden for supporting the military option and appearing duplicitous before the attack, Eisenhower and Dulles wanted no connexion to old-style imperialism. As Eisenhower said on 29 October, 'we should let them know at once of our position, telling them that we recognize that much is on their side in the dispute with the Egyptians, but that nothing justifies double-crossing us' [Document 12]. At the UN, the secretary general, Dag Hammarskjöld, and the Canadian foreign minister, Lester Pearson, resolved the crisis (Melady, 2006). Anglo-French forces would withdraw, replaced by UN peacekeeping troops to separate the Israelis and Egyptians. Britain's climb down proved a spectacular failure.

Figure 5.1 Dwight Eisenhower and Anthony Eden, Washington, DC, 1956
© Everett Collection Historical / Alamy

Anglo-American relations weakened. Eden felt betrayed by Dulles (Avon, 1960) for blocking the Aswan loan and then stymieing Anglo-French actions. Indeed, Dulles and Eden had had only a working relationship since before the Geneva Conference, the lack of friendship coming from Dulles holding unfavourable views of the British Empire (Louis, 1990). Still, thinking the Relationship could augment British policy, Eden had erred. For someone with long diplomatic experience, it constituted a signal failure. He also misjudged the potency of Nasser and other emerging Third World leaders such as Nehru. In January 1957, undermined by his Cabinet and citing illness, he resigned; his chancellor of the Exchequer, Harold Macmillan, succeeded him. Eden's personal misfortune proved minor compared to the broader results of British failure. Overnight, Britain's image as the leading Middle Eastern Power evaporated – protection of its interests there would now require American support (Petersen, 2008). More important, again almost immediately, a general international view developed that Britain ceased to be a major Power (Lucas, 1996). No one had doubted that by 1945 it was the least of the Big Three, and its severe post-war economic and financial difficulties had diminished its international strength. But despite withdrawing from Greece and beginning decolonisation, British leaders had defended their sizable remaining strategic interests – in Malaya, Korea, involvement in NATO, CENTO, and SEATO, and working with the emerging Commonwealth. Whether British international power had constituted a mirage is debatable; but Britain, whether guided by Attlee-Bevin or Churchill-Eden, had had influence. Suez put in stark relief its limitations. A new era for Britain had begun.

Britain, America, and the problem of the Middle East, November 1956–November 1968

Despite the Relationship's changed dynamic, Macmillan and other British leaders resolved to maintain Britain's remaining position in the wider world and, realistically, knew they required American support. Britain could remain an effective American ally and, where Anglo-American strategic interests intersected, help sustain them and those of the United States. It meant repairing the Relationship, which Eisenhower wanted. The first real opportunity came in the Middle East.

On 5 January 1957, in a 'Special Message' to Congress, Eisenhower indicated that any Middle Eastern Power could seek American economic assistance or even military support 'against overt armed aggression from any nation controlled by International Communism' (Hahn, 2006: 38–47). Mentioning Russia's Middle Eastern strategic ambitions – 'true of the Czars and it is true of the Bolsheviks' – he committed America to post-Suez regional stability. Appealing to the Arab states – and Israel – disconcerted about Nasser's ambitions in the guise of pan-Arab nationalism, Eisenhower's doctrine stood as an expression of containment for a region vital to

66   Cold War and limited war, 1945–2015

the American and Western economies. If the oil-producing states fell to the Russians or their proxies, those economies would suffer greatly. Until this moment, Britain had had the lead in safeguarding Western interests in Iraq, Jordan, and other Arab states. Now with CENTO beginning to unravel, America had to step in. Adding to their Europe-first strategic commitment, the Americans now had a commitment in the Middle East. Although initially it was difficult to persuade Israel and leading Arab states of the doctrine's utility, America stood as the Western leader in the region.

Within two years, Eisenhower used his doctrine twice. In April 1957, Jordan's King Hussein confronted a revolt by dissident army factions supporting his opponents and, more important, supported by Syria. Hussein put down the revolt and, over the next year, accepted American economic aid to bolster his government and contain Syria. It constituted a precursor to a deeper crisis in Lebanon in summer 1958. On 1 February 1958, Egypt and Syria united to form the UAR, a product of Nasser's pan-Arab appeal and a desire to stymie communist strength within Syria; Nasser became UAR president. Iraq and Jordan countered on 14 February with their own union, the Arab Federation, of which Nuri became premier. In reality, the Federation had only shared foreign and defence policies – domestic issues remained with each government.

These competing political visions collided in a threatened civil war in Lebanon. Pro-Western Lebanese Christians controlling the government looked favourably on the Baghdad Pact; Moslem Lebanese looked to join the UAR, which purportedly supplied Moslem rebels with arms via Syria. When pan-Arabs overthrew Nuri on 14 July and further threatened Lebanon – the Arab Federation collapsed – Camille Chamoun, Lebanon's president, wanted American help. Eschewing allied support, Eisenhower despatched 14,000 troops to assist Chamoun's government. The rebellion collapsed, and the Americans left in August. Lebanese elections in September saw a new Western-oriented Christian president and, for the time being, a stable regime.

In March 1957, Macmillan began healing the Relationship, or at least providing a public face to Anglo-American amity, in meetings with Eisenhower in Bermuda to discuss Anglo-American nuclear interdependence ('Editorial Note about the Bermuda Conference', 1955–1957). The two men had known each other since the Second World War. Macmillan's first substantive opening to repair transatlantic relations and demonstrate Britain's value in defending common strategic interests came with the Jordanian side of the Lebanese crisis. Nuri's overthrow suggested the fragility of Hussein's regime. Hussein sought military support, but Dulles remained uncertain – the king's domestic position might weaken from Western involvement. Nonetheless, to entrench Hussein as well as British interests in Jordan – and provide a lesson more widely in places such as Kuwait – Macmillan's Cabinet agreed to send forces to assist Amman in July 1958. Cognisant of Suez, it meant working with Washington. On 17 July, two days after Eisenhower ordered American forces to Lebanon, British troops began arriving in Jordan. Before and during this operation, the British and Americans closely collaborated – over airlift, smoothing relations with Israel, and American financing for the mission. Dulles remained suspicious of the British ('Memorandum of a telephone conversation', 1958). Still, without appearing submissive, Macmillan and John Selwyn Lloyd, the foreign secretary, used every opportunity to highlight publicly transatlantic cooperation and, more important, Britain remaining a Power with some influence.

Suez and its aftermath reinforced the truism that for the United States, decolonisation evolved in ways different from which American leaders earlier believed it would. The post-1945 developing world did not always see America as a beacon of liberal democracy or tolerant values. One reason was ideological. Rebelling against capitalistic socioeconomic systems and racism, national liberation movements and the regimes they sometimes created found Marxist prescriptions more appealing – even if more authoritarian than those they replaced. For the same Cold War reasons devolving from steadfast anti-communism in American politics, Truman, Acheson, Eisenhower, Dulles, and other leaders refused to work with them. Non-recognition of the PRC was the most important manifestation of this tendency, but so was American policy towards North Vietnam and North

Figure 5.2 Harold Macmillan and John F. Kennedy, Nassau, December 1962
© Keystone Pictures USA / Alamy

68   Cold War and limited war, 1945–2015

Korea. Consequently, Washington backed anti-communist strongmen such as Diem in South Vietnam and Syngman Rhee in South Korea. Even emerging non-communist governments saw the unbridled capitalism promoted by Washington and corporate America as inimical to the societies they were building and did not share American foreign policy views or interests. States as diverse as Nehru's India and Nasser's Egypt are examples.

Within America's own sphere, Caribbean and Latin American anti-communist leaders received support; their opponents, many non-communist but opposing the excesses of American capitalism and the socioeconomic inequalities it generated, were anathema in Washington. Thus, anti-communist credentials, rather than any commitment to liberal democracy, qualified regional leaders for American support. Fulgencio Batista, who led a brutal regime in Cuba; Carlo Castillo Armas in Guatemala, put in power in 1954 by the Americans after overthrowing a democratically elected government; and other Latin American dictators helped form an informal empire backed by US military power (Argote-Freya, 2006). Of course, not all developing states allied with the Americans were authoritarian. Israel and the Philippines are examples. However, decolonisation proved a mixed blessing for America. Protecting and extending America's interests outside the Western Hemisphere, where it had decided control, required support from its major allies, especially Britain, to ensure stability and contain Russian and increasing PRC inroads.

In the decade after the Jordan-Lebanon crises, Arab-Israeli rivalry fostered instability in the Levant that threatened to expand to the whole Middle East. Although the UAR collapsed in September 1961 due to Syrian antipathy to Egyptian dominance of the government (Jankowski, 2002), Nasser's pan-Arabism continued. Anti-Western after Suez, Nasser aligned Egypt with Russia to construct Aswan, stand against the Americans, and prepare his military for an eventual war to annihilate Israel. He also endeavoured to demonstrate Egypt's position as the leading regional Power. In 1964, when republican rebels deposed the Yemeni king, he sent more than 50,000 troops to support the new regime and bring Yemen into the Egyptian orbit (Ferris, 2013). Jordan and Saudi Arabia, both monarchies, took the other side; Israel sent arms to the royalists; and the struggle became deadlocked. Important in this process was British willingness to send troops to help royalist forces, now fighting a guerrilla war against the new government. Britain had controlled Aden, adjacent to Yemen, since the early nineteenth century; and even after announcing that it would leave Aden by 1968, *realpolitik* dictated blocking Egyptian influence in the southern Arabian Peninsula rather than reconciling with Yemen's republican government (Jones, 2004). The Egyptians withdrew without winning in 1967; so did the British. British Aden became the People's Republic of South Yemen. But foiling Nasser – although the Russians later established a naval base in the new state – British involvement backed Western interests in Yemen from 1964 to 1967.

Cold War to détente, 1954–1968   69

Israeli-Egyptian antagonism in Yemen was part of a broader Arab-Israeli rivalry that the Western Powers could not ignore. After the 1949 armistices, despite UN peacekeeping forces, numerous Israeli-Arab border clashes occurred. Although Syria concluded a defence agreement with Egypt in late 1966, inter-Arab relations were uneasy – the Jordanians complained about a lack of Egyptian support against Israeli raids on Palestinian guerrilla bases in its territory; the PLO had been founded in 1964. Moreover, the region divided between Israel and Russian-backed Egypt and its allies. The situation worsened in May 1967, when, concerned about its client state's security, Moscow provided intelligence to Cairo that Israeli troops were massing on the Syrian border. It did not want armed conflict in the Middle East, and subsequent events showed 'grave miscalculations and . . . Soviet inability to control the Arabs, rather than a conspiracy' (Bar-Noi, 2007). Nasser overreacted: massing Egyptian forces in the Sinai on Israel's border on 16 May, expelling UN peacekeepers on 19 May, and having his troops occupy their position above the Straits of Tiran off Sinai. Israel had long asserted that closing the straits would justify a response, including war. On 30 May, a week after closing the straits to Israeli shipping, Egypt signed a defence agreement with Jordan. Israel responded on 1 June with a national unity government composed of all major parties that after three days' debate decided to take the offensive. On 4 June, it authorised a pre-emptive air strike that decimated Egypt's air force and, with air superiority, struck its Arab neighbours with armour and infantry.

Lasting just six days until a UN-brokered ceasefire, the war produced a resounding Israeli victory that devastated Arab forces and saw Israel acquire the Golan Heights from Syria, the Gaza Strip and Sinai Peninsula from Egypt, and the West Bank from Jordan; Israel also acquired sole control of Jerusalem. Concurrently, Israel acquired about one million Palestinians in the occupied territories. Israel had withered its enemies and stood as the major Power in the Levant.

After Suez, Washington looked for regional balance – Lebanon a case in point. But for nearly the next decade, given Nasser's policies and Israel's search for security, balance proved increasingly difficult. In the genesis of the 1967 war, with the emergence of the Israeli-American 'special relationship' pursued successfully by Eban, now foreign minister, and other Israeli leaders, plus Russian influence with Egypt, Washington confronted difficulty. Should it enforce the Eisenhower Doctrine or accept possible Israeli action? Ultimately, President Lyndon Johnson and his advisors supported the latter. With Israel's battlefield success, Johnson's Administration pushed for a ceasefire to obviate a decisive Arab defeat that could lead to Russian intervention. Although Egyptian propaganda that the Americans aided Israel saw several Arab governments break relations with America, Washington wanted to avoid alienating pro-Western Arab states such as Saudi Arabia. Johnson, however, would not pressure Israel to abandon the occupied territories. That could occur only if the armistice produced a peace settlement – which never

70 Cold War and limited war, 1945–2015

came. Israel had become a firm American ally, and American efforts to find balance to produce regional security were limited.

Thus, whether its leaders liked it or not, in the long process of Middle Eastern decolonisation the United States emerged as the dominant Western regional Power. Like American policy in the Middle East, Britain's policy in the Middle East after 1958 coupled containment with narrow self-interest: protecting oil interests, Arab investment in Britain, and access to populous Arab markets. London understood its weakened position after 1956 and, like Washington, pursued stability. In the early 1960s, with classic balance-of-power reasoning, Macmillan's government provided Israel with weapons. 'We do not give the Israelis arms because they are pro-Western or because we admire their achievement', Macmillan remarked in 1960. 'We give them arms because our interest in the Middle East is to keep the place quiet and to prevent war' (Gat, 2006: 69). Either Israeli or Egyptian victory in such a war would damage British interests. If Israel repeated its 1948 to 1949 military achievements, Arabs generally would blame Western imperialism, including Britain, for their failures. As with Yemen, Egyptian victory could see the fall of Western-supported regimes and jeopardise oil supplies. Accordingly, Israeli victory in 1967 affected Britain adversely – Arab states closed accounts in British banks and restricted petroleum exports; thus, a new Labour government led by Harold Wilson decided on a more overt pro-Arab stance, especially to protect oil supplies (McNamara, 2003). Two weeks after the war ended, Wilson's foreign secretary, George Brown, demanded that Israel return territories won in the war (Brenchley, 2005). Despite Anglo-Israeli relations cooling afterwards, the United States retained Israel as an ally, Britain cultivated better relations with the Arab states, and a new Middle Eastern balance emerged.

European defence and the German question, 1954–1968

Unlike in the decolonising world, Anglo-American relations in Europe after 1954 remained close and cooperative. As always, Germany remained the focus. The Korean War brought American demands that Western Europeans assume greater responsibility for their defence – NSC-68 had limitations. In 1950, the French foreign minister, Robert Schuman, proposed a plan to ease intra-European – really, Franco-German – rivalry by pooling their coal and steel industries. In July 1952, the ECSC – composed of France, West Germany, Italy, and the Benelux – began operating (Kipping, 1990). When Washington proposed West German rearmament to augment European defence outside of NATO, the spectre of a rearmed Germany caused concern in Britain and Western Europe. However, ECSC economic cooperation suggested a military equivalent. In October 1950, the French premier, René Pleven, proposed that the ECSC Powers form a single army and, after difficult negotiations, the EDC Treaty was produced in May 1952. Its essential element entailed a European army with eventual West German

Cold War to détente, 1954–1968   71

involvement under a single European authority (Laurendeau, 1988). All that was required was ratification. The proposed treaty met decided opposition in France, where, with great irony and much delay, the National Assembly rejected it on 30 August 1954. Deputies supporting the French nationalist politician Charles de Gaulle argued against putting French forces under foreign command. Rejection was a bombshell.

London and Washington wanted a rearmed West Germany – Churchill's Cabinet earlier overcame concerns about this possibility. Eden and Dulles were prepared to move without France, and, in early September, Eden struck upon means to do so (Dockrill, 1991): West Germany should sign the Brussels Treaty and then join NATO. In a London conference later that month, all of this was agreed. Moreover, Eden announced that British troops would remain in Europe for 50 years, and the Americans reaffirmed promises made to the EDC: economic, financial, or military aid for their allies. Bonn agreed not to develop ABC weapons – atomic, biological, and chemical – and would have no strategic air force. Ratifying the EDC, the West German government secured the end of the Allied occupation in return for a guarantee not to unify Germany by force –NATO forces would remain in West Germany. Confronting isolation, the French buckled. West Germany joined the Brussels Treaty in October 1954 and, in May 1955, NATO (Ruane, 2002). Critical of the EDC and West German rearmament, Moscow countered on 14 May with the Warsaw Pact, which constituted a military fig leaf: Red Army dispositions, strategy, and command would dominate in Eastern Europe, including East Germany (Gavrilov, 2012). Nevertheless, West German rearmament stood as a major advance by the British and Americans in containing possible communist aggression in Europe after Korea.

In June 1953, three months after Stalin died, anti-government rioting in East Germany produced a hard-line crackdown; this domestic discord reflected the fragility of all Soviet-backed regimes in Eastern Europe. The post-Stalin Russian power struggle saw the advent of Nikita Khrushchev as effective Soviet leader by early 1956. An element of Khrushchev's rise to power involved distancing Moscow from Stalinism to win the hearts and minds of both the Russian people and those of its Eastern European empire. No intention existed of ending communist rule, only provision for a more human face and, as the Warsaw Pact showed, no intention to weaken Red Army dominance. In February 1956, Khrushchev delivered a speech heavily criticising Stalin's methods of governance and perversions of Marxism-Leninism (Jones, 2005). Sensing a less brutal policy towards Russia's satellites, some Eastern European Powers moved towards reform. In the summer after the death of Poland's hard-line communist leader, Polish workers – who were facing food and consumer goods shortages, pitiable housing, and shrinking wages – demonstrated for better economic management; some were killed, many more wounded; but prosecutions were lenient (Kemp-Welch, 1996). By October, nationalist riots in Warsaw and other places had seen the desecration of Soviet monuments and calls for

72   *Cold War and limited war, 1945–2015*

change – not the end of Marxism-Leninism. A reform-minded communist leadership emerged, talked to Moscow, pledged allegiance to the Warsaw Pact, and began to tackle the economy.

Hungary proved more challenging. Also facing national economic inefficiencies, students and workers inspired by Polish unrest began demonstrating on 23 October; unlike the Poles, Hungarian protesters added changed political conditions to demands for food and better wages; calls also came for abolishing the secret police and ending Russian control of the country (Gati, 2006). A strongly nationalist dissident communist regime took power under Imre Nagy, forced a Red Army withdrawal, and allowed a multiparty political system. This was a chance for America to help roll back communism, by backing the new government. Eisenhower's Administration did nothing, however, because of possible confrontation with the Warsaw Pact. Thus, the Red Army re-entered Hungary, suppressed the rebellion, and imprisoned Nagy and his supporters. The Hungarian uprising tarnished the Soviet image in Western Europe and other places, even amongst communists who felt that Moscow had betrayed Marxist-Leninist ideals. Khrushchev and others in the Soviet leadership ended the 'liberalism' engendered by de-Stalinisation, and Europe's Cold War divisions returned stronger than ever.

Germany again became a major issue. Churchill attempted to thaw the Cold War after Stalin's death by arranging a Great Power summit in Geneva in July 1955 (Bischof, 2000). Eisenhower, Eden, the French premier, Edgar Faure, and Khrushchev examined German unification, security, arms limitation, and improvement of East-West relations. West German membership in NATO complicated German unification; and Khrushchev sought to end NATO and the Warsaw Pact through a new collective security arrangement. Follow-up foundered because of Suez. For the Russians, prosperous and vibrant West Berlin challenged Moscow and its East German client because it was a clear contrast to drab communist East Berlin. More important, because Berlin was essentially an open city, East Germans – including well-educated people needed for East German economic survival – could easily emigrate to the West via Berlin. Between 1953 and 1958, an average of 252,000 people a year went this route ('East-West German immigration statistics', 1961–1990). This steady loss of human resources animated Khrushchev to protect East Germany at Geneva.

As Cold War tensions in Europe and the wider world deepened after 1956, Khrushchev moved. In November 1958, demanding Western withdrawal from Berlin in six months, he sought Western recognition of East Germany (Zubok, 1993). The three Western Powers were determined to maintain their presence in Berlin. The West German government opposed any recognition of East Germany or agreement concluded at West German expense (Granieri, 2003). The deadline passed, but, visiting America in October 1959, Khrushchev revived the issue. These talks accomplished little, although West German chancellor Konrad Adenauer remained uncertain of American policy. The Russians wanted a separate peace treaty for

East Germany, which would give East Germany recognition. Although the Powers scheduled a summit at Paris on 14 May 1960, the shooting down of an American reconnaissance plane over Russia on 5 May ended any Soviet-American discussions as long as Eisenhower held office – he could not run in presidential elections scheduled for November. Boycotting the Paris Summit, Khrushchev waited, embarking on bilateral talks with Eisenhower's successor, John F. Kennedy, in June 1961 on issues relating to Southeast Asia, arms limitation, and Berlin. Kennedy tried to find a way around the impasse caused by Adenauer's hard line over East Germany (Williamson, 2012). It was too late. With the East Germans losing another 207,000 émigrés between 1959 and summer 1961 ('East-West German immigration statistics', 1961–90), the situation could not continue. On 13 August 1961, East Germany built a wall separating the two Berlins. East-West tensions reached a new high.

Along with ensuring a British voice on the continent, Macmillan used Berlin as part of his strategy to improve the Relationship and demonstrate Britain's value in defending common strategic interests. As Britain's security interests centred on European stability – echoing the balance of power – he sought to reduce East-West confrontation and resolve the interminable German question. Britain could build diplomatic bridges. Thus, in February 1959, Macmillan held talks with Khrushchev in Moscow to ease tensions over Berlin – not productive over Berlin, they produced agreement in principle to stop nuclear tests and hold a Great Power summit (Ashton, 2006). Macmillan followed with discussions with Adenauer and the new French president, De Gaulle. Having learnt the lesson of Suez, he kept Eisenhower and Dulles fully apprised in meetings at Washington later in March. Eisenhower proved cautious: 'We should make no concessions nor agree to any changes in the present arrangements except as part of a larger agreement out of which we would get something' ('Memorandum of conversation', 1959). Macmillan's efforts led to the calling of the Paris Summit – although Adenauer and De Gaulle became critical of British motives, and De Gaulle opposed any discussions with the Russians. That the summit proved abortive was beyond Macmillan's control. Eisenhower's Administration remained sceptical of any arrangement that might give the Russians an advantage; Khrushchev's boycott proved to be the summit's death knell.

The Berlin Crisis ended in June 1963 when Kennedy and Khrushchev each travelled to the city and delivered speeches upholding the status quo. Kennedy confirmed America's commitment to Germany, liberal democracy, and a West German–American partnership (Daum, 2008: Chapter 3). However, augmented by tensions in Germany and Southeast Asia, a Soviet-American confrontation over Moscow's placing of missiles in Cuba came close to nuclear war – in Berlin, Russian and American tanks even faced one another across the Wall. It suggested to both Powers that issues such as Berlin must cease as flashpoints. The West Germans, still led by Adenauer, who was scheduled to retire in October, had misgivings about what this

74 Cold War and limited war, 1945–2015

portended for German unification. Nonetheless, West Germany stood firmly in the Western bloc, Soviet expansionism remained contained, and new West German leaders would build policy on this fact.

The British did not want a military confrontation with the Soviets; thus Macmillan's efforts in February–March 1959. Some see this and subsequent British policy as appeasing both the Americans and the Russians (Hughes, 2014). This is wide of the mark. Britain's commitment to NATO and containment had not diminished. Admittedly, in various discussions about Germany between 1959 and 1963, London seemed willing to give *de facto* recognition to East Germany, accept the Soviet-defined Polish–East German border, and open dialogue with Moscow, to which the Russians reacted favourably (Newman, 2007). However, Macmillan never once was willing to weaken the Relationship to do so. He might have thought that Kennedy and Eisenhower had weaknesses in foreign policy (Horne, 1989: 231), but 1956 had changed the Special Relationship and Britain's place in it. Britain might pursue its own security interests over Germany after 1958 – which London saw as Anglo-American interests – but when the crunch came between 1961 and 1963, it remained a firm American ally, more firm than either France or West Germany (Mahan, 2002). The next 15 years, from *détente* to the return of Cold War tensions, would show it.

6 From détente to renewed Cold War, 1965–1979

As Britain's position transformed between the mid-1960s and late 1970s – its receding international presence increasingly Eurocentric – its Special Relationship role also evolved. In December 1962, Macmillan said 'Mr. Acheson has fallen into an error which has been made by quite a lot of people in the course of the last 400 years, including Philip of Spain, Louis XIV, Napoleon, the Kaiser and Hitler.' His outburst responded to comments that the retired Acheson had made a few days earlier:

> Great Britain has lost an empire and has not yet found a role. The attempt to play a separate power role – that is, a role apart from Europe, a role based on a 'special relationship' with the United States, a role based on being head of a 'commonwealth' which has no political structure, or unity, or strength – this role is about played out.
>
> (McDonald, 1974)

Acheson dealt with more about international politics, observing that Britain 'is now attempting, wisely in my opinion, to re-enter Europe, from which it was banished at the time of the Plantagenets, and the battle seems about as hard fought as those of an earlier day.' That reporters took his remarks out of context and ignored the European comment annoyed Acheson (Brinkley, 1990). Britain's new role was emerging. Kennedy's Administration distanced itself from Truman's former secretary of state, and London and Washington moved on.

A temporary flashpoint, Acheson's comments said much about the Relationship as *détente* emerged in international politics (Hanhimäki, 2013). From early 1963 until the late 1970s, the major Western Powers and Moscow consciously avoided direct challenges to prevent further crises such as Berlin and Cuba. Rivalry, searching for strategic and material gain, propaganda campaigns, and ideological struggle did not abate. Nevertheless, a Cold War hiatus occurred. A Sino-Soviet split saw Moscow and Beijing compete for communist world leadership; with the 1957 Treaty of Rome, the ECSC transformed into the EEC; and important areas of the developing world remained unstable as Russia, China, and the Western Powers competed for advantage. That America remained the leading Power within the

76   Cold War and limited war, 1945–2015

Western alliance system was indisputable. That it needed its principal allies to help defend Western and American narrow interests remained equally true. But De Gaulle, who was seeking to regain power for France, was unreliable (Reyn, 2010). Given the burden of the Nazi legacy and discomforted by the continuing division of their country, the West Germans were sometimes ambivalent. In this strategic equation, the Relationship retained its importance (Bange, 2008). Britain remained *primus inter pares* amongst America's major allies and, even if some American leaders did not understand – and British leaders did not always make it easy – the Relationship was symbiotic and entrenched the interests of each English-speaking Power.

Britain and American involvement in Vietnam, January 1965–April 1973

The greatest international crisis of the 1960s and 1970s came from American military involvement in Vietnam. As America drifted into the morass of war in Southeast Asia, the Relationship helped contain the communist Powers and ensure international stability. Before *détente*, working with Eisenhower and, then, a more willing Kennedy, Macmillan played a major role in repairing Anglo-American relations. Yet, as the Relationship since Churchill and Roosevelt demonstrated, transatlantic links went beyond high-level personal relationships, occasional and even deep discord, and shared cultural, economic, and political traditions. The Relationship also found basis on bureaucratic connexions, the embassies in London and Washington working well with their host governments, and, whilst never abandoning their own interests, recognising shared strategic ones. The three years in which Kennedy and Macmillan were in power are seen as the 'Golden Days' of a renewed Relationship, 'The House that Jack and Mac Built' (Dumbrell, 2006: 49–74; cf. Ashton, 2006: 691n2).

Meeting differences together demonstrated the durability of Britain and America's Relationship. In October 1957, Eisenhower and Macmillan created Working Groups to examine Anglo-American nuclear issues, economics, information, trade, and some regional problems such as Syria (Jones, 2003). These proved ineffective given wrangling in Washington over surrendering too much to London, something Kennedy's advent did not allay. Despite Roosevelt promising Churchill in 1944 to share atomic knowledge, in 1946 Congress prohibited cooperative ventures with any Power, including Britain. Britain nonetheless developed its own atomic bomb, tested successfully in October 1952 (Baylis, 1995). By 1957, with worldwide advances in missile technology, Britain needed a modern delivery system. After the Suez Crisis, it was apparent that better Anglo-American defence collaboration was also needed. British-developed missiles – the Blue Steel and Blue Streak ICBM – would be ineffective against a Russian first strike. Acquiring faster-firing American-developed Skybolt air-launched missiles suggested a good substitute – Macmillan called it 'interdependence'; Anglo-American cooperation would strengthen transatlantic ties, although some Britons

Détente to renewed Cold War, 1965–1979 77

worried about American control of joint nuclear defence. Still, Macmillan won Eisenhower's permission in 1960 to buy Skybolt (Freedman and Gearson, 1999). Tied to these efforts was Macmillan's determination to start parallel nuclear arms limitation discussions beginning with the Russians – raised in his 1959 visit to Moscow.

However, Kennedy cancelled Skybolt development in November 1962 because of technological problems. Also concerned that a future Anglo-Russian crisis with nuclear weapons in the background could draw America into a quarrel not its own, Washington wanted to discourage separate development and control of nuclear weapons (Schwartz, 1993). Kennedy and Robert McNamara, his defence secretary, endorsed a MAD strategy to deter the Russians. Given effective new sea-launched American missiles – Polaris – Kennedy's Administration supported an MLF of NATO-manned Polaris-armed warships and submarines under a 'dual-key' system: each Power had to agree to fire them. The 'dual-key' system would give Washington MLF-control. America offered Britain 'dual-key' submarine-launched Polaris missiles, but Macmillan's government wanted an independent British deterrent. In December 1962, Kennedy relented, to preserve the Relationship: Britain would buy Polaris and, with no 'dual-key', use its own warheads. Although beholden to American technology, Macmillan thus secured nuclear independence for Britain, which annoyed some Americans and caused difficulty with De Gaulle, who was looking to develop French nuclear forces (Neustadt, 1999). Some critics, especially Americans, suggest the Skybolt-Polaris issue was a failure (Newhouse, 1999: 45). For them, it was. American pre-eminence did not matter. Just as Washington had interests beyond the Relationship, so did London.

The 'Golden Days' unknowingly provided the Relationship's backdrop as America's Southeast Asian commitment escalated beginning in the early 1960s. After Suez, some State Department advisors wanted Britain to end acting like a global Power – a result of its reduced economic and military strength – and move towards Europe. Accordingly, when Macmillan's government applied for EEC membership in 1961, Washington supported it – in 1955, Eden's government had withdrawn from the negotiations leading to the Rome treaty thinking that Britain could prosper without joining (Pagedas, 2000). However, in January 1963, De Gaulle vetoed Britain's application. The British, he surmised, would promote American policies within the organisation; thus, Britain's ability to shape Europe's economy and benefit from EEC membership disappeared again (Mangold, 2006). De Gaulle's motives had little to do with Europe's economy. Vengeful, he wanted an independent French nuclear force; Macmillan had initially backed him but, ultimately, achieved an advantage by acquiring Polaris. Preventing British EEC membership would strengthen France politically and economically within Europe. In this calculus, Washington had to accept that despite Britain and the European Great Powers weakening since 1945 by decolonisation, lesser economies, and reduced military capabilities, they would resist Washington's dominance over them.

78   Cold War and limited war, 1945–2015

During the Anglo-American missile diplomacy, Kennedy said privately, 'there had to be control by somebody. One man had to make the decision – and as things stood that had to be the American President. He couldn't share that decision with a whole lot of differently motivated and differently responsible people in Europe' (Ashton, 2006: 702). Uncontested decision-making, however, was impossible; getting everything Washington wanted a non-starter; and suasion indispensable. Macmillan suffers criticism that his nuclear and EEC endeavours weakened Britain by antagonising Paris and Bonn (Mangold, 2006: 216–19). However, British interests were not necessarily those of France or West Germany; and as the record since at least 1949 showed, the Powers quarrelled as much as they cooperated. Whilst Britain would do what it best judged, even opposing America on some issues, the Relationship anchored British foreign policy whether or not it was close to Europe. Some American leaders might have disliked the situation; but they needed to accept that 'differently motivated and differently responsible people' existed. Certainly, presidents from Truman to Kennedy appreciated British responsibilities. Vietnam and the problems it spawned created difficulties for the Relationship without diminishing Britain's role as America's chief partner.

The slow escalation of American involvement in Southeast Asia began after the 1954 Geneva Conference, devolving from two inter-related issues: containing Soviet and PRC influence by opposing their regional proxies – North Vietnam and communist guerrilla groups in Cambodia and Laos; and failing to understand the nationalism linked to decolonisation. Eisenhower enunciated the 'domino theory' respecting Southeast Asia just before Geneva ('Eisenhower Doctrine', 1957) [Document 11]. Mentioning Indochina, Burma, Thailand, the Malayan Peninsula, and Indonesia, the fall of one to communism, he said, would lead to the loss of all. Kennedy echoed this view in April 1963 ('President Kennedy's news conference', 1963). Thus, after supporting France in Indochina before 1954, an extension of containment, American policy transformed into propping up the region's anti-communist domino-like regimes. In South Vietnam, it produced support for Diem under the rubric of 'nation building', especially after Saigon blocked the national unification vote in 1956: the communists would have triumphed by the appeal of Ho's brand of nationalism opposing domination by any outside Power including Russia and the PRC (Duiker, 1976). North Vietnam then worked to destabilise the South by guerrilla warfare and terrorism – its instrument was the Northern-led Vietcong. With nationalist support in the South and a supply route running from North to South in western Laos and western Cambodia, the 'Ho Chi Minh' trail, the Vietcong made significant inroads. The Eisenhower and Kennedy Administrations stepped up economic support for Diem with, by 1963, 15,000 American military advisors (Logevall, 2012).

Whilst the Vietnam dimension of containment increased incrementally, Laos became a flashpoint in 1961. Civil war had broken out. Eisenhower's Administration supported the anti-communist general Nosavan Phoumi.

Détente to renewed Cold War, 1965–1979 79

As the communist Pathet Lao controlled territory along the Laotian–North Vietnamese frontier, Vietcong use of the Ho Chi Minh trail added North Vietnam to the mix. When Kennedy took office, Eisenhower told him that Laos seemed the first domino. Lacking popular support, Phoumi appeared near defeat but, even then, the civil war would not abate. The Soviets wanted a neutral, not necessarily communist government to bring stability, something discussed at the Kennedy-Khrushchev June 1961 summit. Ignoring SEATO – weakening its effectiveness – Kennedy asked Macmillan in their first meeting for a British military commitment (White, 1999). Facing great pressure and over opposition from the Cabinet, Foreign Office, and defence chiefs, Macmillan agreed – for reasons of alliance solidarity – to joint Anglo-American planning on possible military intervention. Ultimately, it did not matter. To avoid committing American ground forces and looking for Russo-American cooperation over Laos that might transfer to Berlin and Cuba, Kennedy's Administration helped engineer a new Geneva Conference that began on 16 May 1961. After tortuous discussions, Laos and 13 Powers – including the two Vietnams, the ICC Powers, the PRC, Russia, Britain, France, and America – reached agreement in July 1962 (Rust, 2014). They would respect Laotian neutrality, avoid interference in Laotian internal affairs, and, echoing the 1954 Geneva Conference, keep Laos out of military alliances. Agreement proved fragile. North Vietnam continued to use the Ho Chi Minh trail; the Americans responded with economic and military support for the Laotian government; and Kennedy's cooperative approach to the Soviets evaporated over Berlin and Cuba. Nonetheless, the Laotian imbroglio found temporary resolution, and Macmillan showed his – admittedly reluctant – willingness to bolster Anglo-American relations.

Vietnam focussed American attention. By 1963, Diem's regime was facing decided domestic opposition through brutality towards dissidents, preferential treatment for Catholics, corruption, and a flagging fight against the Vietcong (Miller, 2013: Chapters 8–9). South Vietnamese–American relations worsened; Washington wanted effective nation building and, on 1–2 November, Diem's generals engineered a coup – assassinating him and his brother, who coordinated secret police activities. With the generals taking over, Washington looked to win South Vietnamese hearts and minds, improve the economy, and invigorate South Vietnam's defence. Three weeks later, Kennedy was assassinated. Johnson, his vice-president, replaced him, and America's commitment to Southeast Asia transformed. Traditional assessments argue that America's subsequent build-up of forces and expansion of the war occurred because Johnson adhered to Kennedy's strategy (Halberstam, 1965). However, McNamara, who served Johnson, later asserted that Kennedy was moving to avoid escalation; instead, McNamara took responsibility given advice that he tendered to Johnson (McNamara, 1995). Regardless, the war intensified. Like Truman, Johnson was a foreign policy novice relying on foreign and defence policy advisors inside and outside government assembled by his predecessor: McNamara, McGeorge

Bundy, the national security advisor; John McCloy, a former American high commissioner in Germany; and others (Goldstein, 2008).

By early 1968, the Americans had decimated the Vietcong in a counterstroke against their offensive during the Vietnamese New Year – Tet. Nevertheless, American media coverage of Tet suggested that the war was lost; massive American aerial bombardment of North Vietnam did not lessen its will to fight, and American public opinion turned against the struggle (Wyatt, 2014). A good indication of the situation came with Johnson's decision in March not to contest the November 1968 presidential election. In the ensuing campaign, Nixon, the Republican nominee, did not disavow plans to get out of the war (Jeffreys-Jones, 1999: 195). Along with hard feelings towards the Democrats, it helped him win the White House. With continuing aerial bombardment of North Vietnam and the Ho Chi Minh trail destabilising Cambodia and Laos, it took until April 1973 to effect an American negotiated withdrawal and Hanoi's agreement for peaceful unification; two years later, a North Vietnamese offensive saw the fall of Saigon and communist-nationalist unification of the two states. The result was the perception inside and outside of America that it had suffered a major defeat (Tucker, 1990). Moreover, since the mid-1960s, anti-Americanism tied to neocolonialism had permeated the developing and first worlds, especially

Figure 6.1 Lyndon Johnson and Harold Wilson, July 1966
© Keystone-France / Gamma-Keystone / Getty

Détente to renewed Cold War, 1965–1979 81

the younger generation in Western Europe, Canada, and the Antipodes (Datta, 2014).

The war also saw a major readjustment of the global constellation of power. In 1967, Nixon published an article, 'Asia after Vietnam', in which he argued that America could no longer alone bear the burden of containment (Nixon, 1967), meaning regional allies had to help. Refinement of these ideas emerged in a speech in July 1969 articulating the Nixon Doctrine. Whilst upholding its alliances, America would provide a nuclear 'shield' to endangered allies or Powers vital to American security. In meeting other kinds of aggression, Washington would supply economic and military aid – not troops – thus, 'the nation directly threatened [had] to assume the primary responsibility of providing the manpower for its defense' [Document 13]. Nixon and Henry Kissinger, his national security advisor, were rebuilding America's international position – in Kissinger's words, 'from dominance to leadership' (Kissinger, 1994: 704; cf. Zanchetta, 2014: 19–34). This strategy saw an American opening to the PRC in 1971, exploiting the Sino-Soviet split (Tudda, 2012). It also witnessed efforts to use *détente* to cooperate with Moscow over nuclear arms, which produced SALT I in May 1972 – on ABMs and limiting sea- and land-based strategic ballistic missile launchers to existing levels (Newhouse, 1989).

In July–August 1975, the apotheosis of *détente* occurred. In Helsinki, 35 Powers including most of the Europeans, Russia, America, Britain, and Canada, signed a series of accords to nurture East-West amity in Europe – in essence, CSCE formally ended the Second World War by recognising Europe's existing territorial status quo, including the East German–Polish border. The signatories also committed to respecting human rights, peacefully resolving disputes, and other nostrums. Kissinger, now secretary of state, told Gerald Ford, Nixon's successor, 'We never wanted it but we went along with the Europeans. It includes some basic principles, something on human contacts, no change of frontiers, and what they call "confidence-building measures"' [Document 15].

In the years of American involvement in Southeast Asia and its aftermath, Britain supported its ally save for despatching troops to Vietnam. These policies fell largely to Wilson's Labour government (1964–1970) and Edward Heath's Conservative ministry (1970–1974) (Colman, 2004; Hill and Lord, 1996). Both Wilson and Heath balanced between strong domestic anti-Americanism over Vietnam and the Relationship's importance to British foreign policy. Bundy told Johnson in 1965 that every 'experienced observer from David Bruce [American ambassador, London] on down has been astonished by the overall strength and skill of Wilson's defence of our policy in Vietnam and his mastery of his own left wing in the process' (Colman, 2004: 88; cf. Young, 2011: 81–100). After 1970, pushing Britain's EEC membership, Heath spoke of a 'natural', not 'special', Relationship (Jones, 1997: 9). However, his foreign secretary, Alexander Douglas-Home, saw the London-Washington nexus as crucial for Britain's wider policy interests.

82   Cold War and limited war, 1945–2015

Without Heath's apparent knowledge, senior Cabinet bureaucrats consulted bimonthly with the State Department 'to keep US-UK relations on an unchanged basis', as 'most politicians and officials were far more concerned to reconcile the European and US relationships than polarise them' (Hill and Lord, 1996: 310).

Substantive British efforts had begun in 1965 – until then, the assumption had been that the Americans would succeed in Vietnam. After 1965, Labour policy was dual-track: support both peace initiatives and American military policy. In 1965, Wilson looked to the Commonwealth to engineer a peace settlement – scotched by Hanoi seeing Britain as an American puppet (Blang, 2011). In February 1967, the Soviet premier, Alexei Kosygin, visited London. Wilson's government attempted to use Moscow as a conduit to North Vietnam, failing because of Hanoi's continued opposition and Washington's reluctance when it thought it had an advantage in the war (Dumbrell and Ellis, 2003). These efforts were co-extensive with limited British support, a policy continued by Heath. Thus, London gave the Americans regional intelligence and, from their Malayan experience, advised American special forces in jungle fighting (Busch, 2002). It also did not block private British citizens and veterans from joining the American forces.

Nonetheless, Johnson sought a broader military commitment from American allies – Australia and New Zealand sent troops – but Britain refused. In 1957, Macmillan's government had restructured Britain's armed forces in the quest for economy: reducing ground forces, building interceptors, and relying more on nuclear weapons, which led to acquiring Polaris (Rees, 1989). In 1967, recognising Britain's global political contraction since 1956, Wilson's government withdrew forces 'East of Suez', including those still in Malaya and Yemen. The prevailing arguments were strategic and pragmatic: increasingly European-focussed, Britain's international influence depended on economic vitality over a global military presence. In one shrewd assessment, this decision 'marked the beginning of Britain's transformation into a modern, medium-sized world power' (Dockrill, 2002: 225–6). Whilst Wilson believed in the Relationship, Johnson reckoned it a weak reed given Britain's reluctance to commit troops to Vietnam and dissociation from American bombing of North Vietnamese targets (Colman, 2010: 72). America perceived a degree of British infidelity in leaving it to take the brunt of the fighting in Vietnam. Given American desires to dominate in the western Pacific after 1945 and its uncooperative tack at Geneva in 1954, this attitude actually constituted a reckoning with its recent regional policies.

With Heath's government turning to Europe, Nixon and Kissinger saw the Relationship as crucial for American foreign policy. They were preoccupied with Vietnam and, in 1973 and 1974, the Middle East during the Yom Kippur War and its aftermath, when Kissinger engineered a settlement that cut all the Powers, including Russia, out of the equation (Quandt, 2001). Still, Washington expected London's support over crucial issues. When Britain and France refused to back an American ceasefire resolution respecting

Détente to renewed Cold War, 1965–1979 83

Yom Kippur, Kissinger – as a lesson in power politics – temporarily ended Anglo-American intelligence-sharing, straining the Relationship (Thomas, 1997: 230n101). However, Heath's EEC policies suggested that in future, Britain would be part of a group of Powers representing Western European interests. What did it mean for the Relationship? With the Southeast Asian crisis and America's unfavourable international image, Washington could not squander the Anglo-American relationship; Kissinger advised Nixon:

> We do not suffer in the world from such an excess of friends that we should discourage those who feel that they have a special friendship with us. I would think that the answer to the special relationship of Britain would be to raise other countries to the same status, rather than to discourage Britain into a less warm relationship with the United States.
>
> (Kissinger, 1979: 91)

Britain, America, and European economic integration, January 1969–December 1979

Britain's drawing closer to Europe during Nixon's presidency actually supported Anglo-American interests in that crucial region. Britain finally joined the EEC in 1973 after agreement about common agricultural policy, sterling holdings, and some other points – but not nuclear collaboration. After De Gaulle's retirement in 1969, a new French president, Georges Pompidou, conceded British membership (Wall, 2013). Since the early 1960s, Britain's economic position had been difficult, with high unemployment, declining exports, increased imports, and an overvalued pound. In 1967 and 1968, with De Gaulle vetoing another British EEC application, a sterling-gold crisis had touched both Britain and America because of sterling's high value – $2.80 to £1.00 – and pressures on the fixed price of gold supporting the dollar (Newton, 2012). International markets connected the two currencies. Wilson's Cabinet devalued the pound to US$2.40, running against IMF strictures on currency control but making British goods more competitive internationally and looking to reduce unemployment. Johnson's presidency saw foreign governments and institutions cash in dollars for gold as Vietnam produced an American deficit and inflation. Fiscal measures by Congress staunched the flow.

Despite its relative economic decline shown by the sterling crisis, however, Britain's movement toward the EEC after 1969 and its improving economy helped it in Europe. Its position in NATO, troops in West Germany, and nuclear arsenal also enhanced its influence. In this context, British policy towards Russia proved central. Despite *détente*, tensions in Europe rose in August 1968; facing a reformist communist government in Prague, the Warsaw Pact invaded Czechoslovakia, purged the Czech leadership, and installed a regime that imposed stark authoritarianism (Bischof et al., 2009). As with Hungary, NATO could do nothing – America was too enmeshed in

84 *Cold War and limited war, 1945–2015*

Vietnam. The Russian leader, Leonid Brezhnev, issued a doctrine mirroring Truman's: 'the borders of Poland, [East Germany] and Czechoslovakia, as well as of any other Warsaw Pact member, are stable and inviolable. . . . protected by all the armed might of the socialist commonwealth' ('The Brezhnev doctrine', 2008).

Although Britain sought improved relations with the Eastern bloc after 1963 through trade, including a $300 million credit for Russia's consumer industry (Bertsch and Elliott, 1988), the invasion of Czechoslovakia prompted hardline British policies. NATO had established a Nuclear Planning Group in 1967. Working with his West German counterpart, Gerhard Schröder, by May 1969 Denis Healey, Wilson's defence minister, had produced a strategic plan towards Russia: whilst nuclear escalation would be limited and intra-allied consultation improved, nuclear weapons would reinforce alliance objectives (Schake, 2004). British reasoning lay partially with ensuring Britain's nuclear independence and strengthening its diplomatic position (Stoddart, 2012). Britain also looked to prevent Moscow from dividing the Western allies (Hughes, 2009: Chapter 6). Despite the Schröder-Healey report, the German chancellor, Willi Brandt, began pursuing *Ostpolitik* to normalise West German–Soviet Bloc relations, especially with East Germany (Fink and Schaefer, 2009: especially Chapter 1). Having left NATO's integrated command in 1966 – De Gaulle wanted an independent France with nuclear forces – Paris looked to refashion bipolar international politics, especially with Moscow, counterbalance Washington, and enhance French influence (Vaïsse, 1998).

British policy by early 1969 had two basic objectives: ensure the American connexion whilst retaining European influence through NATO and moving towards the EEC; and pursue a separate policy towards Russia and the Eastern Bloc, to prevent possible isolation by Soviet-American cooperation such as had led to SALT. The means to realise both objectives came with preparations for what became the CSCE. In October 1969, the Warsaw Pact proposed a European Security Conference to include all Pact and NATO members and the other European states (Hakkarainen, 2011: 91) – a Soviet invitation in 1954 ignored the Americans to divide NATO as West German rearmament proceeded. This fresh one looked in part to blunt *Ostpolitik* regarding East Germany. Initial Anglo-American assessments were unfavourable; such a conference could divide the Western Powers and, given Russia's record suggesting no substantive policy changes – Czechoslovakia being a case in point – prove hollow (Bozek, 2013). Moving towards European economic integration, however, British perceptions of such a conference changed. The Foreign Office saw it 'essential for a process of gradual change to be carried out unobtrusively within a stable European system, and without actively or publicly seeking the break-up of the Soviet Union, or provoking Moscow into retrograde or dangerous reactions' (Bozek, 2013: 444). Co-operation also offered the possibility of influencing Brandt's *Ostpolitik*.

Détente to renewed Cold War, 1965–1979   85

Accordingly, Britain took an active role in NATO and the EPC, created by the EEC in 1970 to foster intra-community political cooperation with new members. A NATO Ministerial Meeting in October 1972 prepared a joint brief for CSCE preparatory talks – the first time EEC Powers in the alliance outlined a united position. Britain influenced the process with a draft document helped by London's obvious willingness to demonstrate EPC effectiveness within NATO (Smith et al., 2014). As Douglas-Home earlier observed, 'Our voice will be more attentively listened to in Warsaw Pact capitals and in NATO if we are seen to be active participants in everything that is going on' (Smith et al., 2014: No. 89). Heath's government looked to affect confidence-building measures, weaken the Brezhnev Doctrine, and strengthen security with diplomatic as much as military endeavours. It also saw value in confronting Russia within larger blocs – such as NATO and the EPC – rather than unilaterally, as Nixon and Kissinger had done.

More than NATO, the EPC became central for the Western Powers (Hebel and Lenz, 2009); Britain again played the leading role (Hamilton, 1998). One reason resided with Heath, who faced opposition from powerful quarters in Britain over EEC membership and a still less-than-robust economy (Young, 1996). He needed successful economic integration – Britain, for instance, could qualify for EEC aid for depressed industries. Additionally, his pro-Europeanism and Anglo-French reconciliation strengthened the EPC. The second reason came from the EPC itself, nine Powers cooperating economically, concerting strategically without wrangling with other great and small Powers in Europe and North America. That Heath's government arrogated for itself a leading position added to its influence.

By the time the CSCE convened, the British possessed an influential voice within the EPC. They remained sceptical of CSCE success – it might augment Russia in Eastern Europe – but the EPC had to respond constructively (Bozek, 2013). Hence, promoting _détente_ and pushing for EPC coordination within NATO, Britain contributed in a major way to common EPC positions on European security; economic, scientific, and technological cooperation; and humanitarian and cultural partnership. Just as important, they added a transatlantic dimension to the EPC and its goals. It began with Kissinger embarking in 1973 on what he called 'the Year of Europe'. Looking to improve America's neglected relations with the EEC by a transformed 'Atlantic Charter' (Robb, 2010: 297–318) – Vietnam, the opening to China, and SALT had preoccupied Washington, whilst Nixon confronted a political scandal that threatened his presidency – Kissinger looked to reassert American leadership in Western Europe. Linking security and economics, Europe had to increase transatlantic military burden sharing, since its financial support would ensure the continuation of America's security umbrella (Hughes and Robb, 2013).

However, with the Europeans, especially Pompidou and Brandt, Heath hesitated. The EEC responded with the 'Declaration on European Identity' in December 1973 ('Declaration on European identity', 1973). The expanded

Figure 6.2 Richard Nixon and Edward Heath, London, October 1970
© Bill Howard / Evening News / REX / Shutterstock

community would ensure a European identity in its foreign relations: a common heritage and degree of unity; cooperation amongst its members; and the active nature of European unification. In June 1974, with Wilson's Labour Party back in office and new leaders in Paris and Bonn, NATO

Détente to renewed Cold War, 1965–1979 87

endorsed the 'Declaration on Atlantic Relations', highlighting America's 'irreplaceable' role in European defence but asserting that greater European unity strengthened the Atlantic alliance [Document 14]. Genuflecting to Kissinger's notion of the EEC as integral to NATO, it avowed independent American and EEC roles. Kissinger was unimpressed: 1973 was 'The Year That Never Was' (Hynes, 2009). He – and Nixon – had difficulty accepting a less-than-passive Europe and its economic-military integration. Criticism of Heath for his foreign policy because Bonn and Paris drew closer to Washington via the Atlantic 'Declaration' is misplaced (Hynes, 2009: Chapter 5). Heath's priority was Europe. The Relationship remained but entered a new phase after 1974.

Soviet Russian expansionism and the Anglo-American response, May 1975–December 1979

From 1974 to 1980, despite CSCE and restructured European-American relations, the Relationship went into suspended animation. Outwardly, Anglo-American amity seemed little changed. Queen Elizabeth II embarked on a highly successful visit to the United States in summer 1976 to mark the American Revolution's two hundredth anniversary. She told President Gerald Ford, 'I am confident that our visit will help to strengthen the ties of friendship between our two countries' ('Elizabeth II to Ford', 1975). Transnational culture also continued to highlight each country to the other. The American motion pictures *Star Wars* (1976), *Rocky* (1977), and *The Deer Hunter* (1979) had wide popularity in Britain; British rock-and-rollers such as the Rolling Stones, Rod Stewart, and Paul McCartney remained leading American record sellers; and actors such as Peter Sellers, Elizabeth Taylor, Richard Burton, and Meryl Streep were major stars on both sides of the Atlantic (Bragg, 1997; Doyle, 2013; Henderson, 1997).

Between governments, however, little of substance happened. In Britain, domestic politics preoccupied Wilson's Labour government and, after he retired in April 1976, that of James Callaghan. By 1973, Britain's financial predicament returned, with inflation outpacing wages. Heath's ministry responded by capping public salaries – including the government-owned mining industry – and suggesting the private sector follow (Cairncross, 1996). Supported by the Trades Union Congress, coal miners worked to rule, reducing supplies just as the Yom Kippur War precipitated increased petroleum prices. To avoid another sterling crisis and greater inflation, Heath's government introduced a three-day week on 1 January 1974, rationed energy supplies, and limited electricity to three consecutive days a week for industry and commerce. The Conservatives lost the 1974 election; the unions believed they won the day but, by summer 1975, the situation worsened. Britain was gripped by stagflation: high inflation, slow economic growth, and increased unemployment. Britain's unfavourable balance of payments and the unions' demand for higher wages exacerbated the crisis.

88 Cold War and limited war, 1945–2015

In March 1976, following forced redundancies in Britain's unprofitable motor industry (Whisler, 1999), the pound's value eroded. Sterling was collapsing and, by September, Callaghan's government had approached the IMF (Burk and Cairncross, 1992). Washington worried that this catastrophe would produce a left-wing siege economy imperilling the EEC and NATO. Thus, using the IMF, Ford's Administration forced Callaghan to institute deep public retrenchment: £2.5 billion in cuts for a $3.9 billion loan. The political cost was high as the unions turned on Callaghan's government, especially in winter 1978–1979 with interminable public-sector strikes (Taylor, 2004; Tomlinson, 2004). The problems of strained industrial relations, the still-weak pound, a poor balance of payments, social instability, and a disunited Labour Party consumed British ministers. So did increasing violence perpetrated by the IRA, which began a terrorist campaign on the British mainland. Labour did not neglect foreign policy. Wilson worked well at the CSCE; Callaghan pressured the former colony of Rhodesia – which had declared unilateral independence in 1965 under a policy of apartheid – to accept all-party talks for a multiracial government. A strong Atlanticist, Callaghan sent his son-in-law, Peter Jay, as ambassador to Washington and established a good working relationship with the Democrat Jimmy Carter, Ford's successor (Kaufman, 2006). With Labour bereft of effective economic governance, however, the Conservatives, now led by Margaret Thatcher, won election in April 1979.

In America, Carter's advent indicated desires for a better presidency. Nixon had resigned in August 1974, after Republican 'dirty tricks', including electoral malfeasance against the Democrats, had been exposed; his record convulsed the country, sharpening Democrat-Republican divisions (Kutler, 1996). In a period when American voters also criticised Washington's high-handedness that had produced the quagmire in Vietnam, Nixon and Kissinger had helped overthrow a democratically elected Marxist government in Chile in 1973 (Queshi, 2009). Although he had tried to overcome Nixon's dishonest and deceitful record, Ford proved unsuccessful. That he bumbled spectacularly during the 1976 election campaign by saying Eastern Europe was not under the Soviet yoke added to Republican misfortunes (Crain, 2009: 276); he was defeated by Carter, who offered a different foreign policy vision. Echoing Woodrow Wilson, Carter asserted that moral principles must gird foreign policy, a clear contrast with Nixon and Kissinger:

> For too many years, we've been willing to adopt the flawed and erroneous principles and tactics of our adversaries, sometimes abandoning our own values for theirs. . . . This approach failed, with Vietnam the best example of its intellectual and moral poverty.
>
> (Brands, 1999: 146)

Carter's misfortune was that morality-based diplomacy produced flawed policy that seemingly did little to counter Russian adventurism in Africa

Détente to renewed Cold War, 1965–1979   89

and South Asia after 1975. Adding to his burden after the Vietnam War, Congress had limited future presidential authority to deal with international crises that might require military deployment: in July 1973, the 'War Powers Resolution' mandated that presidents secure congressional approval for either a declaration of war or an authorising action – and funding – within 60 days of committing forces (Henry, 1984). Still, early in his Administration, Carter and his secretary of state, Cyrus Vance, had some success. In 1978, building on Nixon's opening to China, they established formal diplomatic relations with the PRC. The same year, Carter brokered the Israeli-Egyptian 'Camp David Accords', which, in 1979, produced a peace treaty formally ending the Yom Kippur War between the two Powers and increased Middle Eastern stability (Quandt, 1986). He also worked with Callaghan regarding Rhodesia (Kaufman, 2006).

Nevertheless, most of Carter's policies added to perceptions of American weakness. To help cleanse his country's image in Latin America, a region long one of American foreign policy's 'intellectual and moral poverty', he agreed in 1977 to end Washington's control of the Panama Canal – anathema to Republicans and conservative Americans (Summ and Kelly, 1988). By 1979, he refused support for the Nicaraguan dictator, Anastasio Somoza, because of human rights violations. This policy saw the advent of the revolutionary Sandinista regime that, linking with Cuba, looked to extend revolutions in Central America (Walker and Wade, 2011). Overall, however, his main problem concerned Russia.

Wanting to entrench *détente* and effect defence-spending cuts, Carter embarked on SALT II negotiations begun during Ford's short presidency (Zanchetta, 2014). Washington wanted numerical equality for each side, reducing delivery vehicles – SALT I froze rather than reduced numbers – and limiting qualitative developments that might threaten future stability. The two Powers' asymmetry in weapons posed the chief obstacle: Russia developed missiles with large warheads; America, smaller ones with greater accuracy (Panofsky, 1979). Problems also concerned new technologies such as MIRVs, with several warheads on a single missile, and the nettled question of verification. In June 1979, nonetheless, Carter and Brezhnev signed the SALT II treaty limiting MIRVs – land- and sea-launched missiles and long-range bombers – to about 2,400 weapons apiece. Carter submitted SALT II to the Senate for ratification, a process that bogged down because of Russo-American tensions.

With the American public wary of overseas commitments due to the Vietnam War, the Russians moved to profit strategically in Africa after mid-1974 as Portugal's empire collapsed in Angola and Mozambique and revolution in Abyssinia produced a Marxist regime (Kalman, 2010; Keller, 1991). It was not that Moscow had complete control over the situation. Cuba moved independently to support the Angolan MPLA both before and after it achieved victory; Fidel Castro, the Cuban leader, sought Soviet support (Gleijeses, 2013). He convinced Brezhnev, who worried Russia's image

90 Cold War and limited war, 1945–2015

would diminish if the Cuban-backed MPLA failed. Signing a Soviet-MPLA treaty of friendship in 1976, some Kremlin leaders saw the opportunity to intervene in the developing world to strengthen Russia's international position and weaken America's (Spence, 1990). Mozambique and Abyssinia added to this policy. In Mozambique, the Russians and the Cubans supported Marxist guerrillas, FRELIMO, which claimed independence in June 1975. The Horn of Africa was no different after Marxist Abyssinia emerged in March 1975 and confronted substantial opposition from armed opponents. Soviet Bloc support materialised – from Russia, East Germany, and North Korea, as well as Cuban troops (Patman, 1993).

Although intervention from South Africa and other Powers vis-à-vis both Angola and Mozambique internationalised these struggles, Carter's Administration found it difficult to intercede because of the 'War Powers Resolution' and public unwillingness to countenance another Vietnam. Thus, even if wanting to do more, Callaghan's government did little other than work with Washington in more humanitarian efforts, such as building opposition to apartheid Rhodesia and South Africa through economic sanctions. Each had limited effect. On bigger issues such as the Middle East, Carter pursued an independent policy that, like Kissinger's, bypassed allies and adversaries alike and produced the Camp David Accords.

The ultimate crisis for Carter came in late 1979. Islamic fundamentalists overthrew the shah's Iranian regime in February, and, in a welter of unadorned anti-Americanism in early November, militants occupied the American embassy in Tehran, taking more than 50 Americans hostage (Bowden, 1985). Following the new leader, Ayatollah Ruhollah Khomeini, Iranian radicals demanded that the shah return to Iran for trial – fleeing, he ultimately came to New York for cancer treatments. The radicals also demanded that Washington apologise for interfering in Iran's domestic affairs – chiefly the 1953 coup – and release assets frozen in the United States. Carter refused this blackmail, and the morality-*realpolitik* dichotomy now confronted his Administration. Vance supported negotiation; Zbigniew Brzezinski, the national security advisor, plumped for active intervention (Bowden, 1985; Brzezinski, 1983: 49). When negotiation faltered and a rescue mission by American special forces failed, Vance resigned. The Iranians achieved a decided propaganda victory, whilst US policies appeared feeble and incompetent. With Iran, given Panama, Nicaragua, and apparent Soviet success in Africa, Carter's vision of a new foreign policy seemed flawed at every level.

Then, on Christmas 1979, Soviet troops entered Afghanistan – ostensibly to aid Kabul in its war against Islamist tribal insurgents (Braithwaite, 2011). In reality, Moscow moved to ensure the security of the Moslem republics within the southern Soviet Union: the possibility of Iran's revolution seeping northwards had importance, as did the apparent weakness of any potential American response. Although Russian leaders anticipated a speedy military victory to underscore the Brezhnev Doctrine, rapid success did not occur.

Détente to renewed Cold War, 1965–1979 91

In line with containment, America and its allies, such as Britain – Thatcher proved a diehard anti-communist – searched for means to coerce Moscow to withdraw. One of Carter's first actions in this regard was to pull SALT II out of the Senate. The United States also blocked American grain deliveries to Russia – which antagonised American farmers – and boycotted the Olympic Games in Moscow in summer 1980. On 23 January 1980, sensing that the Russians sought hegemony in the oil-rich Persian Gulf, Carter proclaimed publicly that Washington would employ armed force to defend American interests in that region. It became the Carter Doctrine, with the key passage written by Brzezinski:

> An attempt by any outside force to gain control of the Persian Gulf region will be regarded as an assault on the vital interests of the United States of America, and such an assault will be repelled by any means necessary, including military force.
>
> (Yetiv, 1995: 56)

Carter moving to active containment proved too little, too late. A principled politician, he discovered the world of *realpolitik* too much for a moralistic approach to foreign policy. *Détente* expired after five years of Soviet adventurism at the expense of a weakened America and a strategically faded Special Relationship. New leaders in Washington and London would have to deal with renewed Cold War.

7 Margaret Thatcher, Ronald Reagan, and the 'Special Relationship', December 1979– December 1988

In the 1980s, with two strongly Atlanticist leaders in London and Washington – Thatcher and Ronald Reagan – the Relationship re-emerged as a major element of international politics. Becoming Conservative leader in 1975, Thatcher heralded decisive change for Britain's society and economy and, crucially, an activist foreign policy allied with America (Moore, 2013; cf. Sharp, 1997) [Document 16]. In January 1976, Thatcher told her countrymen, 'In the Conservative Party we believe that our foreign policy should continue to be based on a close understanding with our traditional ally, America. This is part of our Anglo-Saxon tradition as well as part of our NATO commitment, and it adds to our contribution to the European Community.' As this speech showed, this policy centred on Russia. Thatcher immediately antagonised Moscow, whose propaganda derisively labelled her the 'Iron Lady'. Wearing this epithet as a badge of honour and, over the next three years as opposition leader, in addition to lambasting Wilson and Callaghan's poor economic performance and subservience to the Trades Union Congress, she argued for a better-armed Britain to oppose Russia and re-engage more fully with the Americans. Never subtle, she rejected Heath's conception of 'natural' Anglo-American relations.

A cinema star from the late 1930s to the early 1960s, Reagan became prominent in American politics for anti-communist activism in 1950s Hollywood, a spokesman for American big business, and governor of California from 1967 to 1975 (Johns, 2015). Although twice failing to win the Republican presidential nomination – in 1968 and 1976 – he won that right in 1980, and his campaign promised to revive both America's economy and its international position, which he argued had enervated under Carter. He vowed a new approach to American politics – supply-side economics and less government regulation domestically and, in foreign policy, a rearmed America that desired peace but was willing to confront and restrain an aggressive Russia. On election eve 1980, American voters learnt:

> But let it also be clear that we do not shirk history's call; that America is not turned inward but outward – toward others. Let it be clear that we have not lessened our commitment to peace or to the hope that

Thatcher, Reagan, and the Relationship 93

someday all of the people of the world will enjoy lives of decency, lives with a degree of freedom, with a measure of dignity [Document 17].

Conflating American notions of liberty with capitalism, Reagan's foreign policy attitude remained clear. Fixed on Russia, his Administration would end the slide in American economic and strategic fortunes that had occurred since Vietnam. With similar worldviews and determined to reverse British economic feebleness, Thatcher's Britain stood as America's natural ally in confronting the Soviets. The Relationship moved out of suspended animation.

Carter, Reagan, and Thatcher: to euromissile deployment in Europe, 1981–1985

The basis for renewing the Relationship began in Carter's last year in office. After Callaghan left office, Carter continued pursuing anti-apartheid efforts respecting Rhodesia and South Africa, his object to enhance America's image in Africa as much as facilitate forcing both Rhodesia and South Africa by economic pressure to implement policies of 'one person, one vote' and regime change. Thatcher's government had a different approach (Thompson, 2001). It recognised that with economically significant allies, such as Israel, and access to the sea, South Africa had a strong strategic position. Disliking apartheid, but willing to move slowly to force reform, Thatcher believed general trade sanctions immoral: they exacerbated Black South African unemployment. Moreover, ignoring sanctions would help economic revival in Britain, South Africa's largest trading partner and foreign investor. South Africa, furthermore, was involved in operations against Cuban-backed Angola, necessary to contain communism in the region. Accordingly, over South Africa, Thatcher broke from Carter. In the first six months of her government, however, landlocked and financially strapped Rhodesia buckled. In September 1979, its apartheid government began talks with Black Rhodesian nationalists in London chaired by Lord Carrington, Thatcher's foreign secretary. Four months later, they achieved a power-sharing agreement for a renamed state, 'Zimbabwe'. Although somewhat tentative, the result was a diplomatic achievement for the new Conservative government (White, 2015).

In the Horn of Africa, Carter's Administration played its own game (Jackson, 2007). But in 1979 and 1980, Carter sought British support in South Asia. In one telling view, 'The Soviet invasion of Afghanistan . . . was a chance for Margaret Thatcher to demonstrate her Cold War credentials and her commitment to US leadership' (Bulmer-Thomas, 2013). Showing fidelity to the Americans – London and Washington mistrusted Moscow – her government's efforts had mixed results (Lahey, 2013). Although further Russian expansionism seemed unlikely in the short term, Moscow could achieve increased regional influence by exploiting weaker Powers such as Afghanistan's neighbour, Pakistan. With Thatcher chairing the Joint Intelligence Committee on 10 January 1980, Whitehall began, first, to show Moscow

94 *Cold War and limited war, 1945–2015*

that its invasion had a price and, second, to consider helping Islamist fighters – *mujahidin* – against the Russians (Smith et al., 2012). Britain ended preferential credits for Moscow, cancelled military exchanges, restricted technology exports, and ended high-level contacts. Still, Thatcher faced continuing domestic economic weakness – her government only beginning to reverse Labour's policies – thus, she endorsed Carter's desire to have NATO assist Anglo-American anti-Soviet efforts in Afghanistan. She pressed the Europeans at NATO meetings in February, but their support was not forthcoming. Annoyed with Thatcher's desire to reduce Britain's share of the EEC budget, Paris and Bonn saw economic and political benefits in Europe devolving from continuing *détente* – the West Germans perceived Russian action in Afghanistan as securing their sphere of interest (Campbell, 2003). Whilst sanctioning a British Olympic boycott, Thatcher could not control British athletes, who decided to compete. Britain's MI6 intelligence service nevertheless began working with the CIA in funnelling arms to the *mujahidin*. Britain also showed solidarity with Pakistan. Thatcher discussed British military aid with Pakistan's foreign minister in June 1980, welcomed Mohammed Zia-ul-Haq, the Pakistani strongman, in London in October 1980, and went to Pakistan the next autumn ('Call by the foreign minister of Pakistan', 1980). As she said publicly during her visit, 'East/West relations cannot be normalised, with all that would mean for the stability of Europe, Asia and beyond, without a settlement of the problem of Afghanistan' (Thatcher, 1981).

Reagan's advent began stronger American efforts to confront Russia – as promised in the election campaign, Reagan and his advisors took the offensive against Russian inroads in the wider world. Although following this policy for three years, at the base of which was massive rearmament, Reagan first articulated it publicly in February 1985. Its principal tenet held, 'We must stand by all our democratic allies. And we must not break faith with those who are risking their lives – on every continent, from Afghanistan to Nicaragua – to defy Soviet-supported aggression and secure rights which have been ours from birth' [Document 24]. Thus, the Reagan Doctrine. Thatcher proved a willing ally; they had corresponded, and he met her several times before November 1980 and, once in the White House, again in February 1981 (Henderson, 1981).

Thatcher was already involved in strengthening Western Europe against the Russians. In the late 1970s, assuming Carter's Administration would not respond, Moscow began replacing its missiles in Europe with new SS-20 MIRVs. However, in December 1979, as things in Afghanistan heated up, NATO adopted a carrot-and-stick 'dual-track' policy: seek agreement with Moscow to limit theatre nuclear weapons but base such weapons – euromissiles – in Western Europe: 464 new cruise and 108 Pershing II missiles capable of striking western Russia (Garthoff, 1985). Agreement evaporated because of Afghanistan and SALT II's withdrawal from Congress. Over the next three years, Thatcher led in enhancing Western Europe's nuclear strength. She said in June 1980, 'The fact is that the Soviet Union has the latest nuclear missile – and it is facing Europe. We must have an effective deterrent' (Campbell, 2003).

Despite questioning by senior Cabinet ministers, including John Nott, the defence secretary, she began negotiations with Washington – successful after Reagan took office – to replace Polaris with new, more potent, and expensive sea-launched Trident missiles [Document 18].

Figure 7.1 Ronald Reagan and Margaret Thatcher, Washington, DC, February 1981
© Bettmann / Getty

96   *Cold War and limited war, 1945–2015*

Her diplomacy had two parts. Britain immediately agreed to base 144 cruise missiles at Greenham Common and Molesworth air bases, an action evincing little initial public reaction. Nevertheless, by 1983, when disarmament groups such as the Campaign for Nuclear Disarmament reckoned a bellicose Reagan might launch a nuclear strike against Russia – in March 1983, he labelled the Soviet Union an 'evil empire' – peace advocates supported by Labour tried to galvanise public opinion against Conservative defence policy (Reitan, 2003). Thatcher proved unbending. The second part involved pressuring the major European Powers, especially Germany and France, but also smaller Powers such as the Netherlands, to base euromissiles over public pressures not to do so (Stoddart, 2015). Concerned about Western determination to meet the SS-20 threat in 1979, Brezhnev offered to freeze weapons deployment – a freeze still providing Russia with a strategic advantage via its newer weapons. When this ploy failed, Moscow initiated a disinformation and propaganda campaign to influence Western European peace movements to undercut the case for deploying euromissiles (Prados, 2011) – its goal involved decoupling America from Europe and weakening NATO. Opposing disarmament advocates, Thatcher pressed for euromissile deployment to ensure NATO strength, reinforce America's connexion to the alliance, and, most important, underwrite Britain's strategic bona fides to the Relationship.

Whilst Reagan proposed a 'zero-zero' policy after taking office – both alliances eliminate INF in Europe (Prados, 2011) – new governments in Bonn and Paris helped Thatcher. Francois Mitterrand, the socialist French president after May 1981, was strongly Atlanticist and wary of Russian policy. Willing to accept American leadership on this issue, he also reckoned that West German euromissiles would tie Bonn closer to the EEC and NATO – Bonn's continuing pursuit of *Ostpolitik* concerned Paris. France possessed its own INF; and, in January 1983, Mitterrand spoke to the *Bundestag*, arguing for West German deployment despite domestic opposition (Cole, 1994: 138; cf. Lellouche, 1983–1984). Whilst West Germany's Social Democratic chancellor, Helmut Schmidt, had been integral to NATO's 'dual track' decision, his party contained dissidents opposed to euromissiles; he seems initially to have seen the threat to deploy as means to get the Russians to the negotiating table (Spohr, 2015). Consequently, West Germany prevaricated. When Schmidt lost office to the conservative Christian Democrats, led by Helmut Kohl, in March 1983 elections, Thatcher – and Mitterrand – found a more amenable NATO ally. Euromissiles were a crucial issue in the elections, one analysis suggesting that West Germans voted more for NATO than to support American policy (Burt, 1983). Whilst the advent of Mitterrand and Kohl helped NATO's strategic position, Thatcher's efforts over euromissile deployment was long-standing and firm; she also thought zero-zero dangerous: it might eliminate basing cruise and Pershing II INF missiles in Europe, which caused some tensions with Reagan (Baylis and Stoddart, 2015). Nonetheless, she had strengthened Britain militarily, pursued NATO cohesion, and, by endorsing American euromissile policy, reinforced the Relationship.

The Falklands War and the strength of the 'Special Relationship', 1982–1983

In the midst of euromissile diplomacy, a major crisis reinforced the Relationship. Since 1832, Britain had controlled the Falkland Islands, which lay 500 kilometres off Argentina's south coast. Although the islands constituted a sparsely populated colony of little strategic value, Argentina long coveted them as part of its national territory. A military junta led Argentina after 1976, its governance proving decidedly inept: economic stagnation and civil unrest produced hardline police-state control. A new junta leadership emerged in December 1981, headed by General Leopoldo Galtieri; its naval member, Admiral Jorge Anaya, surmised the moment ripe to seize the Falklands (Middlebrook, 2009). A recent defence review by Nott proposed withdrawing the only British naval vessel in the region, suggesting to Anaya that Britain would not defend the Falklands (Dorman, 2001). A successful invasion would distract Argentinian public opinion from the economic crisis and human rights imbroglio and, building on patriotism, strengthen junta legitimacy. Thatcher's government never anticipated an Argentinian invasion – with the Falkland Islanders wishing to remain British, London was involved in desultory UN-based discussions that looked for some compromise over Argentinian access (Kacowicz, 1994).

On 19 March 1983, a group of visiting Argentinian metal merchants that included Argentinian marines in mufti raised the Argentinian flag on South Georgia, one of the Sandwich islands, 2,400 kilometres east of the Falklands (Freedman, 2005). Britain countered by sending its sole naval vessel from the port of Stanley on East Falkland and despatched south two submarines and a supply ship on 29 March, and the junta responded by invading the Falklands on 2 April. Admiral Sir Henry Leach, the chief of the naval staff, had counselled Thatcher and senior ministers that 'Britain could and should send a task force if the islands are invaded' and, on 1 April, ordered a flotilla exercising in the Mediterranean to ready for deployment to the South Atlantic ('. . . An attempt to understand The Falklands War', 2014). Reacting to the invasion the next day, Thatcher's Cabinet approved retaking the islands, a decision backed immediately by the Conservative-controlled House of Commons.

The military course of the Falklands War is well known (Freedman, 2005; Smith, 1989). Britain's victory was not assured – its forces had to traverse 13,000 kilometres of ocean and, with aerial cover, land and dislodge the invaders. On the islands, greater, well-armed Argentine troops quickly overran the small British garrison and colonial administration. Britain's essential military tool was the Task Force – a 143-vessel fleet of warships, including two aircraft carriers, supply ships, auxiliary merchantmen, and several thousand troops. RAF deployment to British-controlled Ascension Island north of the Falklands provided additional air support, although Argentina's warplanes outnumbered those of Britain. On 2 April, London declared

98 Cold War and limited war, 1945–2015

a 200-nautical-mile 'Maritime Exclusion Zone' around the Falklands within which British submarines could attack Argentinian naval vessels. On 30 April, a 'Total Exclusion Zone' followed: all vessels and aircraft from any Power might suffer attack without warning. Awaiting Britain's counteroffensive, the reinforced Argentinians dug in.

Naval exchanges in early May ended any possibility of a political settlement. On 2 May, with Cabinet approval, a RN submarine sank the Argentinian light cruiser, *General Belgrano*, with a loss of 323 hands. It proved a strategic victory, as all Argentinian warships retreated home for the duration of the conflict. Two days later, however, Argentinian fighter aircraft unleashed a missile attack on the HMS *Sheffield*, a destroyer patrolling the Task Force perimeter – immobilised, the ship sank a week later; 20 crew died. This attack roused the British will to continue.

On 25 April, British forces recaptured South Georgia. This was followed by bombing of Argentinian targets on the Falklands from Ascension. Another Argentinian strategic weakness was that, as the Falklands' airstrips were inadequate for modern warplanes, their air force operated from the mainland. Task Force carriers, thus, gave the British an advantage in the air war. On May 21, after British special forces captured the air base on a nearby island, 4,000 British troops landed on the northwest coast of East Falkland to establish a bridgehead: their goal was Port Stanley. Facing air attacks, British forces won control of the west side of East Falkland before moving eastwards to Stanley. After a parachute regiment defeated a larger Argentinian force on 28 May in the southwest, 5,000 British reinforcements arrived and, despite air attacks on their supply ships, consolidated the British position. This paved the way for an assault on 11 June against Stanley. After three days of heavy fighting, the Argentinians capitulated, almost 10,000 troops surrendered, and the conflict ended.

Military operations provided the backdrop for the conflict's diplomacy. Britain immediately brought the matter before the UN Security Council; condemning the invasion, Resolution 502 demanded Argentina's withdrawal (1982). Whilst the Commonwealth and EEC also supported Britain – the latter with economic sanctions against Argentina – some Latin American Powers backed Buenos Aires. However, as this was a Cold War crisis, the positions of America and Russia were critical. Abstaining from the UN vote, the Russians privately indicated to Galtieri's regime that they would offer aid for junta support on matters from Afghanistan to Central America – Reagan's Administration had taken a strong line against Sandinista Nicaragua and its Cuban ally (Carothers, 1991). Reckoning the political cost too high, Buenos Aires received no Soviet military or intelligence support (Gustafson, 1998). With its forces mired in Afghanistan, Moscow could actually do little.

Washington still worried about Soviet intervention of some sort, its initial reaction centring on mediation. Reagan's secretary of state, Alexander Haig, a retired general and former NATO supreme commander, believed the

Thatcher, Reagan, and the Relationship 99

British could not succeed militarily. In the NSC on 30 April, he described the situation as 'tragic, with both sides similar to a demented man on a ledge ready to jump, reaching for help but unable to grab our hand.' He then described 'the elements of the American [mediation] plan, which in effect would give ultimate sovereignty to Argentina but under evolutionary conditions which the Islanders could ultimately accept' [Document 19]. Haig was a senior Administration official with little sympathy for the Relationship; the influential American UN ambassador, Jeanne Kirkpatrick, was more concerned about Argentina as an American ally. In her view, Galtieri's regime would now accept UN intervention, something 'hard for the British to turn down because this time the U.N. will be evenhanded.' Reagan concluded, 'after all these years, the U.N. could accomplish something as constructive as averting war between the U.K. and Argentina'.

Thatcher's determination not to surrender jettisoned any notion of an American-brokered settlement, the sinking of the *Belgrano* and the *Sheffield* accentuating the nature of the conflict. Moreover, given British policy concerning Russia, appeasement would imperil Western strength. Haig had embarked on shuttle diplomacy between London and Buenos Aires in April to resolve the crisis (Holmes and Rofe, 2012), his willingness to give Argentina 'ultimate sovereignty' showing either an inability to understand Thatcher's position or a belief that Washington could force an unpalatable solution on London. On 30 April, with Buenos Aires rejecting American mediation, Reagan's Administration blocked arms sales to Argentina and provided material and intelligence support to Britain.

Working with Britain's ambassador to Washington, Sir Nicholas Henderson, who was friendly with Reagan, Thatcher's government embarked on a campaign to publicise its position in America (Davis, 2015). This effort supplemented Thatcher's concerted efforts to use personal diplomacy within the Relationship to ensure Reagan's undiluted support for British policy. It was not that Reagan underestimated her determination. On the eve of the invasion, he warned Galtieri, 'If the only option is a military invasion. . . . Ms. Thatcher is a decisive woman and she will have no choice but to fight back.' (Wynia, 1986: 15) Yet American policy for the first month of the crisis lacked consistency, suggesting infidelity to its principal European ally. Thatcher had taken the fight for euromissile deployment to her political cost with British opinion and NATO allies. As late as 31 May, before the final assault on Stanley, Reagan sought a peace that would not humiliate Argentina. Thatcher responded unambiguously: 'I didn't lose some of my best ships and some of my finest lives, to leave quietly under a ceasefire without the Argentines withdrawing' [Document 20]. Reagan conceded politely.

Washington's problem lay in choosing between two friendly Powers. Reagan first worried about Britain succeeding and, when it was certain it would, the impact on American policy in Latin America (Wappshot, 2007) – although some Latin American Powers, such as Chile, Argentina's rival, supported Britain. The transition to coherence meant supporting one or the other. As

100   Cold War and limited war, 1945–2015

so often happened in transatlantic relations, *realpolitik* ruled: the choice had to be Britain, given its connexion to America in NATO, in European and wider security issues, and the Relationship. Lawrence Eagleburger, an influential State Department official, explained this transition best: 'I was driven essentially by one very simple argument – an ally is an ally. I believed . . . that one of our serious general foreign policy problems is a growing perception – correct perception – that we are no longer reliable partners and allies as we were, [and] under those circumstances in a case that was so important to Mrs. Thatcher . . . we had no choice' (Desch, 2008: 151). Caspar Weinberger, the anglophile defence secretary, also strongly supported Thatcher (NSA, 1982). Argentina's defeat added to Britain's international gravitas and, with its important position within the Western alliance, the Relationship's strength.

Thatcher, Reagan, and Mikhail Gorbachev: the weakening of Soviet Russia, 1983–1988

In the first half of the 1980s, communist control of Eastern Europe seemed to intensify; in Poland, for instance, martial law was declared in December 1981 to stymie worker dissent channelled through an independent nationalist trade union movement, Solidarity (Kramer, 2010). In these circumstances, ironically, Thatcher and Reagan confronted a Kremlin that lacked stable leadership. Brezhnev died in November 1982, his successor Yuri Andropov died in February 1984, and Andropov's successor, Konstantin Chernenko, died in March 1985 (Brown, 2009: Chapter 20). Representing the Communist Party's old guard, having matured politically under Stalin, these leaders shared philosophical beliefs about inevitable Marxist-Leninist success outside Russia and international capitalism's unavoidable collapse. More practically, they sought to counter the Americans and their allies wherever possible, protect their Eastern European empire, and shepherd the Russian-dominated Soviet Bloc economy to underpin domestic solidarity, the cost of Russian armed forces, and the strength of Russian foreign policy. Their tools were stark authoritarianism at home and, within Eastern Europe, the Red Army to guarantee obedient Warsaw Pact allies. With little reform since Khrushchev's time, the old guard stubbornly supported an increasingly sclerotic political system in Russia and Eastern Europe, a command economy weakening daily by intractable central planning, high defence spending, and a war in Afghanistan that further enfeebled the economy and stretched Russian military resources (Lundestad, 2012: 135–7). Furthermore, whilst Angola remained firmly Marxist, Mozambique and Abyssinia faced instability that Soviet aid could not solve. Younger Party leaders – prominent after Stalin's death – reckoned that the old governance had to change for Russia to remain a Great Power; this generational division further compounded instability in Moscow. In 1984, by selecting Chernenko, the old guard blocked the younger generation's rising star, Mikhail Gorbachev. When Gorbachev

Thatcher, Reagan, and the Relationship   101

became the Party's general secretary hours after Chernenko's death, a watershed for Russia occurred.

Gorbachev and his supporters intended to reform the Party and government and, recognising the economy's weakness, rebuild this crucial element of Soviet power (Brown, 2009: Chapter 24). They never intended to end one-party rule, abandon Marxism-Leninism, or surrender any advantages to the Western Powers – instead, they sought to promote openness and democratisation in government (*glasnost* and *demokratizatsiya*), restructure the government and economy (*perestroika*), and accelerate economic development (*uskoreiye*). Reagan – from the moment he took office – used American economic and financial resources and technological superiority to prepare America's armed forces to confront the Russians. His strategy involved escalating the Cold War – for instance, by supporting the *mujahidin* in Afghanistan and anti-Marxist forces in Africa and Central America – and a propaganda campaign, including the 'evil empire' speech, to convince Americans and others 'that communism is another sad, bizarre chapter in human history whose last pages even now are being written' [Document 21] (Cohen, 2015). Given Russian economic limitations, Moscow would have to yield in the face of Western rearmament, including euromissile deployment. Moreover, Reagan and Weinberger promoted SDI as the linchpin of their anti-Russian policies. Marrying American financial resources to superior technology would provide a satellite-based ABM system to defeat any Soviet attack. It also meant abandoning Kennedy and McNamara's MAD strategy in favour of an American first strike. For Moscow, a nuclear arms agreement with the Western Powers became a necessity.

Thatcher was one of the first Western leaders to see Gorbachev as someone 'we can do business with' (Coffey, 2009: 373–4; cf. Sharp, 1997: Chapter 10). She met him in March 1984, when he seemed Chernenko's likely successor. As she told the BBC, 'I like Mr. Gorbachev. We can do business together. . . . we have two great interests in common: that we should both do everything we can to see that war never starts again, and therefore we go into the disarmament talks determined to make them succeed' (17 December 1984). No doubt, Gorbachev was mounting a charm offensive – he also impressed Mitterrand (Coffey, 2009). Nevertheless, despite sensing that change in Russia's leadership could engender nuclear arms limitation, Thatcher proved cautious. She did not want Britain's nuclear arsenal sacrificed on the altar of good relations, something that could lessen Britain's international status increased by the Falklands War. In fact, in a June 1983 general election, domestic opposition to Thatcher melted away in the aftermath of victory, Labour ran a poor campaign, and the Conservatives increased their majority (Butler and Kavanaugh, 1984).

A realist, Thatcher knew that Britain had to balance between Moscow and Washington. She did all possible, therefore, to work within the Relationship. It was not always easy. For instance, in October 1983, American forces invaded the eastern Caribbean island state of Grenada in response

102 *Cold War and limited war, 1945–2015*

to perceptions that its Marxist government was falling under Cuba's influence. Strategically, the American invasion and overthrow of Grenada's government constituted part of the wider regional conflict involving Reagan's America, its Central American and Caribbean allies, and its Cuban and Sandinista adversaries. Washington saw a Cuban-built airport in Grenada as a potential transport hub for Soviet penetration of the region; moreover, as America's first intervention abroad since Vietnam, Grenada provided an opportunity to restore confidence in Washington's ability to intervene successfully abroad in an area judged essential to American national security. In Reagan's view, 'I understood what Vietnam had meant for the country, but I believed the United States couldn't remain spooked forever by this experience to the point where it refused to stand up and defend its legitimate national security interests' (Reagan, 1990: 451). Other Powers, chiefly Russia, had to know that a new era in American foreign policy existed.

Nevertheless, as Grenada was a Commonwealth member, Britain had some responsibility. Reagan told Thatcher the day before the invasion that he was only contemplating action (Reagan telegram to Thatcher, 1983). Her foreign secretary, Geoffrey Howe, immediately told Parliament that the government knew of no American plans. The intervention thus surprised the British as much as anyone else. Thatcher later wrote, 'I felt dismayed and let down by what had happened. At best the British government had been made to look impotent; at worst we looked deceitful' (Thatcher, 1993: 331). Knowing that American action had caught London unaware, Reagan telephoned the day after the invasion [Document 22] ('Grenada: No.10 record of telephone conversation', 1983). As Thatcher suspected as bogus American claims that the speed of events precluded consultations and that Reagan had purposely kept her uninformed, he told her that the Organisation of East Caribbean States had suddenly asked for American help: 'We have had a nagging problem of a loose source, a leak here. At the same time we also had immediate surveillance problem [*sic*] – without their knowing it – of what was happening on Cuba to make sure that we could get ahead of them if they were moving[,] and indeed, they were making some tentative moves'. Although Thatcher put her concerns on record – 'I know about sensitivity, because of the Falklands. . . . The action is underway now and we just hope it will be successful', each leader said nothing to impair the Relationship. Indeed, Reagan proved particularly apologetic: 'We regret very much the embarrassment caused you'. Even so, the Americans had acted in their own interest; Britain had to accept that fact.

Another lesson for Britain in dealing with the far more important Russian question came forth as well. For Britain's security, its wider defence within NATO, and the foreign policy voice that Thatcher was securing, London could not lag over any nuclear agreement. Here, SDI proved nettlesome as, if successful, it might undermine the long-established strategy of deterrence by diminishing Britain's Trident and euromissile forces. In December 1984, after Grenada and her first meeting with Gorbachev, Thatcher and a

Thatcher, Reagan, and the Relationship   103

high-level British delegation met Reagan and senior US officials at Camp David. Although they discussed a range of issues including Central America and the Middle East, Thatcher's focus lay on SDI and nuclear negotiations with Moscow.

> Saying she didn't wish to debate strategic theory, Mrs. Thatcher noted that some claim SDI would be an incentive for the Soviets to produce more offensive systems and could encourage the Soviets to launch a pre-emptive first strike. From our point of view, said Mrs. Thatcher, deterrence remains our fundamental objective.
>
> (Document 23; cf. Brown, 2010: 26)

Reagan's secretary of state, George Schultz, who replaced Haig in July 1982, and his national security advisor, Robert McFarlane, disagreed. McFarlane pointed out that 'her remarks are based on the assumption that offensive deterrence in its present form can and will endure. . . . In recent years the character of Soviet offensive systems has changed dramatically; they are more mobile and carry increased warheads, making verification a near impossible task.' Still, looking to protect Britain's nuclear independence, she won Reagan's approval that America was not 'attempting to regain [its] superiority through SDI' alone – euromissiles remained important (Hughes, 1990). Although the Western Powers could do business with Gorbachev – which she emphasised – Washington and London had to approach Moscow prudently.

Reagan accepted Thatcher's surmise about working with Gorbachev over nuclear arms reductions – with SDI development and Western assistance to the *mujahidin* in the background. In November 1984, immediately after his re-election, he had invited Chernenko's government to resume negotiations on strategic, intermediate, and defensive weapons – START negotiations he promoted in May 1982 that the Russians had essentially abandoned because of SDI. The Russians accepted in January 1985, but Chernenko's death and Gorbachev's subsequent consolidation of power delayed productive talks. Although the Russians continued to develop and deploy new weapons, their economy could not withstand an arms race. In July 1985, Gorbachev suspended Russian nuclear testing, which did nothing to reduce existing deployments: Reagan refused to reciprocate – testing remained central to SDI and American nuclear modernisation – which put additional pressure on Moscow. In November 1985, Reagan met Gorbachev at Geneva in friendly but unproductive talks. The Russians would have to make real concessions. Gorbachev understood. In January 1986, he outlined a three-part proposal for nuclear disarmament over 15 years, which Reagan and his advisors rejected as too slow.

Bargaining continued until the autumn. Responding to supposed Russian treaty violations in May, Reagan renounced American commitments to SALT I and II on strategic offensive weapons. Wedded to SDI, he followed

104 *Cold War and limited war, 1945–2015*

his SALT announcement with an effort to outmanoeuvre Gorbachev by suggesting the abolition of all nuclear missiles. Because it gave America a strategic advantage, Gorbachev rejected it; but the two Powers continued negotiations. These efforts constituted the genesis of a Russo-American summit at Reykjavik in October 1986 – Reagan and Gorbachev talked privately about eliminating all nuclear weapons. Whilst doing so proved impractical, Reykjavik produced agreement on eliminating European INF – cruise and Pershing missiles – and cutting strategic offensive weapons by one-half. Finding agreement on SDI within the ABM Treaty proved barren.

In early 1987, Reagan was engulfed in a scandal after it was revealed that US officials had secretly helped sell arms to Iran, using the profits to support anti-Sandinista 'Contras' in Nicaragua (Byrne, 2014). An arms control agreement could benefit Reagan's falling approval ratings. Facing economic constraints and reckoning that SDI would take time to become operational, Gorbachev broke. He offered to separate INF from strategic talks, including SDI. It was a significant climb-down for Russia, leading to an INF agreement signed at Washington in December 1987 (Watson, 2011). This agreement included improved verification – Reagan had said 'trust but verify' – whilst eliminating a class of nuclear weapons. Efforts towards a strategic agreement continued into 1988. Despite the earlier INF success, however, the Powers failed to resolve remaining differences over interpreting the ABM Treaty and the nature of offensive/defensive weapons under START. And one major issue respecting the both Russia's reality and its willingness to accommodate occurred: on 20 July 1987, announcement came that Russian troops would withdraw from Afghanistan (Braithwaite, 2011: Part III). When the last Soviet troops departed on 15 February 1989, the Americans and their allies shared a signal achievement.

In this convoluted diplomacy, Thatcher remained concerned about America's connexion to European security given Red Army numerical superiority over NATO – cruise and Pershing missiles were a deterrent. She, therefore, concentrated on three intertwined policies: working with Britain's Western European allies, keeping lines of communication open with Gorbachev and Eastern Europe, and, given Russo-American dialogue, pressuring Reagan to remain committed to Western European defence. The main effort concerning Western Europe occurred within the WEU, reborn in 1984. At a council meeting in April 1986, whilst supporting Russo-American arms-limitation efforts, the WEU emphasised the importance of independent British and French nuclear forces for deterrence (Bloed and Wessel, 1995). Nonetheless, conventional forces had a role, and Britain and the WEU wanted ongoing conventional force talks in Vienna to ensure asymmetrical cuts: given its numbers, the Red Army should withdraw more troops than NATO. Meeting Reagan again just after Reykjavik, Thatcher secured his agreement to recognise Western Europe's defence priorities: 'We confirmed that NATO's strategy of forward defence and flexible response would continue to require effective nuclear deterrents based upon a mix of systems. . . . reductions in

Thatcher, Reagan, and the Relationship   105

nuclear weapons would increase the importance of eliminating conventional disparities' ('Press Conference after Camp David talks', 1986). Whilst sacrificing INF – cruise missiles left Britain in March 1991 – Trident remained essential to British deterrence.

With unified European defence hingeing on NATO, Thatcher faced differing West German–French views about nuclear arms limitation and its portent. Bonn remained uneasy about euromissile deployment in West Germany given that Germany would be the probable European nuclear battleground. On 26 August 1987, Kohl announced that his government would remove all Pershing and cruise missiles if the Americans and Russians did the same (Graham and LaVera, 2003). Facing domestic opposition and seeking better Russian relations touching *Ostpolitik*, he looked to better any bargaining position with Gorbachev. As befitted their desire for 'security independence', the French took the opposite position (Fraudet, 2006: 104–7). Euromissiles linked France to America's nuclear umbrella and allowed for French nuclear forces. American weapons also boosted French security.

Thatcher's government took a middle stance. Reluctant to withdraw euromissiles, it understood the Reagan Administration's position. Thatcher had won Washington's commitment to continued Western European security, lobbied for realistic conventional forces to oppose the Warsaw Pact, and retained Trident as part of Western deterrence. With the British also supporting the *mujahidin*, she met with Gorbachev a few times. In March 1987, for instance, she did not hold back: 'communism is striving to dominate everywhere. . . . Yemen, Ethiopia, Mozambique, Angola, Nicaragua, Cuban troops in some African countries' [Document 25]. Gorbachev had to understand that the Western Powers – implying a strong Anglo-American axis – would not relent in those places or Europe. Moreover, Moscow should reform its relationship with Eastern Europe and move towards a capitalist economy – accepting the political repercussions for its empire.

Poland was an example. In the early 1980s, Thatcher's government balanced between the Polish government and the reformist Solidarity movement, the latter supported by the anti-communist Polish pope, John Paul II, who had become pontiff in 1978 (O'Sullivan, 2006). Part of the reason was to avoid regional instability that could prompt Russian intervention; the other to increase British trade to aid political liberalisation (Poggiolini, 2012). British and EEC trade with Poland increased after 1983, but the Polish government–Solidarity relationship remained uneasy. In 1986, tinged with Polish nationalism, that relationship soured further because of the imprisonment of Solidarity activists and the regime's hard domestic line. Britain's ambassador in Warsaw warned that the consequences for 'Poland's relations with the West and thus for East-West relations, for Mr. Gorbachev's own reform programme and for human rights in Poland would be very serious' (Poggiolini, 2012: 272). In the 1981–1982 Polish crisis, pursuing a hard line against the Russians and the Warsaw Pact, Washington

106   *Cold War and limited war, 1945–2015*

thought the Europeans weak over sanctions against them. Reagan told the NSC, 'this is the last chance of a lifetime, that this revolution started against this "damned force", we should let our Allies know that they, too, will pay a price if they don't go along; that we have long memories' (Saltoun-Ebin, 2010: 108). British and EEC trade with Russia, however, dwarfed that of America. Thatcher's restraint provoked some difficulties with Washington – for instance, over a Siberian pipeline being built by Western corporations to deliver gas to Western Europe. The Kremlin would spend profits in Western Europe, creating greater Russian dependence on these markets. Accordingly, Thatcher used trade to liberalise Eastern Europe whilst ensuring the hardest anti-Soviet line in Western Europe. Reagan's view was that 'he had been hasty and that [Thatcher] had made him aware of the fact' (Thatcher Foundation, 1981–1982; cf. Aldous, 2012: 61–2). Nonetheless, along with SDI and support for the *mujahidin* – the gas problem abating – the Americans increased economic sanctions against Russia in areas such as technology transfers.

By March 1987, meeting Gorbachev and in a televised debate with Russian journalists, she took a more activist line. After endorsing increased Soviet-Western contact, she pointed out that there would be no appeasement. 'We believe – I think as you believe', she remarked, 'that every nation has the right to defend its own security' ('TV interview for Soviet television', 1988). To increase East-West contact, she travelled to Poland just before American presidential elections won by Reagan's vice-president, George H.W. Bush. On 3 November 1988, she made plain publicly: 'Freedom and responsibility go hand in hand. . . . That is why it is so vital that there should be a real dialogue with representatives of all sections of society, including Solidarity' (Thatcher, 1988; cf. Domber, 2014: 217, 279). A day later, she spoke at Gdansk, Solidarity's birthplace: 'I believe very strongly with you that the next generation should be brought up knowing the glories of the past and the great battles of history that have been won so that we might continue to live our own way of life in our own countries' (Thatcher, 1988). She received thunderous applause. With American military and economic revival, Britain supported the policy that progress for Poland had to include Solidarity and its ambitions. Polish liberalisation was essential, mirroring Gorbachev's reforms in Russia; it would enhance the Western Powers' strategic position in Europe – if not the wider world. And what was true for Poland remained true for all of Eastern Europe.

Six weeks earlier, Thatcher had outlined the goals of British foreign policy in Europe in a speech at Bruges [Document 26]. Opposed to full European integration, Britain was committed to Europe. Despite quarrelling over matters including the EEC budget, Britain's 'destiny is in Europe, as part of the Community'. Yet, the American connexion remained central to the success of democracy and capitalism on the continent: 'We must strive to maintain the United States' commitment to Europe's defence, their allies should bear the full part of the defence of freedom, particularly as Europe grows wealthier.' Notwithstanding her difficulties with Washington since Carter's time, British foreign policy under Thatcher's watch had striven for effective European defence and married it to American interests. Britain had a generally sympathetic and effective listener in Reagan. Whilst the major European Powers might not always be on side – a function of anti-American sentiment stretching back to the late 1940s – Britain was. Vigilance against the Russian threat and, perhaps, weakening Moscow's control over Eastern Europe to establish a more integrative Europe as a guarantee of continued peace and prosperity remained essential. The Relationship had helped define the 1980s in international politics.

8 The Special Relationship and the new international order, 1989–2015

In the quarter century after 1989, the Relationship gradually lost its strategic relevance – although its cultural and transnational dimensions remained. The reason stems from the breakdown of the bipolar international order – Soviet Russia and its Eastern European empire had collapsed by 1991. In the new international order, seemingly facing few adversaries, Republican and Democratic administrations pursued increasingly unilateral foreign policies to protect American interests – echoing Paul Wolfowitz, a former diplomat and defense official under Reagan and Bush, they perceived an American-dominated unipolar world. It is not that Britain and other American allies lacked utility. In crises in the Balkans, the Middle East, and South Asia, the Americans joined or constructed coalitions of Powers sharing their interests, looked to reinforce American pre-eminence, and, given persistent anti-Americanism abroad, sought political cover to override criticism overseas and domestically about nakedly enhancing American interests. Overall, however, Washington saw little use for permanent allies – implicit in the Relationship. Yet, beliefs in American omnipotence were flawed, as the new order witnessed the military and economic rise of the PRC, a revived Russia, the EU – the restructured EEC – and asymmetrical threats in the form of effective terrorist organisations that endangered Western concepts of liberal democracy as well as more substantial economic and strategic interests. American leaders lacked understanding of the nature of transitions from one international order to another since at least the mid-seventeenth century – that America had become just another Great Power, admittedly potent, in a new multi-Power order (McKercher, 2015). In many ways, the post–Cold War era constituted a return to the pre-1939 world.

George H.W. Bush, Margaret Thatcher, and the end of the Cold War, 1989–1990

Thatcher established a cordial working relationship with Bush after he took office. They probably disagreed on domestic economic policies – Bush once called Reagan's supply-side proposals 'voodoo' economics and, as president, sought to soften their hard edges (Sloan, 2004). To weaken Britain's class

The new international order, 1989–2015   109

structure and promote individual initiative – marrying social and economic policy – Thatcher continued relentlessly to limit government spending and deregulate and privatise national industries, as she had shown she could by successfully confronting the Miners Union in the mid-1980s (Vinen, 2009).

But in foreign policy, Bush and Thatcher agreed about Russia and Western security. Bush had been a Second World War fighter pilot, a congressman, an ambassador to the UN and China, and director of the CIA. Understanding the hard edge of foreign policy from lengthy experience, he followed Reagan in seeking to weaken Russia. As a German audience learnt in May 1989: 'We seek self-determination for all of Germany and all of Eastern Europe' (Bush, 1989). Like Thatcher, he then travelled to Eastern Europe – Poland and Hungary. Western security and its linchpins of liberal democracy and capitalism stood central to strategy. More insightful than Reagan, Bush believed that the distribution of power in international politics – balance – remained vital to stability (Maynard, 2008). His foreign policy put diplomacy before force. Taking away Russia's eastern empire would create instability, so Gorbachev and the new Kremlin leadership would have to abandon it of their own accord.

As Bush took office in January 1989, Gorbachev's reforms were not reviving Russia's economy. Defence costs diverted spending from consumer goods. *Glasnost* emboldened Russian dissidents who promoted CSCE-defined human rights, something that Russian casualty rates in Afghanistan accentuated. Gorbachev told the Politburo as early as May 1987, 'I told you about my meeting with Thatcher. She said they were afraid of us; that we invaded Czechoslovakia, Hungary, and Afghanistan' ('Anatoly Chernyaev's notes (excerpts) from the Politburo Session . . .', 1987). His response involved strengthening 'our policy for humanization of international relations with our actions', a key being asymmetrical Red Army cuts in Eastern Europe to show the Warsaw Pact as defensive rather than offensive. Building consensus in the Kremlin, he announced unilateral reductions in Eastern Europe in December (Kramer, 2012). Later that month, the Politburo learnt that without reduced defence spending and force reductions, Russia would 'never be able to sustain a long-term economic and social policy'. Although Eastern Europe received encouragement to institute *glasnost* and the rest, all depended on each regime's willingness to reform. Little consistency existed. Poland and Hungary were trying – seen in Bush and Thatcher's visits; East Germany and Czechoslovakia were not. Each Warsaw Pact member's leadership faced a dilemma: Moscow's old guard emplaced them; Gorbachev's reforms and Red Army reductions threatened their existence. In June 1989, in free elections, Solidarity won a large number of seats at Communist Party expense (Castle, 2003: Chapter 6). The Red Army stayed in its barracks. At a Warsaw Pact meeting in July, it was formally announced that the Brezhnev Doctrine was dead.

East Germany proved important. Its regime had long been oppressive – building the Berlin Wall and brutally controlling its people through its

110 Cold War and limited war, 1945–2015

secret police. Gorbachev pushed reforms for East Germany in April 1987, angering its leader, Erich Honecker (Gedmin, 1992). Nevertheless, East Germany's economy faltered under heavy debt and, in local elections in May 1989, communist electoral fraud increased unrest, made starker by Poland's largely free elections the next month (Childs, 2001). Public demonstrations began, producing state-sponsored violence against the protesters. More ominous and recalling the time before the Berlin Wall, large numbers of East Germans travelled ostensibly on vacation to liberalising Hungary but, with Budapest's acquiescence, crossed into Austria and the West. By early October, finding travel to Hungary blocked, several thousand journeying to Prague had received asylum on West Germany's embassy grounds. A month earlier, describing themselves as not political parties, various fora had emerged to call for change in the political system (Kukutz, 2009). Accordingly, when Gorbachev came to East Berlin on 7 October to celebrate the fortieth anniversary of the regime, a crossroads emerged. Gorbachev indicated that Honecker should retire (Kramer, 2012). Honecker was gone in days, but the new government could not cope with the changing domestic situation. On 9 November, because of an error by East Germany's government, East Germans unexpectedly received permission to cross into West Berlin without papers. They did so in numbers. The Wall fell.

To a large degree, 9 November ended the Cold War. The two Germanys united socially and economically in July 1990; in October, they reunified politically (Kettenacker, 2009). Supplanting other Eastern Bloc communist regimes occurred as quickly (Saxonberg, 2001). Most transitions were peaceful, although Romania's strongman, Nicolae Ceaucescu, died by firing squad on Christmas 1989. Soviet Russia lasted little longer. Having unleashed forces beyond his control, Gorbachev tried to decentralise power – hardliners who preferred the status quo attempted a coup in August 1991. A senior politician, Boris Yeltsin, defeated the hardliners, ousted Gorbachev, and, on 26 December, the Russian Federation replaced the Soviet Union (Plokhy, 2014). Few former Soviet republics joined. The Baltic states, Byelorussia, Ukraine, and several Central and South Asian republics opted for independence.

In this process, America sought balance. After January 1989, Bush, his secretary of state, James Baker, and his national security advisor, Brent Scowcroft, crafted a cautious but firm strategy to assist Eastern Bloc disintegration. Restructuring foreign policy decision-making with new advisors, Bush struck upon a new strategy for Russo-American relations (Maynard, 2008: Chapter 1). Whereas Reagan had concentrated on nuclear arms, Bush looked to transform Central and Eastern Europe. As his restructuring took time, a 'pause' emerged in Russo-American relations; Gorbachev complained to Thatcher in April that the 'pause' had frozen East-West discussions around arms control and other issues ('Record of conversation between Gorbachev and Thatcher', 1989). Thatcher responded, 'Bush is a very different person from Reagan. . . . Bush is a more balanced person, he gives more attention to detail. . . . he will continue the Reagan line, including on Soviet-American relations'.

Thus, nuclear arms limitation slowed as Washington confronted the fast-moving situation in Eastern Europe. Instead of pushing to end Russian control, the Americans let events take their course and then met them. In April, for instance, as Poland prepared for June elections, Bush suggested special assistance for Poland [Document 27]. In August, new elections ended single-party rule in Poland. Moreover, Baker established a personal relationship with Gorbachev's foreign minister, Eduard Shevardnadze. Meeting in Europe and the United States, they resolved a range of issues – for instance, chemical weapons verification inspections (White House memorandum, 1989).

Centring on possible reunification, the German question remained fundamentally important. Thatcher and Mitterrand were distrustful. Meeting Gorbachev in Moscow in September 1989, Thatcher said, 'We do not want a united Germany. This would lead to a change to postwar borders, and we cannot allow that because such a development would undermine the stability of the whole international situation and could endanger our security' ('Record of conversation between Mikhail Gorbachev and Margaret Thatcher', 1989). Like Bush, she had apprehensions about stability should communism collapse too quickly, but underneath lay unease over what a reunited Germany portended for Europe and Britain (Watt, 2003; cf. Thatcher, 1993). Bush, Baker, and Scowcroft, conversely, sought not only German union; they wanted a united Germany committed to NATO. Towards this end, they would need to allay Russian fears and overcome allied misgivings about greater Germany (Cox and Hurst, 2002). Accordingly, caution overlaid Bush's determination, for example, when the Wall fell, welcoming 'the decision by the East German leadership to open the borders' (Sarotte, 2014: 162). Profusions of victory would have been counterproductive to improving Russo-American relations. More important, Bush and his advisors saw the event as only a milestone on the road to ending the Eastern Bloc. These attitudes suffused Bush's diplomacy in supporting German reunification over the next 11 months. Supported by Kohl's government, Washington had a vision for post–Cold War Europe; reluctant allies such as Britain would have to accept it.

The same determination animated Bush's Russian policies until December 1991. Just after the Wall fell, on 2 December 1989, Bush and Gorbachev finally held talks at Malta to deal with nuclear disarmament and improving trade ('The President's meetings with President Gorbachev', 1989; 'Soviet transcript of the Malta Summit', 1989). Announcing publicly the Cold War's end, they agreed to manage Russo-American relations to redistribute power (Bush and Scowcroft, 1998). Bush's purpose involved assuring Gorbachev that Washington supported *perestroika*, linking it to Kremlin leniency in Eastern Europe. Gorbachev looked to end American policies that weakened Russia; Russo-American cooperation was essential. As Gorbachev said: 'It

112 *Cold War and limited war, 1945–2015*

is clear that we are moving from a bipolar to a multipolar world' (The American record does not mention this comment). For both men, it produced efforts to build close personal ties, à la Baker and Shevardnadze, to help their respective diplomacies (Cairo, 2004). Malta set the tone until Soviet Russia ended: a successful nuclear arms agreement by June 1990, German reunification, the rise of more Western-defined democratic regimes in Eastern Europe, and maintaining NATO whilst the Warsaw Pact disappeared (Cox and Hurst, 2002; Kramer, 2012; Maynard, 2008). Russia's demise was largely an American success, assisted by Kohl and the Germans. More widely, the Russians could do little to prevent it; and, significantly, Soviet collapse largely by-passed the Relationship.

The 'Special Relationship' and the Gulf War, 1990–1992

Whilst the Cold War was ending, the Western Powers unexpectedly faced a Middle Eastern crisis: on 2 August 1990, Iraq invaded Kuwait. Baghdad's strongman, Saddam Hussein, wanted Iraq to be the dominant regional Power; with Kuwaiti oil fields – combined with Iraq's, Baghdad would control almost 200 billion barrels of world proven reserves – he could underwrite his ambition by producing about 4.6 million barrels daily (www. opec.org/library/Annual%20Statistical%20Bulletin/interactive/2004/FileZ/XL/T33.HTM). From 1980 to 1988, Saddam had fought a vicious war against Iran to aggrandise Iraq; it ended in deadlock. Given parlous Iranian-American relations, and despite declaring neutrality and the Iran-Contra Affair, Reagan's Administration provided arms and intelligence to Baghdad (NSA, 25 February 2003).

Controversy exists over the genesis of the Kuwait crisis. Although Iraqi-American tensions had accrued by mid-1989 – for example, Saddam alleged that Washington and Tel Aviv encouraged Kuwait to reduce oil prices to weaken Iraq – Bush sought to conciliate Baghdad. A Senate delegation in April looked to better relations. Bush followed with a letter to Saddam, delivered by the American ambassador to Baghdad, April Glaspie, on 25 July. Meeting the Iraqi leader, she said: 'We have no opinion on your Arab-Arab conflicts, such as your dispute with Kuwait. . . . Baker has directed me to emphasize the instruction, first given to Iraq in the 1960's [*sic*], that the Kuwait issue is not associated with America' (www.globalresearch.ca/gulf-war-documents-meeting-between-saddam-hussein-and-ambassador-to-iraq-april-glaspie/31145). Saddam, the argument goes, received a 'green light' to settle the Kuwait question (Aburish, 2000: 282); eight days later, Iraq invaded.

It was not that Bush had always shunned military options. In December 1989, American forces invaded Panama to depose its drug-trafficking leader, General Manuel Noriega, who threatened American access to the Canal promised in Carter's transfer of authority (Taw, 1996). But in early August 1989, Bush's tendency to use diplomacy before force unwittingly

The new international order, 1989–2015   113

gave Saddam the 'green light'. Iraq's swiftly successful invasion threatened the regional balance. Because an Iraqi presence in Kuwait threatened Saudi oil fields, the security of Western interests and Middle Eastern depended on getting Iraq out. Looking for international diplomatic, economic, and military support, America immediately blockaded Iraqi trade (National Security Directive 45, 20 August 1990). When Bush telephoned Thatcher to inform her of his effort, he later recalled, 'she listened to my explanation, agreed with the decision, but then added these words of caution – words that guided me through the Gulf crisis, words I'll never forget as long as I'm alive. "Remember, George", she said, "this is no time to go wobbly"' (Bush, 1992).

As much as protecting Western access to oil and re-establishing regional stability, defence of narrow British interests guided Thatcher. Although British forces left the Gulf in 1971 with the withdrawal 'East of Suez' – except two air bases in Oman – London retained political and economic influence by investment, trade, recasting political agents in each polity as ambassadors, and treaties of friendship (Petersen, 2015). Still, Britain's problem in 1989 involved limited regional military presence. American efforts to dominate in the Middle East since at least the Yom Kippur War had given Washington such a presence, plus almost unrivalled political influence with a range of Middle Eastern Powers. Under Carter and Reagan, bases in Diego Garcia in the Indian Ocean, Egypt, Oman, and Saudi Arabia allowed American forces to protect Middle Eastern petroleum supplies. Along with military agreements with Saudi Arabia and several Gulf States, Bush fashioned an effective military response. Thirty-four Powers comprised the resultant coalition, although only 29 of them despatched troops, weapons, medical support, and aid. Under an American supreme commander, America mustered almost 697,000 personnel with sophisticated weaponry; the other major contributors with modern arms were Saudi Arabia (100,000 troops), Britain (45,400), Egypt (33,600), France (14,600), and Syria (14,600). Other members contributed between 9,900 (Kuwait) and 50 troops (Norway and Hungary) ('Gulf War Coalition Forces: Countries compared', n.d.). Moreover, Powers other than America contributed to coalition funding: Saudi Arabia ($16.8 billion), Kuwait ($16.01 billion), and Japan ($10.74 billion) (Papp, 1996: 26). Iraqi troops were 300,000 strong, with weaponry that included older missiles – SCUDs – and chemical and biological components (Anonymous, 1993: 5; cf. Wedgwood, 2006).

When diplomacy failed to resolve the crisis – Saddam fruitlessly employed this time to hasten nuclear weapons production (Wedgwood, 2006) – the coalition began bombing Iraqi military targets on 17 January 1991 (Allison, 2012; Head and Tilford, 1996). With the bulk of coalition forces in Saudi Arabia, sporadic skirmishing also began; following a scorched-earth policy, the Iraqis started destroying Kuwaiti oil installations and dumping crude oil into the Persian Gulf. Iraq also attempted to unite Arab nationalists and Islamic militants in what Saddam characterised as *jihad* – a holy

114   *Cold War and limited war, 1945–2015*

war – against his enemies. American pressure and supply of anti-missile defences restrained Israel, which suffered some SCUD attacks. On 24 February, after Baghdad ignored an ultimatum to withdraw from Kuwait or face ground attack, the coalition moved forward. It triumphed spectacularly – British and French armoured forces scored important victories. On 28 February, the Iraqis retreated from Kuwait and Bush called for a ceasefire.

Apart from high Iraqi civilian and combat deaths caused by air raids and battlefield combat, two principal criticisms surround this war. First, detractors brandishing moral imperatives charged the conflict as one of 'blood for oil'. They were correct. Yet their sub-theme is flawed: 'The U.S. freely used bribery and intimidation to create the anti-Iraq coalition' (D'Amato, 2000–2001). The Western Powers and Japan could not accept Iraqi control of a substantial proportion of world oil production or that oil-rich Saudi Arabia might be Iraq's next target. The security of the Gulf States was also imperative, especially since financial and security arrangements tied them to Powers like America and Britain. Saudi Arabia, Egypt, and Syria, let alone Israel, would forbear Iraqi expansion to their strategic detriment. With the Falklands in mind, Thatcher told Bush: 'First, aggressors must never be appeased. . . . if Saddam Hussein were to cross the border into Saudi Arabia he could go right down the Gulf in a matter of days. He would then control 65% of the world's oil reserves and could blackmail us all' (Hughes, 2014: 120).

Second, Bush's decision for a ceasefire before toppling Saddam's regime suggests a lost chance to reshape the Middle East (Indyk, 1992). American neoconservatives assert that an early ceasefire disallowed an opportunity for stability (Frontline, n.d.). Heavily ideological, neoconservatives believe in laissez-faire democracy domestically and promoting external interests, including by military power; they disdain what they see as radicalism – not only communism and socialism, but also American liberalism personified by the Democratic Party and Republicans with whom they disagree (Fuller, 2012). However, Bush and Scowcroft were realists, writing later, 'We were concerned about the long-term balance of power at the head of the Gulf' (*Time*, 2 March 1998). Accordingly, even a weakened post-war Iraq could balance against Iran, see Saudi and Gulf State security braced, Western and Japanese economic and strategic interests entrenched, and Egypt, Israel, and Syria less threatened.

On 29 January 1991, with Soviet Russia crumbling and war over Kuwait imminent, Bush told Americans that international politics were transforming. 'What is at stake is more than one small country; it is a big idea: a new world order, where diverse nations are drawn together in common cause to achieve the universal aspirations of mankind – peace and security, freedom, and the rule of law' [Document 28]. America had to lead. Beyond platitudes about peace and cooperation, nothing altruistic existed in his message. Less strident than neoconservatives like Wolfowitz, his message had similar intent: 'We . . . have the will at home and abroad to

The new international order, 1989–2015 115

do what must be done – the hard work of freedom'. It would be American-defined freedom. In this emerging new order, Thatcher pushed for a robust Western response to Saddam, and Britain contributed to the coalition. She later said she thought the war ended too soon (*Telegraph*, 21 February 2001), but in an unexpected political turn to help the Conservatives in an anticipated election in 1991 or 1992, her own party drove her out of office in November 1990, chiefly because many disliked her authoritarian leadership style, her programme cuts, and her proposed poll taxes (Campbell, 2003). Nonetheless, she transformed Britain and strengthened the Relationship as the core of British foreign policy. But as the Gulf War showed, the situation was changing. Thatcher's successors would have to deal with the new international order and American leaders less willing to accept a leading British role in international politics.

Britain, America, and the Balkans, 1992–1998

Until he was succeeded by the Democrat Bill Clinton in January 1993, Bush continued to seek international balance ('World proven crude oil reserves by country', 1980–2004). Without support from Moscow, former allies of Russia, such as Cuba and Nicaragua, withered economically or saw the advent of moderate pro-American regimes. Indeed, in Latin America, generally, old-style right-wing Cold War dictatorships gave way to moderate, market-driven, and democratically elected governments because of domestic opposition to – and the fading American imperative to support – the old regimes (Mainwaring and Scully, 2010). Nonetheless, American policy in the 'new world order' had a flaw: Bush failed to devise a strategy to replace containment. His efforts respecting Russia, Eastern Europe, and Iraq were *ad hoc*: letting events take their course and then meeting them. This weakness manifested itself in a crisis in the Balkans – an issue that confronted America in the transition from Bush to Clinton and affected European security, thereby also involving Britain and NATO.

Eastern Europe's general transition to independence was peaceful. Ironically, never part of the Soviet Bloc, Yugoslavia was the exception. In a polity of culturally diverse Serbs, Croatians, Slovenians, Bosnian-Herzegovinians, Albanians, and Macedonians professing differing faiths, particularism had been tempered and unity brokered by Josip Broz Tito, leader of Yugoslavia from 1945 until his death in 1980 (Beloff, 1985; Haug, 2012). After the late 1940s, Tito pursued independent foreign and economic policies that balanced between Moscow and the West. A Croat, he won support from the Serbian majority and the other nationalities for being even-handed. After Tito's death, however, Serb Yugoslavs began dominating the government; national unity ebbed. In 1991, as Yugoslavia splintered, Slobodan Milosevic became first president of sovereign Serbia. Cynically manipulating Serb nationalism and Orthodox Christianity, his regime used Serbian forces and paramilitaries to squelch separatism and ensure a greater

Figure 8.1 John Major, George H.W. Bush, and Bill Clinton, March 2008
© ITAR-TASS Photo Agency / Alamy

Serbia. Consequently, throughout the 1990s, former Yugoslavia was rocked by a series of ethnic wars marked by barbarity on every side, although Serbs proved most excessive (Bieber et al., 2014). The Balkans gave imbalance to south-eastern Europe in the new order inherited by Clinton and European leaders like John Major, Thatcher's successor.

With long-standing Balkan complexities – ethnic distrust, religious and cultural intolerance, and shifting political alliances – Slovenia and Croatia declared independence in 1991. Thereafter, smaller polities sought independence by military means or with diplomatic support from European and other Powers. In this inchoate atmosphere, two intensely violent struggles – Bosnia in 1994 and 1995 and Kosovo in 1999 – warranted outside intervention.

When new Serbia and Croatia looked to take Bosnian territory after 1991, British and American policy mirrored that of the major European Powers: use minimal numbers of UN peacekeepers – the UN Protective Force [UNPROFOR] – and avoid outside intervention. A belief existed amongst the Western Powers that Milosevic's regime would bring stability, and diplomacy might quicken it (Glaurdić, 2011). By January 1993, an informal Anglo-American effort led by Cyrus Vance, now a UN special envoy, and EU representative David Owen, Callaghan's former foreign secretary, produced a peace plan: with UN backing, Bosnia would be divided into ten semi-autonomous regions (Owen, 2013). The Bosnian Serbs rejected it. When Owen suggested using military force to impose the plan, Major hesitated: 'We could not unite the international community behind such a proposal' (Owen, 1995; cf. Kaufman, 2002). He pressed for humanitarian aid with 'intensified pressure on all the parties to halt the fighting and negotiate seriously' (Owen, 1995: 16).

Clinton's Administration had little of substance to offer beyond supporting UNPROFOR – the prevailing view was that the situation in the Balkans was a European problem, not an American one – and the Defence and State departments disagreed on policy. The Defence Department wanted to avoid committing forces to what might become protracted anti-guerrilla operations; the State Department desired consultations with NATO's principal Powers and Russia along with 'lift and strike' – lifting a general arms embargo that disadvantaged Bosnian Croats and Moslems whilst launching air strikes against Serb forces (Brands, 2008). Major's caution irritated Clinton and his advisors nonetheless. In preparing to meet Major in spring 1993, 'Clinton aides joked, "Don't forget to say 'special relationship' when the press comes in." "Oh, yes", Clinton said. 'How could I forget? The special relationship!" He then threw his head back and laughed' [Document 29].

Anglo-American division devolved from growing American unilateralism to protect and extend American strategic interests. Clinton took office intent on utilising a new grand strategy, 'Democratic Enlargement'; bowing to Wilsonianism, it entailed three mutually reinforcing goals: sustain national security, bolster the economy, and promote democracy (Søndergaard, 2015). As America never participated in UN peacekeeping, it would mean going it alone. In this context, Washington raised questions about Britain's continued possession of a permanent UN Security Council seat. Douglas Hurd, Major's foreign secretary, responded tartly that American ideas about a new world order were fallacious; 'Once-fashionable talk of a "New World Order" dawning was utopian folly . . . because "the phrase promised more than we shall ever be able to perform"' [Document 30], because Britain had its own international role and interests to protect.

In February 1994, the UN secretary general had sought NATO air support for UNPROFOR, to which the Americans, British, French, and Germans agreed (Burg and Shoup, 1999: Chapter 7). A Croatian-Bosnian peace agreement occurred within weeks with territorial adjustments, but combat between Serb paramilitaries and NATO-supported UNPROFOR stretched into 1995 as diplomacy failed to resolve the crisis. The situation in Bosnia worsened dramatically in July 1995 with the genocide of over 7,000 Moslem men by Serb-supported forces at Srebrenica, a supposed safe area (Gendercide Watch, 1995). Losing international support after Srebrenica and fighting UNPROFOR-NATO had forced the Serbs to the peace table, where it was agreed that a 60,000-strong NATO-led Implementation Force would deploy to Bosnia-Herzegovina (NATO, 2014). Serbian expansionism ended.

118   *Cold War and limited war, 1945–2015*

The Relationship was further frayed. With beliefs about American omnipotence confirmed by Soviet Russian collapse, the Bush and Clinton administrations looked to enhance American interests abroad that each conflated with American-defined international peace and security. Other Powers, especially Britain, had different interests, such as ensuring a leading role in both the UN and regional bodies such as the EU. They did not necessarily mesh with American ones. Whilst Major still saw the Relationship as central to British policy along with Britain's European role (Major, 2011), Clinton seemed willing to ignore it.

George Bush, Jr., Tony Blair, the war against terrorism, and changing international politics, 2001–2007

In May 1997, the Labour Party, led by Tony Blair, won office in a general election. Having learnt the lesson that the 'old' Labour policies had been political poison with most British voters, Blair had created 'new' Labour after becoming party leader three years earlier. New Labour moved to the political centre, accepting Thatcher's notion of free markets – but mitigating some of its harder edges over crime, the environment, and social policy – and a willingness to curtail 'tax and spend' policies (Faucher-King and Le Galès, 2010). Not all Labour supporters accepted this orientation, but electoral success suggested a fresh approach remained essential. Most important, New Labour saw a robust foreign policy as crucial to ensure Britain a leading place in the post–Cold War order (McCourt, 2011). Here, Blair looked to revitalise Anglo-American relations. In Chicago in April 1999, he outlined a 'Doctrine of the International Community':

> We are all internationalists now, whether we like it or not. We cannot refuse to participate in global markets if we want to prosper. We cannot ignore new political ideas in other countries if we want to innovate. We cannot turn our backs on conflicts and the violation of human rights within other countries if we want still to be secure [Document 31].

Although waxing on international cooperation by all Powers and international organisations to preserve peace and security, his focus lay with America.

Just as Thatcher used the Falklands to cement her Great Power credentials and commitment to the Relationship, Blair used Kosovo's longstanding desire to secede from Milosevic's Yugoslavia. Wanting improved Anglo-American relations, his government backed a Clinton-led initiative to support Kosovo's breakaway. Protecting its Balkan interests, Russia vetoed UN efforts to intrude in the conflict, so Washington appealed to NATO. In doing so, Clinton's Administration needed congressional approval and, realising unilateralism's limitations, European support (Phillips, 2012). The effort was successful, and NATO forces bombed Serbia between March and June 1999. Tying intervention to humanitarianism, Blair aligned British and

The new international order, 1989–2015 119

American policy, although he was first to advocate sending in ground troops (Daalder and O'Hanlon, 2000). Kosovo's independence – military intervention forcing a sovereign state to disgorge a portion of its territory – came from the Americans (Daalder and O'Hanlon, 2000: Chapter 5).

In January 2001, the Republican George W. Bush, son of George H.W. Bush, succeeded Clinton as president. Although purporting to admire Churchill ('Remarks on accepting . . .', 2012), Bush Junior was not an anglophile. Unlike his father, he was a deeply conservative domestic politician, had rarely travelled abroad, and populated his Administration with neoconservatives such as Dick Cheney, the vice-president; Donald Rumsfeld, the secretary of defence; and Paul Wolfowitz, now deputy secretary of defence. These leaders, too, were not anglophiles; Cheney even denied publicly Thatcher's 'do not be wobbly' admonition to denigrate London's strong reaction over Iraq in 1990 (Bowers, 2013). Within months of taking office, the Bush Administration made clear that it was interested less in European defence than in East Asia and that Washington 'was committed to a defense system against limited missile attack [on the homeland rather than Europe]' (Ricks, 2001: 31; Hodge, 2002: 166). Europe could accept it or not. America would look after its own interests with or without its ostensible allies. The long-pursued 'Europe first' strategy had disappeared.

However, on 11 September 2001, the Islamic terrorist group Al Qaeda, based in Taliban-controlled Afghanistan, attacked the United States; commandeering American airliners, it flew them into the World Trade Center in New York and into the Pentagon in Washington. Led by a Saudi dissident named Osama bin Laden, the members of Al Qaeda were apoplectic that infidel American forces, still containing Saddam's Iraq, remained in Saudi Arabia adjacent to the holy cities of Mecca and Medina. It also opposed Western notions of democracy, free speech, women's rights, and other issues reckoned to run counter to *Koranic* teachings. In response to the attack, Bush's Administration prepared to invade Afghanistan, overthrow the Taliban, and decimate Al Qaeda; Britain immediately signed on, as a tangible expression of the 'Doctrine of the International Community'. As Blair told the Labour Party, supporting Washington was the only means for Britain to influence its more powerful ally (Daalder, 2003).

On 7 October, after the Taliban-controlled Afghan government refused American demands to hand over Al Qaeda leaders, destroy terrorist camps, and allow American on-site inspections, Anglo-American forces launched air attacks from bases in the region, especially Diego Garcia and Saudi Arabia ('Blair statement in full', 2001). Britain had aligned with America militarily and diplomatically. As NATO joined the British and Americans in Afghanistan, the Taliban was defeated and allied ground forces began an anti-guerrilla campaign reminiscent of Russian operations after December 1979 (Auerswald and Saideman, 2014). Nonetheless, by December 2001, the allies had emplaced a pro-Western regime in Kabul and began a difficult war to legitimise the new government. Ironically, American forces

120 *Cold War and limited war, 1945–2015*

had earlier trained and armed their anti-Western opponents, the *mujahidin*, including bin Laden. As with Vietnam, members of the American-led coalition faced criticism at home, especially in Britain. Still, Britain was in the struggle for the long haul.

Bush's Administration then decided to remove Iraqi president Saddam Hussein from power. Cheney and Rumsfeld were adamant in this regard – discarding Bush Senior's strategic imperative to leave a weak Iraq balancing Iran. American neoconservatives, including the president, wanted long-delayed victory over Iraq to show American strength in the region and hem in Iran. They struck upon Saddam's bluster about producing WMD as justification for doing so: Iraq's possession of WMD supposedly threatened pro-American Powers in the region such as Saudi Arabia and Israel. Saddam's WMD propaganda looked to deter an American-led attack. Although UN inspections would later find that Iraq had no effective WMD, Washington – through a propaganda campaign led by Cheney – asserted it did (Council on Foreign Relations, May 2005). In this equation, relying on doctored American intelligence assessments that supported Bush Administration charges and shared with the British and others (Phythian, 2008), Blair had British troops join the anti-Iraq coalition.

The British public opposed the move. In London on 16 February 2003, more than one million people rallied against the war; similar demonstrations occurred in Glasgow and Belfast ('Million march against Iraq war', 2003). Much of this opposition flowed from disbelief about Iraqi possession of WMD. Disapproval also devolved from negative views about Bush's foreign policy. In September 2001, just after the World Trade Center and Pentagon attacks, Bush had announced the 'war on terror' would not end 'until every terrorist group of global reach has been found, stopped and defeated' [Document 32]. He had followed in January 2002 with a declaration that America would undermine an 'axis of evil' in the new international order, specifically listing North Korea, Iran, Cuba, and Iraq [Document 33]. Outside of Whitehall, these arguments found little support in Britain – two-thirds of the public opposed war (IPSOS MORI, 2003). Although this dissent was complex – some also opposed New Labour economic policies – it fixed on Bush because of his stridency over phantom WMD; and, confident after re-election in June 2001, Blair thought he could convince his public of the justness of overthrowing Saddam (Dyson, 2012).

With operations in Afghanistan unfinished, the invasion of Iraq began on 19 March with Anglo-American forces reinforced by contingents from other Powers 'to disarm Iraq of weapons of mass destruction, to end Saddam Hussein's support for terrorism, and to free the Iraqi people' (Ramos, 2013: 116). Baghdad fell on 9 April, Saddam went into hiding, and coalition forces began operations against remaining resistance. WMD were not found, undermining a key Bush-Blair assertion about the enterprise in both countries (NSA, 2004). Moreover, although the Americans led a transitional government from 2003 to 2005, when a new Iraqi government took office

The new international order, 1989–2015 121

with American support, in 2005 it confronted armed opposition from a range of Islamist dissidents bolstered by anti-Western *mujahidin*, some of whom were supported by Iran (Gregg, Rothstein and Arquilla, 2010).

When Bush left office in January 2009, the Afghanistan and Iraq wars had yet to end despite formidable American-led Western forces and economic aid to legitimise the new regimes in Kabul and Baghdad. In these circumstances, the Relationship crumbled further. It was not that the British and Americans lacked foreign policy successes. For instance, in a humanitarian intervention that brought some stability to West Africa, Blair had involved Britain in Sierra Leone's civil war after 2000 (Dorman, 2009). Bush had created the President's Emergency Plan for AIDS Relief, a five-year $15 billion programme to combat AIDS, especially in Africa (Library of Congress, 2007). But a war on two fronts – in Afghanistan and Iraq – casualty rates on each side, and the meretricious handling of WMD darkened both leaders' reputations at home and abroad. In Britain by 2008, the majority of people – 53 to 27 percent – believed that Washington might intervene against other Powers: 'the public saw the Bush administration as an especially aggressive regime' (Dyson, 2012: 37–8). Moreover, developing nuclear weapons, Iran remained in place. With the Americans absorbed by matters in the Middle East, the PRC strengthened, the new Russia looked to recapture its former international position, and other centres of international economic power, such as the EU and other organisations, continued their incremental growth. Notwithstanding Blair's intentions, a weaker Britain had little influence over America. The new international order was transforming; other Powers and organisations were generating global and regional power.

Barack Obama, Gordon Brown, and David Cameron: challenges old and new after 2007

An unforeseen result of the new international order after 1991 was the rise of those new centres of international economic and international power. The supposition that America could, in Wolfowitz's words, 'prevent the re-emergence of a new rival' proved barren and brought new foreign policy challenges. The EU prospered, buttressed by an organisation-wide currency, the euro. By investment, trade, and several former Eastern Bloc Powers joining, the EU's writ extended into Eastern Europe (Baldwin, 1995: 474–81). As important was the growth of East and South Asian economies, especially the PRC and India, which competed successfully with both America and the EU for regional and international trade, development, and commodities such as metals, grain, and petroleum. Other regional trading blocs, such as ASEAN and Latin America's Mercosur, also impeded American economic power in the wider world. In the 1990s, bereft of the Cold War, globalisation of the international economy occurred apace – the World Bank defining globalisation as 'the growing integration of economies and societies around the world' ('Globalization', n.d.).

122 *Cold War and limited war, 1945–2015*

The growth of economic rivals mirrored political ones. No Power was as potent as the United States, but some had unquestionable strength and looked to pursue their national and international interests. Thus, building on its growing economic and financial strength, the PRC arrogated for itself a leading position in East Asia and, by fostering aid and other agreements with developing states in Africa and Latin America, its global influence (Shih and Huang, 2016). In these calculations, the Chinese increasingly portrayed America as their principal adversary. Despite a violent suppression of human and civil rights dissenters in China in June 1989, the two Powers sought to keep relations steady – the Americans finally supporting the PRC's application to join the new World Trade Organisation tendered in 1995; given American pressures, Beijing helped reduce a growing Sino-American trade imbalance and encouraged American investment in the PRC (Xuefeng, 2006). The Americans, nonetheless, did not intend to appease a more robust PRC strategically. In 1995 and 1996, for instance, the PRC conducted a series of missile tests in the seas surrounding Taiwan, to pressure its KMT government. Clinton responded by despatching an American carrier to the Taiwan Straits (Xuefeng, 2006). Given American dominance in the western Pacific since 1945, there were limits to PRC territorial pretensions, including Tibet ('Press Briefing by National Security . . .', 1997).

Britain's response to the changing East and South Asian balances of power reflected policies followed since ending its military presence east of Suez. As in the Gulf States, Britain's position in the 1990s came from investment and trade guaranteed during decolonisation and, through globalisation and Thatcher's economic policies, the City of London's resurgence as a money market and its traditional place as an international investment and insurance centre (Hilpert and Kecker, 2008). As its economy expanded, the PRC became progressively important for British economic diplomacy and private-sector considerations (House of Commons Library, 2012). Hong Kong is a case in point. By an 1898 treaty, Britain had a 99-year lease of Hong Kong. As early as December 1984, Thatcher signed an agreement with Beijing that set 1 July 1997 as the transfer-of-power date and, importantly for her, codified the so-called 'One Country, Two Systems' principle: rather than immediately adopting PRC socialism, Hong Kong would enjoy capitalism and its economic benefits for 50 years ('Record of a meeting . . .', 1984). Although Major thought Thatcher too compromising with Beijing, it made little difference. On 1 July 1997, Hong Kong became a Special Administrative Region of the PRC, with a capitalist economy and one-party control (Horlemann, 2003). Britain helped ensure political stability and, perhaps better than might be expected, protect its trade and investment in East Asia.

Britain and America came to pursue separate policies concerning the new centres of economic and political power in the wider world after the Gulf War. These policies reflected strategic developments since 1945 – America's determination to retain its leading global place; Britain ensuring

The new international order, 1989–2015   123

its economic – not necessarily military – position after decolonisation. In both circumstances, separate development is understandable. Respecting the Relationship, it highlighted increasingly dissimilar interests and uncoordinated policy.

Gordon Brown, Labour's chancellor of the Exchequer, succeeded Blair in June 2007. Over the next three years, further shifts occurred in British and American leadership. In January 2009, the Democrat Barack Obama succeeded Bush; and in May 2010, the Conservative David Cameron became premier in a Conservative–Liberal Democrat coalition. Starting in 2008, furthermore, an economic crisis rivalling that of the 1930s dislocated the international community. Both America and Britain had to concentrate on their domestic economies and improve trade and investment (Cheng, 2012; Vaitilingam, 2009). The distracted governments rarely produced harmonised diplomatic action.

Nonetheless, in Afghanistan and Iraq, Britain continued a military commitment to sustain the regional balance. Obama won the 2008 American presidential election partly by promises to find peace built around establishing effective pro-Western governments in Kabul and Baghdad – and, more important, bring American troops home. It was not a straightforward process. In both theatres, American military levels increased to achieve victory in 2010 (Pfiffner, 2011). Nevertheless, in April 2009, British forces withdrew from Iraq; American forces departed in December 2011; by late 2014, most Western contingents had left Afghanistan. Some troops remained, to protect embassies and other installations, but military withdrawal had occurred. Anglo-American military cooperation ended.

Willing to allow British integration with the American missile system, Brown had a formal but less than friendly connexion with Bush (Dumbrell, 2013). Although supporting the Relationship, Brown – unlike Blair – had no intention to allow Washington to determine British strategic interests – Blair's domestic political Achilles heel. British troops left Iraq under his watch. And whilst Cameron respected the Relationship's political side, his government believed that its military dimension lay beyond Britain's financial capacity (Parsons, 2012). Brown and Cameron's problem was that for Obama, an African American politician born in Hawaii, American strategic interests lay in the Pacific and East Asia. The PRC's increasing political and military strength and its desire to be a Great Power – with other Powers seeking to benefit from Chinese economic growth – threatened American interests (Mingjiang and Kemburi, 2014). Indeed, Beijing had bought American government bonds, whilst the United States incurred a massive trade deficit with the PRC.

When Cameron visited Washington in March 2012, he and Obama published an article in the *Washington Post*: 'Not just special, but an essential relationship' [Document 34]. As British and American interests did not now coincide on several issues, it constituted platitudes rather than practical politics. In the western Pacific and East Asia, America strengthened

124   *Cold War and limited war, 1945–2015*

economic and strategic ties with Powers such as Australia and the Philippines and organisations such as ASEAN, to counter Chinese inroads (Seng, 2014). It also confronted a PRC-backed bellicose North Korea. British efforts towards good trading and political relations with the PRC continued as they did after in the transfer of Hong Kong. Hence, in October 2008, reversing policy, Brown's government acknowledged Tibet as an integral part of the PRC ('HMG recognizes Tibet as an . . .', 2008). Even after Cameron met with the Dalai Lama in May 2012, his chancellor of the Exchequer, George Osborne, went to Beijing the next year to cement business agreements (Sudworth, 2013).

What was so for East Asia was the same for the Middle East. Iran's desire to build nuclear weapons and support Shia Islamic forces in Lebanon and the Gaza Strip and against Israel and Sunni states backed by Saudi Arabia saw massive economic sanctions against Tehran – since 1979 by the Americans, after 2006 by the UN. Finally, after difficult bargaining with the five permanent members of the UN Security Council, as well as Germany, in July 2015, Iran agreed not to produce nuclear weapons for ten years and allow Western on-site inspection of its nuclear facilities; in return, sanctions would end (Broad and Peçanha, 2015). Yet, the Americans and the five Powers remained divided. The Europeans, Russians, and Chinese saw potential for trade and investment; America was ambivalent, given Republican opposition to Obama's foreign policy and the still-virulent anti-Americanism of Iran's regime ('Britain eyes business opportunities in wake of Iran nuclear deal', 2015; Broad and Peçanha, 2015; 'Khamenei: Opposition to US persists after nuclear deal', 2015). Moreover, Tehran still armed proxies to do its fighting.

Despite Washington's long-term policy of being the dominant Western Power in the region, revolutions in Moslem states in North Africa and the Middle East from late 2010 to mid-2012 saw Britain and the Europeans – the old colonial masters with economic interests to protect – take the lead in supporting the insurgents. Looking to reduce Islamic anti-Americanism fanned by Iraq and Afghanistan, Obama's Administration stood aside for other NATO Powers to overthrow Libya's dictatorship of Muammar Gaddafi (Daalder and Stavridis, 2012). When America got involved with Syria, Obama warned the Syrian government that a 'red line' existed over which it could not cross in combating rebels. But he did nothing when Damascus used chemical weapons against its own people (Mardell, 2013). Cameron unsuccessfully pressed the UN for action in Syria, and Parliament would not condone a major military involvement ('Syria crisis', 2013). When Islamic militants – ISIS – emerged in 2014 to create a caliphate out of portions of a weakened Iraq and a disintegrating Syria with the most rebarbative tactics and threatened the regional balance of power, the Americans, NATO, and the EU enforced economic sanctions and mounted air strikes to degrade ISIS and help Iraqi and Kurdish ground forces. There was no hint of using Western ground troops, and bilateral Anglo-American cooperation was

The new international order, 1989–2015   125

non-existent – Britain participated through its NATO and EU memberships. London and Washington each looked after their own strategic interests: the Americans to protect Iraq; the British to help Arab states with which it traded (Boot, 2014; Joshi, 2014).

Concurrently, a resurgent Russia under a new authoritarian, Vladimir Putin, attempted to re-establish Moscow's control over several former Soviet territories on its periphery. In the Crimea and Ukraine after 2012, Putin used Russian military power, as well as proxies such as pro-Russian Ukrainian nationalists, to take territory (Herszenhorn, 2015). Building on Great Russian nationalism allied with the Orthodox Church, and employing propaganda that the Americans and NATO were seeking to destroy Russia, he rearmed and improved its nuclear forces. Russia also pressured the Baltic states and Poland, both NATO members. Because the new Russia still faced a degree of Western economic sanctions, Putin moved to align his country with the PRC, reversing Nixon's 1972 policy (Schoen and Kaylan, 2014). In this equation, the Western Powers divided somewhat. The Americans pursued a hard line against Putin's policies – using strong economic sanctions and deployments of small numbers of troops for deterrence – whilst the EU was more permissive, given its Eastern European markets and reliance on Russian natural gas exports (European Commission, 2011; Hunt, 2015). NATO also moved to deter with limited deployments – Britain sent 75 troops to Ukraine – and Cameron talked of the need for a tougher Western response (Parker, 2014). But given EU diffidence and British defence cuts, a new status quo ensued. With Washington's Pacific and East Asian focus, any new American efforts in Europe were unlikely. Unlike in early Cold War Europe, the Kennedy-Macmillan years, or the 1980s, the Relationship offered little towards a joint strategic response to preserving European security in the face of a Russian threat to Western interests.

Global power – Bush Senior's strategic balance – diffused by the end of the 1990s. America remained pre-eminent, but in a multipolar world. Whether Democrat or Republican, Washington could not limit other rivals – Powers and international organisations. In essence, America's alliances became progressively *ad hoc* – for instance, during NATO involvement in Iraq; and differing perceptions of common interests became the norm. Britain gradually and obviously became secondary in American thinking beginning with German unification in 1990. It was also increasingly European, despite some domestic opposition to the EU asserting that Brussels imperilled British sovereignty. With America more concerned with the Pacific and East Asia, the Relationship waned. The Anglo-American strategic partnership was no longer necessary. Stability in the evolving international order would now come from other diplomatic means. Emotion and sentiment might still suggest some sort of Anglo-American ties, but they did not entail a close diplomatic and military relationship.

Part IV
Epilogue

9 The Anglo-American 'Special Relationship' and international politics since 1941

An appraisal

In America's 2012 presidential elections, the Republican candidate, Mitt Romney, outlined his foreign policy objectives a month before voting. Criticising Obama's diplomacy, he looked at American problems: the Middle East, Afghanistan, continuing terrorist threats (although American special forces had assassinated bin Laden months earlier), defence cuts, freer trade, foreign assistance without substantive reciprocation, and 'friends and allies across the globe' wanting more American leadership. Never specifying which 'friends and allies', he asserted: 'The 21st century can and must be an American century. . . . to steer it onto the path of freedom, peace, and prosperity.' Even admitting electioneering hyperbole, Romney offered a message about America's pre-eminence. Critical of Romney's remedies – 'still stuck in a Cold War time warp' – Obama had earlier highlighted the Democrats' foreign policy record:

> Around the world, we've strengthened old alliances and forged new coalitions to stop the spread of nuclear weapons. We've reasserted our power across the Pacific and stood up to China on behalf of our workers. From Burma to Libya to South Sudan, we have advanced the rights and dignity of all human beings – men and women; Christians and Muslims and Jews.
>
> ('Remarks by the President . . .', 2012)

For Democrats or Republicans, pre-eminent America would guide the world, and in their views about foreign policy, neither man mentioned Britain. The Special Relationship had become a relic of history, declining after the end of the Cold War and gone by 2012, if not earlier.

Nonetheless, the Anglo-American strategic partnership had been the basis of the Western alliance for 50 years as leaders in London and Washington recognised its diplomatic and military utility; collaborating offered the best means to protect and extend each Power's perceived national interests and, thereby, better ensure international stability. Although long developing transnational emotional and sentimental ties underpinned the Relationship, it always constituted a strategic alliance. It emerged after 1939

130   *Epilogue*

in circumstances of expediency and *realpolitik* to defeat common enemies, and, after 1945, successive leaderships in London and Washington sustained it through recognising its diplomatic and military utility in meeting Russia's threat to Western interests in Europe, plus Russian and other adversarial threats in other regions of the globe.

The Relationship's course was not always easy. Roosevelt drove hard bargains with Churchill before and after 1941 over issues such as the destroyers-for-bases deal. Most important, whilst seeing their formal and informal dominance over Puerto Rico, Hawaii, the Philippines, and other territories and polities as something nobler than empire, Americans disparaged British colonialism. It became a leitmotif of Washington's war aims that America would encourage the decolonisation of not only the British Empire but also those of the other European Powers. Roosevelt endorsed Churchill's peripheral strategy immediately after Pearl Harbor – beginning America's 'Europe first' orientation – and, in the process, overcame key advisors, such as Marshall, who questioned American power propping up the British Empire. Whilst the need for military victory delayed decolonisation until later, it remained a firm objective of Roosevelt's Administration.

Nonetheless, the Churchill-Roosevelt partnership produced a political and structural foundation for a strategic alliance. The Atlantic Charter, agreed in August 1941 before America joined hostilities, provided an Anglo-American blueprint for the post-war world – and their war aims after Pearl Harbor – although each Power interpreted differently the promotion of self-government. Out of the Atlantic Charter arose the UN, the IMF and World Bank, German and Japanese disarmament, freer trade, and more. Unseen, its intent to restore self-government and have territorial changes respect the wishes of their populations ultimately engendered strain with Russia in Eastern and Central Europe and helped plant the seeds of the Cold War. Arcadia's creation of the CCS and Roosevelt's acceptance of 'Europe first' proved critical for the Anglo-American direction of the war and success in North Africa, Italy, northwest Europe, and the Pacific theatre. Equally significant, despite strain over the cross-Channel invasion, close and constant contact between British and American politicians, diplomats, and commanders in running the Western war effort created the basis of what later became Anglo-American collaboration in the post-war world and in strategic alliances such as NATO. When Churchill and Roosevelt departed the scene in 1945, the foundation for continued Anglo-American strategic cooperation was in place outside of any personal diplomacy.

Would new leaders continue the strategic partnership after peace returned? In the new international order, marked by the advent of atomic and thermonuclear weapons, London and Washington shared perceptions of Russian and communist aggression in Iran, Turkey, and Greece, as well as Germany and Central and Eastern Europe; it proved the diplomatic catalyst for perpetuating the wartime relationship. After 1945, America emerged as the Relationship's dominant partner – thus the Americans led and, through

The Relationship and politics since 1941   131

initiatives like the Truman Doctrine and Marshall Plan, began containing Russia – a renewed Europe-first strategy. In the military sphere, however, Britain's participation in occupying Germany, its central role in the Brussels Pact and WEU, and its contributions to the Berlin Airlift gave London a strong voice in containment. That Bevin proved central in creating NATO only added to British gravitas and influence. Truman and Acheson, particularly, understood Britain's still important role.

The American problem concerned decolonisation. As Britain under economic and domestic pressures began decolonising – first, India and Palestine and, later, in Africa and Southeast Asia – Washington saw its long-term desire for ending the great European empires realised. Britain's decolonisation proved relatively peaceful – that of France, especially in Indochina, much less so. But contrary to suppositions going back to Roosevelt, the Americans did not enjoy unadorned success in the developing world; they encountered problems such as the Indo-Pakistani dispute over Kashmir and Arab hostility to Israel. Washington had to choose sides. America never won India's friendship. In the Middle East, Israel, along with a few Arab states like Saudi Arabia, gradually became allied with America; other Arab Powers – Egypt, Syria, Iraq, and Jordan – were ultimately either ambivalent or hostile towards America. And when American-led UN forces fought in Korea, the unresolved war that led to the 1954 Geneva Conference saw Anglo-American dispute – a quarrel between Eden and Dulles – over shaping post-war stability. It ultimately produced Anglo-American membership in SEATO, but the PRC, North Vietnam, and Laotian and Cambodian instability complicated American determination to maintain post-war influence in East Asia. Quite simply, American efforts to harness decolonisation in their favour produced a blemished record, one in which Britain's contrasting successes such as the Colombo Plan and defeating communist insurgents in Malaya aided East Asian containment.

Transforming Trizonia into West Germany, remilitarising West Germany, and backing Western European economic integration between 1952 and 1957 made American containment effective militarily and economically. Britain's role in supporting these objectives other than in the Treaty of Rome proved important. Its acquisition of atomic weapons in 1952 augmented Western military strength in Europe. Given Europe-first and East Asian problems, and helping keep the shah on his throne in 1953, the Americans let Britain handle the Middle East because of its long experience and commitment to the region. However, the 1956 Suez crisis created a major fissure in the Relationship. Misjudging Anglo-French military capacity, collaboration with the Israelis, the reaction of former colonies such as India, and American willingness to acquiesce in Nasser's defeat, Britain and its ally France were unsuccessful in their attempt to reacquire the Suez Canal by armed force. Eden and Eisenhower each felt double-crossed by the other; the more powerful America saw Eden's resignation. Far more important, both Britain's supposed status as a Middle Eastern Power and, more stunningly, any claim as a global Power evaporated within days.

132 *Epilogue*

As Macmillan moved to repair the Relationship and revive Britain's international position, he and his government demonstrated Britain's value to America albeit its now-permanent status as the lesser partner. One element of this strategy involved assisting Middle Eastern stability, in Jordan and later Yemen. Macmillan's focus, however, lay in Europe. He won Eisenhower's support to use the American Skybolt missile for Britain's nuclear deterrent against Russia. He also embarked on diplomacy involving Moscow, Paris, and Bonn over nuclear arms limitation via a proposed Great Power summit in May 1960 that collapsed when Russo-American relations worsened after the downing of an American reconnaissance plane over Russia.

Kennedy's advent saw the development of a strong relationship between leaders over containing the Russians. With Skybolt's technological demise, the centrepiece was Macmillan winning an independent British nuclear force built around American sea-launched Polaris missiles with British warheads. Some American officials were annoyed; but the Relationship re-emerged from Suez: founded on bureaucratic connexions, the embassies in London and Washington working well with their respective host governments, and, whilst neither side abandoned its own interests, continuing recognition of shared strategic ones. The final Berlin Crisis in 1961 and 1962 was a case in point. In various discussions about Germany between 1959 and 1963, Macmillan's government seemed willing to give *de facto* rather than *de jure* recognition to East Germany, accept the Soviet-defined Polish–East German border, and open dialogue with Moscow. However, Macmillan never once weakened the Anglo-American relationship to do so. Britain proved an effective European ally, as when it backed the Americans and NATO in the wake of the Berlin Wall's construction.

Some observers portray the Kennedy-Macmillan years as 'Golden Days' for Anglo-American relations. They were; and they provided the strategic background to the international crisis caused by America's involvement in Vietnam, its ultimate blemish in meeting decolonisation. As the Kennedy and Johnson Administrations slowly bogged down in Southeast Asia, British governments from Macmillan to Wilson to Heath supported Washington in several ways except despatching troops. The British economy faced difficulties. To cut defence spending, Wilson's government withdrew British forces 'East of Suez' in 1967; strategically Britain had increasingly become a European Power – with an independent nuclear deterrent – and its international influence depended more on its economic vitality than a global military presence. Johnson was unimpressed, but Nixon and Kissinger saw transatlantic ties important as they wrestled with Vietnam and renewed crisis in the Middle East in 1973 and 1974. On the British side, as Heath talked of a 'natural', rather than special, Relationship and pursued EEC membership for Britain, Douglas-Home ensured bureaucratic links between the British Cabinet and the State Department 'to keep US-UK relations on an unchanged basis' (Hill and Lord, 1996: 310). America's failure in Vietnam devolved from its leaders' long-term mishandling of decolonisation – assuming their

The Relationship and politics since 1941   133

pre-eminence and national values would bolster their interests – and desire to dominate the western Pacific and East Asia. As in other areas of the globe, anti-Americanism existed in South and East Asia – and in Latin America and other places – because of Washington's choices and the dictatorial regimes it supported. But even when London proved unsupportive – for instance, when Kissinger sought a ceasefire in the Yom Kippur War – Britain was America's steadfast European ally, which Kissinger and Nixon understood.

The Relationship went into suspended animation after 1974. On the American side, Nixon's fall from grace produced a concentration on domestic politics, less interventionist post-Vietnam foreign policy, *détente* with Russia leading to CSCE, Carter-Brezhnev arms talks that created SALT II, and Carter initiating a moralistic foreign policy. For the British, continuing economic malaise, trade union unrest, high unemployment, and stagflation forced Britain to the IMF. After 1975, the Russians reckoned they had a free hand in the developing world that could strengthen them strategically: in Mozambique, Angola, and the Horn of Africa. When crisis in Iran in 1979 – also showing the weakness of Carter's morally based diplomacy – threatened to spill into the southern Moslem Soviet republics and Kabul seemed at risk of falling out of Russia's orbit, the Red Army invaded Afghanistan. With *détente* dead, the Cold War returned. Although Carter now looked to contain Russian power – he had a staunch Atlanticist ally in Thatcher after April 1979 – it was too late for him.

Reagan took office in January 1981 and, with strong personal ties to Thatcher, the two leaders brought the Relationship to a new high. With similar worldviews, they fixed on the Russian question. Thatcher led at seeking European support for basing euromissiles on the continent, buttressing NATO. She acquired the new American-developed, British-controlled Trident strategic missile to replace Polaris and, in so doing, reinforced the Relationship. For his part, Reagan and his advisors determined to reverse Soviet inroads in the wider world, stand by democratic allies such as Britain and, from Afghanistan to Nicaragua, resist Soviet-sponsored aggression. Accordingly, together with the British, the Americans supported the anti-Russian *mujahidin* in Afghanistan to bleed the Red Army and deplete Moscow's treasury. Alone, Washington embarked on anti-communist offensives with proxies in Central America and the Caribbean. Most crucial, Reagan's Administration began to develop SDI, joining American wealth with superior technology to accentuate the re-emergent Cold War and force Moscow into an arms race in which it could not compete.

The 1982 Falkland Islands crisis strengthened the Relationship, as well as Thatcher and Reagan's personal bonds. Accordingly, Anglo-American efforts brought the Russians to the bargaining table. In March 1985, after three years of unstable leadership, a new generation of Russian leaders, headed by Gorbachev, recognised the economic and political decay of the Soviet system. Pursuing domestic reforms, they decided they needed to reduce military spending. Seeing Gorbachev as a man 'we can do business with', Thatcher

134   *Epilogue*

convinced Reagan to negotiate seriously with the Kremlin whilst maintaining pressure on Russia. Reagan did so and, by December 1987, there was agreement to eliminate INF in Europe. In this process, Thatcher kept Britain's independent Trident forces, continued support for the *mujahidin*, and exploited weak points in the Eastern Bloc, particularly Poland.

By 1989, when Bush Senior succeeded Reagan, the Russians were withdrawing from Afghanistan, seeking strategic nuclear limitation, and pushing Gorbachevian reform on its Eastern European empire. Gorbachev, however, had unleashed forces that the Kremlin could not control, such that the Eastern Bloc began to fracture; in Polish elections in June 1989, spectacularly, Solidarity took seats from the Communist Party and, unlike in Hungary in 1956 and Czechoslovakia in 1968, the Red Army did nothing. The Brezhnev Doctrine ceased to exist. Thatcher and Bush travelled to reforming countries such as Poland and Hungary to proselytise liberalisation. Although the willingness of Soviet Bloc regimes to implement reform varied, East Germany proved pivotal. In light of electoral corruption, a poor economy, and an authoritarian record, the East German public demanded change. Gorbachev had forced the inflexible Honecker from office by mid-October; on 9 November, the Berlin Wall fell; the Cold War ended; and, within a year, as independence came to Central and Eastern Europe, a united Germany emerged. The Bush Administration stood back from these events – Russia would have reacted unfavourably to forceful action – but supported change when it appeared; for instance, by giving economic aid to Poland. In December 1991, with Gorbachev eclipsed, Soviet Russia dissolved. The strategic threat uniting Britain and America since 1945 no longer existed.

Bush talked about a 'new world order' in January 1991. Initially within this order, it seemed that the Relationship would continue – for instance, protecting its own regional interests, Britain supported America in 1990 and 1991 to force the occupying Iraqis out of Kuwait and away from the bulk of world petroleum reserves. Concurrently, however, the new order witnessed Bush and his advisors promoting German unification and, once that was achieved, having united Germany remain in NATO. Although opposing a greater Germany, Britain and other American allies such as France had to acquiesce in this decision. Convinced of America's pre-eminence in international politics, the Bush Administration increasingly fashioned strategic policy and action without reference to traditional (or, at least, traditional since 1941) US allies in Europe. Thatcher left office in November 1990. Despite her successors' inclination over the next 20 years to work with American administrations whether Democrat or Republican, American leaders slowly distanced themselves from effective collaboration with Britain – and other allies – in crises as diverse as those in the Balkans in the 1990s and those in Afghanistan and Iraq after 2001.

Some British leaders still saw value in the Relationship, such as Blair, who advised the Labour Party in 2001 that supporting Washington was Britain's only means to influence it (Daalder, 2003). Blair's military commitment in

The Relationship and politics since 1941   135

Afghanistan and Iraq endeavoured to demonstrate this assertion. It failed in Iraq, which the British public began questioning on the eve of the war against Saddam. The next decade only added to disfavour amongst new British leaders and the public – lack of Iraqi WMD underscored the issue. Shorn of the Russian threat after 1991, American leaders were confident in a growing unilateralist approach to foreign policy; as Bush Junior's Administration told its European allies in spring 2001, America would look after its interests with or without them. Obama agreed; new and important threats in East Asia and the Pacific, primarily the PRC, informed American strategy. Britain had no place in these calculations.

Thus, the Special Relationship evaporated even though effusive words emanated from Washington and London (Obama and Cameron, 2011). Building on increasing transnationalism by 1939, the Relationship that emerged after Pearl Harbor had at its centre strategic interest in defeating the Axis Powers. The Relationship existed as long as there were common adversaries – Nazi Germany, fascist Italy, and Japan in one international order; Soviet Russia in the next. When working together offered the best means to protect and extend Britain and America's perceived national interests and, thereby, better ensure international stability, the Relationship had strategic value. When it did not, its reason for being disappeared.

Part V
Documents

Document 1

Churchill, 'The lights are going out' [Broadcast to the United States from London], 16 October 1938

I avail myself with relief of the opportunity of speaking to the people of the United States. I do not know how long such liberties will be allowed. The stations of uncensored expression are closing down; the lights are going out; but there is still time for those to whom freedom and parliamentary government mean something, to consult together. Let me, then, speak in truth and earnestness while time remains.

The American people have, it seems to me, formed a true judgment upon the disaster which has befallen Europe. They realise, perhaps more clearly than the French and British publics have yet done, the far-reaching consequences of the abandonment and ruin of the Czechoslovak Republic. I hold to the conviction I expressed some months ago, that if in April, May or June, Great Britain, France, and Russia had jointly declared that they would act together upon Nazi Germany if Herr Hitler committed an act of unprovoked aggression against this small State, and if they had told Poland, Yugoslavia, and Rumania what they meant to do in good time, and invited them to join the combination of peace-defending Powers, I hold that the German Dictator would have been confronted with such a formidable array that he would have been deterred from his purpose. This would also have been an opportunity for all the peace-loving and moderate forces in Germany, together with the chiefs of the German Army, to make a great effort to re-establish something like sane and civilised conditions in their own country. If the risks of war which were run by France and Britain at the last moment had been boldly faced in good time, and plain declarations made, and meant, how different would our prospects be today!

Source: *[excerpt]: http://teachingamericanhistory.org/
library/document/the-lights-are-going-out/*

Document 2

'Atlantic Charter, August 1941': Avalon Project

The President of the United States of America and the Prime Minister, Mr. Churchill, representing His Majesty's Government in the United Kingdom, being met together, deem it right to make known certain common principles in the national policies of their respective countries on which they base their hopes for a better future for the world.

First, their countries seek no aggrandizement, territorial or other;

Second, they desire to see no territorial changes that do not accord with the freely expressed wishes of the peoples concerned;

140   *Documents*

Third, they respect the right of all peoples to choose the form of government under which they will live; and they wish to see sovereign rights and self government restored to those who have been forcibly deprived of them;

Fourth, they will endeavor, with due respect for their existing obligations, to further the enjoyment by all States, great or small, victor or vanquished, of access, on equal terms, to the trade and to the raw materials of the world which are needed for their economic prosperity;

Fifth, they desire to bring about the fullest collaboration between all nations in the economic field with the object of securing, for all, improved labor standards, economic advancement and social security;

Sixth, after the final destruction of the Nazi tyranny, they hope to see established a peace which will afford to all nations the means of dwelling in safety within their own boundaries, and which will afford assurance that all the men in all lands may live out their lives in freedom from fear and want;

Seventh, such a peace should enable all men to traverse the high seas and oceans without hindrance;

Eighth, they believe that all of the nations of the world, for realistic as well as spiritual reasons must come to the abandonment of the use of force. Since no future peace can be maintained if land, sea or air armaments continue to be employed by nations which threaten, or may threaten, aggression outside of their frontiers, they believe, pending the establishment of a wider and permanent system of general security, that the disarmament of such nations is essential. They will likewise aid and encourage all other practicable measure which will lighten for peace-loving peoples the crushing burden of armaments.

Source: *[excerpt]: http://avalon.law.yale.edu/wwii/atlantic.asp*

Document 3

Casablanca Conference: unconditional surrender. Roosevelt radio address, 12 February 1943

In an attempt to ward off the inevitable disaster, the Axis propagandist are trying all of their old tricks in order to divide the United Nations. They seek to create the idea that if we win this war, Russia, England, China, and the United States are going to get into a cat-and-dog fight.

This is their final effort to turn one nation against another, in the vain hope that they may settle with one or two at a time – that any of us may be so gullible and so forgetful as to be duped into making 'deals' at the expense of our Allies.

To these panicky attempts to escape the consequences of their crimes we say – all the United Nations say – that the only terms on which we shall deal with an Axis government or any Axis factions are the terms proclaimed at Casablanca: 'Unconditional Surrender.' In our uncompromising policy we mean no harm to the common people of the Axis nations. But we do mean to impose punishment and retribution in full upon their guilty, barbaric leaders. . . . It is one of our war aims, as expressed in the Atlantic Charter, that the conquered populations of today be again the masters of their destiny. There must be no doubt anywhere that it is the unalterable purpose of the United Nations to restore to conquered peoples their sacred rights.

Source: *[excerpt]: www.ibiblio.org/pha/policy/1943/430212a.html*

Document 4

Roosevelt and Churchill to Stalin on Allied strategy, 21 August 1943

In our conference at Quebec, just concluded, we have arrived at the following decision as to military operations to be carried out during 1943 and 1944.

The bomber offensive against Germany will be continued on a rapidly increased scale from bases in the United Kingdom and Italy. The objectives of this air attack will be to destroy the German air combat strength, to dislocate the German military, industrial, and economic system, and to prepare the way for a cross channel invasion.

A large-scale buildup of American forces in the United Kingdom is now underway. It will provide an initial assault force of British and American divisions for cross channel operations. A bridgehead in the continent once secured will be reinforced steadily by additional American troops at the rate of from three to five divisions per month. This operation will be the primary British and American ground and air effort against the Axis.

The war in the Mediterranean is to be pressed vigorously. Our objectives in that area will be the elimination of Italy from the Axis alliance, and the occupation of that country as well as Sardinia and Corsica as bases for operations against Germany.

Our operations in the Balkans will be, limited to the supply of Balkan Guerrillas by air and sea transport, to minor raids by Commandos, and to the bombing of strategic objectives.

We shall accelerate our operations against Japan in the Pacific and in Southeast Asia. Our purposes are to exhaust Japanese air, naval, and shipping resources, to cut the Japanese communications and to secure bases from which to bomb Japan proper.

Source: *[excerpt]: http://avalon.law.yale.edu/wwii/q004.asp*

Document 5

Roosevelt avoids commitment of American forces in post-war Europe: 'Radio address at a dinner of the Foreign Policy Association', 21 October 1944

I speak to the present generation of Americans with a reverent participation in its sorrows and in its hopes. No generation has undergone a greater test, or has met that test with greater heroism and I think greater wisdom, and no generation has had a more exalted mission.

For this generation must act not only for itself, but as a trustee for all those who fell in the last war – a part of their mission unfulfilled.

142   *Documents*

It must act also for all those who have paid the supreme price in this war –
lest their mission, too, be betrayed.

And finally it must act for the generations to come – that must be granted
a heritage of peace.

I do not exaggerate that mission. We are not fighting for, and we shall
not attain a Utopia. Indeed, in our own land, the work to be done is never
finished. We have yet to realize the full and equal enjoyment of our freedom. So, in embarking on the building of a world fellowship, we have set
ourselves a long and arduous task, which will challenge our patience, our
intelligence, our imagination, as well as our faith.

That task, my friends, calls for the judgment of a seasoned and a mature
people. This, I think, the American people have become. We shall not again be
thwarted in our will to live as a mature Nation, confronting limitless horizons.
We shall bear our full responsibility, exercise our full influence, and bring our
full help and encouragement to all who aspire to peace and freedom.

Source: *[excerpt]: www.presidency.ucsb.edu/ws/?pid=16456*

Document 6

The United States commits to ensuring the peace settlement after the Second World War: 'The Berlin (Potsdam) Conference, July 17–August 2, 1945'

The Governments of the United Kingdom, the United States and the U.S.S.R.
consider it necessary to begin without delay the essential preparatory work
upon the peace settlements in Europe. To this end they are agreed that there
should be established a Council of the Foreign Ministers of the Five Great
Powers to prepare treaties of peace with the European enemy States, for sub-
mission to the United Nations. The Council would also be empowered to
propose settlements of outstanding territorial questions in Europe and to consider such other matters as member Governments might agree to refer to it.

Source: *[excerpt]: Avalon Project, http://avalon.law. yale.edu/20th_century/decade17.asp*

Document 7

Truman's secretary of state shows ambivalence about Iran: 'Report by Secretary Byrnes, December 30, 1945, on Moscow Meeting'

The Foreign Ministers reached understanding on all important items placed
on our agenda with the exception of Iran. At one time it looked as if we
might agree on a tripartite commission to consider Iranian problems which
have been accentuated by the presence of Allied troops in Iran. Unfortu-
nately, we could not agree. I do not wish to minimize the seriousness of the
problem. But I am not discouraged. I hope that the exchange of views may

Documents 143

lead to further consideration of the grave issues involved and out of such consideration a solution may be found.

Source: [excerpt]: Avalon Project, http://avalon.law. yale.edu/20th_century/decade19.asp

Document 8

'President Harry S. Truman's address before a Joint Session of Congress, March 12, 1947'

I believe that it must be the policy of the United States to support free peoples who are resisting attempted subjugation by armed minorities or by outside pressures.

I believe that we must assist free peoples to work out their own destinies in their own way.

I believe that our help should be primarily through economic and financial aid which is essential to economic stability and orderly political processes.

The world is not static, and the status quo is not sacred. But we cannot allow changes in the status quo in violation of the Charter of the United Nations by such methods as coercion, or by such subterfuges as political infiltration. In helping free and independent nations to maintain their freedom, the United States will be giving effect to the principles of the Charter of the United Nations.

It is necessary only to glance at a map to realize that the survival and integrity of the Greek nation are of grave importance in a much wider situation. If Greece should fall under the control of an armed minority, the effect upon its neighbor, Turkey, would be immediate and serious. Confusion and disorder might well spread throughout the entire Middle East. . . . It would be an unspeakable tragedy if these countries, which have struggled so long against overwhelming odds, should lose that victory for which they sacrificed so much. Collapse of free institutions and loss of independence would be disastrous not only for them but for the world. Discouragement and possibly failure would quickly be the lot of neighboring peoples striving to maintain their freedom and independence.

Source: [excerpt]: Avalon Project, http://avalon.law. yale.edu/20th_century/trudoc.asp

Document 9

Kennan proposes the strategy of containment: 'Telegram, George Kennan to George Marshall ["Long Telegram"], February 22, 1946'

Everything possible will be done to set major Western Powers against each other. Anti-British talk will be plugged among Americans, anti-American talk among British. Continentals, including Germans, will be taught to abhor both

144   *Documents*

Anglo-Saxon powers. Where suspicions exist, they will be fanned; where not, ignited. No effort will be spared to discredit and combat all efforts which threaten to lead to any sort of unity or cohesion among other [word missed] from which Russia might be excluded. Thus, all forms of international organization not amenable to Communist penetration and control, whether it be the Catholic [word missed] international economic concerns, or the international fraternity of royalty and aristocracy, must expect to find themselves under fire from many, and often [word missed]. . . . We must formulate and put forward for other nations a much more positive and constructive picture of sort of world we would like to see than we have put forward in past. It is not enough to urge people to develop political processes similar to our own. Many foreign peoples, in Europe at least, are tired and frightened by experiences of past, and are less interested in abstract freedom than in security. They are seeking guidance rather than responsibilities. We should be better able than Russians to give them this. And unless we do, Russians certainly will.

Source: *[excerpt]: www.trumanlibrary.org/whistlestop/*
study_collections/coldwar/documents/pdf/6-6.pdf

Document 10

Churchill's 'Iron Curtain Speech'

Now, while still pursuing the method of realising our overall strategic concept, I come to the crux of what I have travelled here to say. Neither the sure prevention of war, nor the continuous rise of world organisation will be gained without what I have called the fraternal association of the English-speaking peoples. This means a special relationship between the British Commonwealth and Empire and the United States. This is no time for generalities, and I will venture to be precise. Fraternal association requires not only the growing friendship and mutual understanding between our two vast but kindred systems of society, but the continuance of the intimate relationship between our military advisers, leading to common study of potential dangers, the similarity of weapons and manuals of instructions, and to the interchange of officers and cadets at technical colleges. It should carry with it the continuance of the present facilities for mutual security by the joint use of all Naval and Air Force bases in the possession of either country all over the world. This would perhaps double the mobility of the American Navy and Air Force. It would greatly expand that of the British Empire Forces and it might well lead, if and as the world calms down, to important financial savings. Already we use together a large number of islands; more may well be entrusted to our joint care in the near future.

Source: *[excerpt]: W. Churchill, The Sinews of Peace,*
in Mark A. Kishlansky, ed., Sources of World History
(New York: HarperCollins, 1995), 298–302.

Document 11

Eisenhower outlines the 'Domino Theory': 'The President's News Conference of April 7, 1954'

Finally, you have broader considerations that might follow what you would call the 'falling domino' principle. You have a row of dominoes set up, you knock over the first one, and what will happen to the last one is the certainty that it will go over very quickly. So you could have a beginning of a disintegration that would have the most profound influences.

Now, with respect to the first one, two of the items from this particular area that the world uses are tin and tungsten. They are very important. There are others, of course, the rubber plantations and so on.

Then with respect to more people passing under this domination, Asia, after all, has already lost some 450 million of its peoples to the Communist dictatorship, and we simply can't afford greater losses.

But when we come to the possible sequence of events, the loss of Indochina, of Burma, of Thailand, of the Peninsula, and Indonesia following, now you begin to talk about areas that not only multiply the disadvantages that you would suffer through loss of materials, sources of materials, but now you are talking really about millions and millions and millions of people.

Finally, the geographical position achieved thereby does many things. It turns the so-called island defensive chain of Japan, Formosa, of the Philippines and to the southward; it moves in to threaten Australia and New Zealand. . . . So, the possible consequences of the loss are just incalculable to the free world.

Source: *[excerpt]: http://coursesa.matrix.msu.edu/
~hst306/documents/domino.html*

Document 12

Eisenhower worries the British might double-cross the United States over Suez: 'Memorandum of a conference with the president', 29 October 1956

The President thought the British are calculating that we must go along with them (he thought they were not banking too heavily on our being tied up in the election, but are thinking in longer range terms.) He thought we should let them know at once of our position, telling them that we recognize that much is on their side in the dispute with the Egyptians, but that nothing justifies double-crossing us. He did not conceive that the United States would gain if we permitted it to be justly said that we are a nation without honor. Admiral Radford thought that this matter must be handled on the basis of principle, and the President agreed. Secretary Dulles said that tomorrow

146   *Documents*

there may well be fighting along the Canal, with the pipe lines broken, and with the British and French moving in.

> Source: *[excerpt]: FRUS, Suez Crisis, July 26–December 31, 1956, Volume XVI, Document 411: http://history.state.gov/historical documents/frus1955–57v16/d411*

Document 13

The Nixon Doctrine

Let me briefly explain what has been described as the Nixon Doctrine – a policy which not only will help end the war in Vietnam, but which is an essential element of our program to prevent future Vietnams.

We Americans are a do-it-yourself people. We are an impatient people. Instead of teaching someone else to do a job, we like to do it ourselves. And this trait has been carried over into our foreign policy.

In Korea and again in Vietnam, the United States furnished most of the money, most of the arms, and most of the men to help the people of those countries defend their freedom against Communist aggression.

Before any American troops were committed to Vietnam, a leader of another Asian country expressed this opinion to me when I was traveling in Asia as a private citizen. He said: 'When you are trying to assist another nation defend its freedom, U.S. policy should be to help them fight the war but not to fight the war for them.' In accordance with this wise counsel, I laid down in Guam three principles as guidelines for future American policy toward Asia:

- First, the United States will keep all of its treaty commitments.
- Second, we shall provide a shield if a nuclear power threatens the freedom of a nation allied with us or of a nation whose survival we consider vital to our security.
- Third, in cases involving other types of aggression, we shall furnish military and economic assistance when requested in accordance with our treaty commitments. But we shall look to the nation directly threatened to assume the primary responsibility of providing the manpower for its defense.

The defense of freedom is everybody's business – not just America's business. And it is particularly the responsibility of the people whose freedom is threatened. In the previous administration, we Americanized the war in Vietnam. In this administration, we are Vietnamizing the search for peace.

> Source: *[excerpt]: http://cf.linnbenton.edu/artcom/social_science/ clarkd/upload/Nixon%20Doctrine.pdf*

Documents 147

Document 14

Europe's NATO members' 'Declaration on Atlantic Relations', 19 June 1974

The members of the Alliance reaffirm that their common defence is one and indivisible. An attack on one or more of them in the area of application of the Treaty shall be considered an attack against them all. The common aim is to prevent any attempt by a foreign power to threaten the independence or integrity of a member of the Alliance. Such an attempt would not only put in jeopardy the security of all members of the Alliance but also threaten the foundations of world peace.

At the same time they realise that the circumstances affecting their common defence have profoundly changed in the last ten years: the strategic relationship between the United States and the Soviet Union has reached a point of near equilibrium. Consequently, although all the countries of the Alliance remain vulnerable to attack, the nature of the danger to which they are exposed has changed. The Alliance's problems in the defence of Europe have thus assumed a different and more distinct character.

However, the essential elements in the situation which gave rise to the Treaty have not changed. While the commitment of all the Allies to the common defence reduces the risk of external aggression, the contribution to the security of the entire Alliance provided by the nuclear forces of the United States based in the United States as well as in Europe and by the presence of North American forces in Europe remains indispensable.

Nevertheless, the Alliance must pay careful attention to the dangers to which it is exposed in the European region, and must adopt all measures necessary to avert them. The European members who provide three-quarters of the conventional strength of the Alliance in Europe, and two of whom possess nuclear forces capable of playing a deterrent role of their own contributing to the overall strengthening of the deterrence of the Alliance, undertake to make the necessary contribution to maintain the common defence at a level capable of deterring and if necessary repelling all actions directed against the independence and territorial integrity of the members of the Alliance.

Source: *[excerpt]: www.nato.int/cps/en/natohq/ official_texts_26901.htm*

Document 15

Kissinger discusses CSCE with Ford: 'Memorandum of a conversation', 15 August 1974

Kissinger:. . . . On CSCE – we never wanted it but we went along with the Europeans. It includes some basic principles, something on human contacts, no change of frontiers, and what they call 'confidence-building measures.'

148 *Documents*

The Soviet Union wants it as a substitute for a peace treaty. They more or less have that. The big hang-up is on freedom of movement. It is meaningless – it is just a grandstand play to the left. We are going along with it.

What you will face is whether to conclude it at the summit level or foreign minister level. My guess is the Europeans will decide on a summit. We have positioned with the Soviet Union, so we look like we are ahead of the Europeans.

The President: What is the timetable?

Kissinger: Maybe next March. The Soviet Union wants it this year, but that is not possible. If you meet Brezhnev in December, they won't want it before that.

There are no decisions to make now. . . . On MBFR – we made an absurd proposal which couldn't fly. Now we are modifying it. The Soviets should cut more than us, but not so much. Then we should add the nuclear package – 32 Pershings, 54 F–4, 1,000 nuclear warheads. It is strategically insignificant, but it does have the consequence of establishing some ceiling on our nuclear forces.

Source: *[excerpt]: FRUS, European Security, Basket III, Volume XXXIX, Document 243: http://history.state.gov/ historicaldocuments/frus1969–76v39/d243*

Document 16

Thatcher, 'Speech at Kensington Town Hall ("Britain Awake")', 19 January 1976

The first duty of any Government is to safeguard its people against external aggression. To guarantee the survival of our way of life.

The question we must now ask ourselves is whether the present Government is fulfilling that duty. It is dismantling our defences at a moment when the strategic threat to Britain and her allies from an expansionist power is graver than at any moment since the end of the last war. . . . A huge, largely land-locked country like Russia does not need to build the most powerful navy in the world just to guard its own frontiers.

No. The Russians are bent on world dominance, and they are rapidly acquiring the means to become the most powerful imperial nation the world has seen.

The men in the Soviet politburo don't have to worry about the ebb and flow of public opinion. They put guns before butter, while we put just about everything before guns.

They know that they are a super power in only one sense – the military sense. . . . We have seen Vietnam and all of Indochina swallowed up by Communist aggression. We have seen the Communists make an open grab for power in Portugal, our oldest ally – a sign that many of the battles in the Third World War are being fought inside Western countries.

And now the Soviet Union and its satellites are pouring money, arms and front-line troops into Angola in the hope of dragging it into the Communist bloc.

Documents   149

We must remember that there are no Queensbury rules in the contest that is now going on. And the Russians are playing to win.

They have one great advantage over us – the battles are being fought on our territory, not theirs.

Source: *[excerpt]: www.margaretthatcher.org/document/102939*

Document 17

Reagan, 'A vision for America', 3 November 1980

Let it always be clear that we have no dreams of empire, that we seek no manifest destiny, that we understand the limitations of any one nation's power.

But let it also be clear that we do not shirk history's call; that America is not turned inward but outward – toward others. Let it be clear that we have not lessened our commitment to peace or to the hope that someday all of the people of the world will enjoy lives of decency, lives with a degree of freedom, with a measure of dignity.

Together, tonight, let us say what so many long to hear: that America is still united, still strong, still compassionate, still clinging fast to the dream of peace and freedom, still willing to stand by those who are persecuted or alone.

For those who seek the right to self-determination without interference from foreign powers, tonight let us speak for them,

For those who suffer from social or religious discrimination,

For those who are victims of police states or government induced torture or terror,

For those who are persecuted,

For all the countries and people of the world who seek only to live in harmony with each other, tonight let us speak for them.

And to our allies – who regard us with such constant puzzlement and profound affection – we must also speak tonight.

Source: *[excerpt]: www.presidency.ucsb.edu/ws/?pid=8519*

Document 18

Reagan to Thatcher, n.d. [but March 1982]

Thank you for your letter of March 11.

I am pleased to confirm that the United States Government is prepared to supply to the United Kingdom TRIDENT II missiles, equipment and supporting services as proposed in your letter, subject to and in accordance with applicable United States law and procedures.

The United States readiness to provide these systems is a demonstration of the great importance which the United States Government attaches to the maintenance by the United Kingdom of an independent nuclear deterrent capability. I can assure you of the United States' willingness to cooperate closely with the United Kingdom Government in maintaining and modernizing that capability.

150 *Documents*

I attach great importance to your assurance that the United Kingdom TRI-DENT II force will be assigned to NATO and that the economies realized through cooperation between our two governments will be used to reinforce the United Kingdom's efforts to upgrade its conventional forces. Such nuclear and conventional force improvements are of the highest priority for NATO's security.

I agree that, as the next step, our two governments should initiate the technical and financial negotiations which you propose.

Source: *[excerpt]: www.reagan.utexas.edu/archives/ speeches/1982/31182b.htm*

Document 19

NSC Meeting, 30 April 1982

Secretary Haig then outlined the current diplomatic situation and what the United States proposes to do now. He began by describing the situation as tragic with both sides, similar to a demented man on a ledge ready to jump, reaching for help but unable to grab our hand. He then described the elements of the American [mediation] plan which in effect would give ultimate sovereignty to Argentina but under evolutionary conditions which the Islanders could ultimately accept. . . .

Secretary Haig added that until now, we had wanted to avoid the U.N. He added that the Argentines have always suspected us of being on the side of the British. Our imperative has always been to get a settlement. The Argentine strategy is to string out the process and hope the weather will prevent the British from taking action. Meanwhile their position remains rigid. Their final offer, if accepted by the British, would cause Mrs. Thatcher's fall. Our proposals, in fact, are a camouflaged transfer of sovereignty, and the Argentine foreign minister knows this, but the junta will not accept it. . . .

The President concluded the meeting approving the specific actions outlined in the press statement and noting it would be nice if, after all these years, the U.N. could accomplish something as constructive as averting war between the U.K. and Argentina.

Source: *[excerpt]: www.thereaganfiles.com/ falkland-island-nsc-meeting.pdf*

Document 20

'Falklands: Reagan phone call to Thatcher (urges ceasefire)', 31 May 1982

Reagan could barely get a word in as the prime minister gushed out a torrent of dismissal. 'I didn't lose some of my best ships and some of my finest lives, to leave quietly under a ceasefire without the Argentines withdrawing,' she said.

Documents 151

'Oh. Oh, Margaret, that is part of this, as I understand it . . .' stammered Reagan, trying to outline a Brazilian peace plan. It called for a ceasefire, Argentine withdrawal and a third-party peace-keeping force in the disputed islands. 'Ron, I'm not handing over . . . I'm not handing over the island now,' insisted Thatcher. 'I can't lose the lives and blood of our soldiers to hand the islands over to a contact. It's not possible.

'You are surely not asking me, Ron, after we've lost some of our finest young men, you are surely not saying, that after the Argentine withdrawal, that our forces, and our administration, become immediately idle? I had to go to immense distances and mobilise half my country. I just had to go.'

Source: *[excerpt]: www.margaretthatcher.org/document/110526*

Document 21

Reagan's 'Evil Empire' speech: 'Remarks at the Annual Convention of the National Association of Evangelicals in Orlando, Florida', 8 March 1983

So, I urge you to speak out against those who would place the United States in a position of military and moral inferiority. You know, I've always believed that old Screwtape [the fictional name for a devil in C.S. Lewis' *The Screwtape Letters* (1942)] reserved his best efforts for those of you in the church. So, in your discussions of the nuclear freeze proposals, I urge you to beware the temptation of pride – the temptation of blithely declaring yourselves above it all and label both sides equally at fault, to ignore the facts of history and the aggressive impulses of an evil empire, to simply call the arms race a giant misunderstanding and thereby remove yourself from the struggle between right and wrong and good and evil.

Source: *[excerpt]: www.reaganfoundation.org/bw_detail.aspx? p=LMB4YGHF2&lm=berlinwall&args_a=cms& args_b=74&argsb=N&tx=1770*

Document 22

'Grenada: Reagan phone call to Thatcher', 26 October 1983

We regret very much the embarrassment caused you, and I would like to tell you what the story is from our end. I was awakened at 3:00 in the morning, supposedly on a golfing vacation down in Georgia. The Secretary of State [George Shultz] was there. We met in pajamas out in the living room of our suite because of this urgent appeal from the Organisation of East Caribbean States pleading with us to support them in Grenada. We immediately got a group going back here in Washington, which we shortly joined, on planning and so forth. It was literally a matter of hours. We were greatly concerned, because of a problem here – and not at your

152   *Documents*

end at all – but here. We have had a nagging problem of a loose source, a leak here. At the same time we also had immediate surveillance problem [sic] – without their knowing it – of what was happening on Cuba to make sure that we could get ahead of them if they were moving and indeed, they were making some tentative moves. They sent some kind of command personnel into Grenada.

Incidentally, let me tell you that we were being so careful here that we did not even give a firm answer to the Caribbean States. We told them we were planning, but we were so afraid of this source and what it would do; it could almost abort the mission, with the lives that could have endangered.

When word came of your concerns – by the time I got it – the zero hour had passed, and our forces were on their way. The time difference made it later in the day when you learned of it.

Source: *[excerpt]: www.margaretthatcher.org/document/109426*

Document 23

Thatcher and Reagan discuss (i) Gorbachev and (ii) European nuclear deterrence, 'Cold War: Thatcher-Reagan Meeting at Camp David', 22 December 1984

Turning to Gorbachev's visit to the UK, Mrs. Thatcher said he was an unusual Russian in that he was much less constrained, more charming, open to discussion and debate, and did not stick to prepared notes. His wife [Raisa Gorbachev] was equally charming. The Prime Minister noted that she often says to herself the more charming the adversary, the more dangerous. . . . Mrs. Thatcher underlined that she had told Gorbachev there is no point in trying to divide Britain from the United States. This ploy will never succeed. Britain is part of the Western Alliance of free nations and the Soviets should drop any illusions about severing Europe or Great Britain from the United States. . . .

We do not want our objective of increased security, opined the Prime Minister, to result in increased Soviet nuclear weapons. Nuclear weapons have served not only to prevent a nuclear war, but they have also given us forty years of unprecedented peace in Europe. It would be unwise, she continued, to abandon a deterrence system that has prevented both nuclear and conventional war. Moreover, if we ever reach the stage of abolishing all nuclear weapons, this would make conventional, biological, or chemical war more likely. Hitler won the race for the rocket; the U.S. won the race for the nuclear bomb. The technological struggle goes on, she observed. There are all sorts of decoys, jamming systems and technological developments such as making the missile boost phase even shorter. All these advances make crisis management more and more difficult. . . . The President agreed and said he is trying to convince the Soviets that we mean them no harm. He often thought that the basic system in Russia had not changed fundamentally, i.e., that their current communist system is another form of the aristocratic system that ruled Russia under the Czar. Gandhi had once said that the Soviets believe more in survival than in communism.

Mrs. Thatcher replied that it is correct to emphasize military balance, not superiority. Balance gives us security. Making a specific reference to SDI, she said research contributes towards maintaining a military balance. We need to explain to our publics that SDI is only a research program, that it does not contravene any existing treaties and if we get to the development stage, many alternative factors will have to be considered at that time. For example, the ABM treaty may have to be renegotiated.

Secretary Shultz stressed our concern is that the current situation is not balanced. The Soviets have many more offensive nuclear systems than foreseen under Salt I [*sic*]. The defensive side is covered under the ABM treaty, but we have essentially dropped the notion of deploying a defensive system around cities and bases. . . . Saying she didn't wish to debate strategic theory, Mrs. Thatcher noted that some claim SDI would be an incentive for the Soviets to produce more offensive systems and could encourage the Soviets to launch a preemptive first strike. From our point of view, said Mrs. Thatcher, deterrence remains our fundamental objective. And like you, we are fearful of the Soviets finding an excuse to walk out of the Geneva talks.

Source: [*excerpt*]: *www.margaretthatcher.org/document/109185*

Document 24

Outlining the Reagan Doctrine: Reagan, 'Address before a Joint Session of the Congress on the State of the Union', 6 February 1985

We cannot play innocents abroad in a world that's not innocent; nor can we be passive when freedom is under siege. Without resources, diplomacy cannot succeed. Our security assistance programs help friendly governments defend themselves and give them confidence to work for peace. And I hope that you in the Congress will understand that, dollar for dollar, security assistance contributes as much to global security as our own defense budget.

We must stand by all our democratic allies. And we must not break faith with those who are risking their lives – on every continent, from Afghanistan to Nicaragua – to defy Soviet-supported aggression and secure rights which have been ours from birth. . . . I want to work with you to support the democratic forces whose struggle is tied to our own security.

Source: [*excerpt*]: *www.presidency.ucsb.edu/ws/?pid=38069*

154 *Documents*

Document 25

Thatcher confronts Gorbachev over the nature of Russian foreign policy: 'Record of conversation between Mikhail Gorbachev and Margaret Thatcher, March 30, 1987, Moscow'

Gorbachev. . . . To be frank, we familiarized ourselves with your March 21st speech in Torquay, which took place a week before this visit. The Soviet leadership sensed a whiff of the spirit of the 1940s-1950s, Churchill's Fulton speech, and the Truman doctrine. We welcomed the Prime Minister's intention to come to Moscow and were ready to discuss the main international and bilateral issues in a friendly and sincere tone, in the spirit of mutual understanding. But what did we see? Again Communism and the Soviet Union were presented as the 'evil forces;' again the same words about the need to grow a position of power in the West. We were very surprised. Frankly, we even thought that the Prime Minister may cancel her visit.

Thatcher. No, you can't have thought that! Nobody thinks that the Soviet Union is weak. The Soviet Union has enormous power. You have superior intermediate-range weapons and strategic offensive weapons, if we count warheads, as well as chemical and conventional arms. You are very powerful, not weak. We do not expect anyone to be weak in protecting their country. I am sure that you would not respect us if we were weak. In the speech you mentioned I did not attribute any evil intent to you. Moreover, I said that Mr. Gorbachev wants to do things frankly and in the spirit of cooperation, just like we do. But you have the superiority in practically everything, maybe with the exception of computers and some scientific research. The Soviet Union adheres to the doctrines of communist world domination, the Brezhnev doctrine I did not mention it in that speech, but naturally such policies cause concern in the West. Of course we have to have ideological battles, it is only natural. But we have to do it the appropriate way. Instead, we see communism is striving to dominate everywhere. Take for example Yemen, Ethiopia, Mozambique, Angola, Nicaragua, Cuban troops in some African countries. And Vietnam? As soon as the American troops left it immediately attacked Cambodia, instead of addressing its own internal affairs. And Afghanistan? That is why we say that communism's foreign policy is aimed at world domination.

Source: *[excerpt]: http://nsarchive.gwu.edu/NSAEBB/ NSAEBB422/docs/Doc%201%201987-03-30% 20Gorbachev-Thatcher%20memcon.pdf*

Document 26

On Britain, Europe, and the Atlantic alliance: Thatcher, 'Speech to the College of Europe', 20 September 1988

The European Community belongs to *all* its members.

It must reflect the traditions and aspirations of *all* its members.

Documents 155

And let me be quite clear. Britain does not dream of some cosy, isolated existence on the fringes of the European Community. Our destiny is in Europe, as part of the Community.

That is not to say that our future lies only in Europe, but nor does that of France or Spain or, indeed, of any other member.

The Community is not an end in itself. . . . My first guiding principle is this: willing and active cooperation between independent sovereign states is the best way to build a successful European Community.

To try to suppress nationhood and concentrate power at the centre of a European conglomerate would be highly damaging and would jeopardise the objectives we seek to achieve. . . . My second guiding principle is this: Community policies must tackle present problems in a *practical* way, however difficult that may be. . . . My last guiding principle concerns the most fundamental issue – the European countries' role in defence.

Europe must continue to maintain a sure defence through NATO.

There can be no question of relaxing our efforts, even though it means taking difficult decisions and meeting heavy costs.

It is to NATO that we owe the peace that has been maintained over 40 years. . . . Let us have a Europe which plays its full part in the wider world, which looks outward not inward, and which preserves that Atlantic community – that Europe on both sides of the Atlantic – which is our noblest inheritance and our greatest strength.

Source: *[excerpt]: www.margaret thatcher.org/document/107332*

Document 27

George H.W. Bush on support for Poland and liberalisation in Eastern Europe: 'Remarks to Citizens in Hamtramck, Michigan', 17 April 1989

For almost half a century, the suppression of freedom in Eastern Europe, sustained by the military power of the Soviet Union, has kept nation from nation, neighbor from neighbor. And as East and West now seek to reduce arms, it must not be forgotten that arms are a symptom, not a source, of tension. The true source of tension is the imposed and unnatural division of Europe. How can there be stability and security in Europe and the world as long as nations and peoples are denied the right to determine their own future, a right explicitly promised by agreements among the victorious powers at the end of World War II? How can there be stability and security in Europe as long as nations which once stood proudly at the front rank of industrial powers are impoverished by a discredited ideology and stifling authoritarianism? The United States – and let's be clear on this – has never accepted the legitimacy of Europe's division. We accept no spheres of influence that deny the sovereign rights of nations. . . . Now the Poles are now taking steps that deserve our active support. And I have decided as your President on specific steps to be taken by the United States, carefully chosen to recognize the reforms

156   *Documents*

underway and to encourage reforms yet to come now that Solidarnosc [Solidarity] is legal. I will ask Congress to join me in providing Poland access to our Generalized System of Preferences, which offers selective tariff relief to beneficiary countries. We will work with our allies and friends in the Paris Club to develop sustainable new schedules for Poland to repay its debt, easing a heavy burden so that a free market can grow.

Source: *[excerpt]: www.presidency.ucsb.edu/ws/?pid=16935*

Document 28

George H.W. Bush outlines the new international order:
'Address before a Joint Session of the Congress on the State
of the Union', 29 January 1991

I come to this House of the people to speak to you and all Americans, certain that we stand at a defining hour. Halfway around the world, we are engaged in a great struggle in the skies and on the seas and sands. We know why we're there: We are Americans, part of something larger than ourselves. For two centuries, we've done the hard work of freedom. And tonight, we lead the world in facing down a threat to decency and humanity.

What is at stake is more than one small country; it is a big idea: a new world order, where diverse nations are drawn together in common cause to achieve the universal aspirations of mankind – peace and security, freedom, and the rule of law. Such is a world worthy of our struggle and worthy of our children's future. . . . The end of the cold war has been a victory for all humanity. A year and a half ago, in Germany, I said that our goal was a Europe whole and free. Tonight, Germany is united. Europe has become whole and free, and America's leadership was instrumental in making it possible.

Our relationship to the Soviet Union is important, not only to us but to the world. That relationship has helped to shape these and other historic changes. . . . We will watch carefully as the situation develops. And we will maintain our contact with the Soviet leadership to encourage continued commitment to democratization and reform. If it is possible, I want to continue to build a lasting basis for U.S.-Soviet cooperation – for a more peaceful future for all mankind.

Source: *[excerpt]: www.presidency.ucsb.edu/ws/?pid=19253*

Document 29

Clinton deprecates the 'Special Relationship': B.M. Seener, 'Report
and Retort: The Special Relationship is not flat', 8 August 2007

John Major and Bill Clinton publicly traded diplomatic blows over Bosnia in the early 1990s. For three years Britain led Security Council opposition

Documents 157

to U.S. intervention against the Bosnian-Serbs. That the United States no longer viewed Britain as a strategic asset also exacerbated the tension. In anticipation of Major's 1993 White House visit, Clinton aides joked, 'Don't forget to say "special relationship" when the press comes in.' 'Oh, yes', Clinton said. 'How could I forget? The special relationship!' He then threw his head back and laughed.

Source: *[excerpt]: National Interest, http://national interest.org/commentary/report-and-retort-the-special-relationship-is-not-flat-1735*

Document 30

Major's foreign secretary characterises the fallaciousness of the New World Order: 'Hurd warning over "slide into disorder": Foreign Secretary backs imperial UN and defends Britain's global role to justify permanent Security Council seat', 28 January 1993

'Chaos and anarchy are the enemies of commerce' and 'they are often accompanied by grotesque abuse of human rights,' Mr Hurd said. The case for a continued high-profile world role was an economic necessity for an island nation such as Britain.

'We live by international trade. Our exports account for 18 per cent of our GDP, compared with just 9 per cent for Japan and 7 per cent for the United States,' he said. 'Our exporters need a stable and predictable world in which to trade.'

Once-fashionable talk of a 'New World Order' dawning was utopian folly, Mr Hurd suggested, because 'the phrase promised more than we shall ever be able to perform'.

With 25 substantial conflicts raging around the world, the best that could be expected of the international community was action 'to avert the continuing slide into disorder'.

The sort of tasks the UN was facing in Somalia, where government had broken down, were akin to 'the traditional imperial role' played by Britain, Mr Hurd said. The difference was that the UN was taking on an imperial role for purely humanitarian objectives rather than to attain power or privilege.

Defending Britain's position as a veto-holding permanent member of the Security Council, Mr Hurd said: 'The Americans have a saying, "If it ain't broke, don't fix it." And I think there is something to be said for that.' In a statement that dismayed the Foreign Office, the US Secretary of State, Warren Christopher, said on Monday that changes should be made to the composition of the council to include Germany and Japan as permanent members.

Source: *[excerpt]: Independent, www.independent.co.uk/news/ hurd-warning-over-slide-into-disorder-foreign-secretary-backs-imperial-un-and-defends-britains-global-role-to-justify-permanent-security-council-seat-1481282.html*

158   *Documents*

Document 31

Blair, 'Doctrine of the International Community', 22 April 1999, Chicago Economic Club

Twenty years ago we would not have been fighting in Kosovo. We would have turned our backs on it. The fact that we are engaged is the result of a wide range of changes – the end of the Cold War; changing technology; the spread of democracy. But it is bigger than that[.]

I believe the world has changed in a more fundamental way. Globalisation has transformed our economies and our working practices. But globalisation is not just economic. It is also a political and security phenomenon.

We live in a world where isolationism has ceased to have a reason to exist. By necessity we have to co-operate with each other across nations. . . . We are all internationalists now, whether we like it or not[.] We cannot refuse to participate in global markets if we want to prosper. We cannot ignore new political ideas in other counties if we want to innovate. We cannot turn our backs on conflicts and the violation of human rights within other countries if we want still to be secure.

On the eve of a new Millennium we are now in a new world. We need new rules for international co-operation and new ways of organising our international institutions . . . Today the impulse towards interdependence is immeasurably greater. We are witnessing the beginnings of a new doctrine of international community. By this I mean the explicit recognition that today more than ever before we are mutually dependent, that national interest is to a significant extent governed by international collaboration and that we need a clear and coherent debate as to the direction this doctrine takes us in each field of international endeavour. Just as within domestic politics, the notion of community – the belief that partnership and co-operation are essential to advance self-interest – is coming into its own; so it needs to find its own international echo. Global financial markets, the global environment, global security and disarmament issues: none of these can be solved without intense international co-operation.

Source: *[excerpt]: www.britishpoliticalspeech.org/ speech-archive.htm?speech=279*

Document 32

George W. Bush inaugurates the war on terror, 21 September 2001

Our war on terror begins with al Qaeda, but it does not end there. It will not end until every terrorist group of global reach has been found, stopped and defeated.

Americans are asking, why do they hate us? They hate what we see right here in this chamber – a democratically elected government. Their leaders are self-appointed. They hate our freedoms – our freedom of religion, our freedom of speech, our freedom to vote and assemble and disagree with each other.

They want to overthrow existing governments in many Muslim countries, such as Egypt, Saudi Arabia, and Jordan. They want to drive Israel out of the Middle East. They want to drive Christians and Jews out of vast regions of Asia and Africa.

These terrorists kill not merely to end lives, but to disrupt and end a way of life. With every atrocity, they hope that America grows fearful, retreating from the world and forsaking our friends. They stand against us, because we stand in their way.

We are not deceived by their pretenses to piety. We have seen their kind before. They are the heirs of all the murderous ideologies of the 20th century. By sacrificing human life to serve their radical visions – by abandoning every value except the will to power – they follow in the path of fascism, and Nazism, and totalitarianism. And they will follow that path all the way, to where it ends: in history's unmarked grave of discarded lies.

Source: *[excerpt]: https://georgewbush-whitehouse.*
archives.gov/infocus/bushrecord/documents/
Selected_Speeches_George_W_Bush.pdf

Document 33

George W. Bush declares that the United States will undermine the international 'Axis of Evil': State of the Union Address, 29 January 2002

Iraq continues to flaunt its hostility toward America and to support terror. The Iraqi regime has plotted to develop anthrax and nerve gas and nuclear weapons for over a decade. This is a regime that has already used poison gas to murder thousands of its own citizens, leaving the bodies of mothers huddled over their dead children. This is a regime that agreed to international inspections, then kicked out the inspectors. This is a regime that has something to hide from the civilized world.

States like these and their terrorist allies constitute an axis of evil, arming to threaten the peace of the world. By seeking weapons of mass destruction, these regimes pose a grave and growing danger. They could provide these arms to terrorists, giving them the means to match their hatred. They could attack our allies or attempt to blackmail the United States. In any of these cases, the price of indifference would be catastrophic.

We will work closely with our coalition to deny terrorists and their state sponsors the materials, technology, and expertise to make and deliver weapons of mass destruction. We will develop and deploy effective missile defenses to protect America and our allies from sudden attack. And all nations should know: America will do what is necessary to ensure our nation's security.

Source: *[excerpt]: http://millercenter.org/*
president/speeches/speech-4540

160   *Documents*

Document 34

Obama and Cameron, 'The U.S. and Britain still enjoy special relationship', 12 March 2012

As two of the world's wealthiest nations, we embrace our responsibility as leaders in the development that enables people to live in dignity, health and prosperity. Even as we redouble our efforts to save lives in Somalia, we're investing in agriculture to promote food security across the developing world. We're working to improve maternal health and end preventable deaths of children. With a renewed commitment to the lifesaving work of the Global Fund for AIDS, TB and Malaria, we see the beginning of the end of the AIDS pandemic. Through our Open Government Partnership, we're striving to make governments more transparent and accountable.

Finally, as two peoples who live free because of the sacrifices of our men and women in uniform, we're working together like never before to care for them when they come home. With new long-term collaborations to help our wounded warriors recover, assist in veterans' transition back to civilian life and support military families, we recognise that our obligations to troops and veterans endure long after today's battles end.

Our troops and citizens have long shown what can be achieved when British and Americans work together, heart and hand, and why this remains an essential relationship – to our nations and the world.

So like generations before us, we're going to keep it up. Because with confidence in our cause and faith in each other, we still believe that there is hardly anything we cannot do.

Source: *[excerpt]: Washington Post, www.washingtonpost.com/ opinions/barack-obama-and-david-cameron-the-us-and- britain-still-enjoy-pecial-relationship/2012/03/12/ gIQABH1G8R_story.html*

Further reading

The historiography of Anglo-American relations in general and the 'Special Relationship' in particular is vast, rich, and disputatious. A range of commentators see the Relationship as complex but cooperative in confronting a disordered world after 1939: for instance, A.R. Holmes and J.S. Rofe, eds., *The Embassy in Grosvenor Square: American Ambassadors to the United Kingdom, 1938–2008* (Houndmills: Macmillan, 2012); P.M. McGarr, *The Cold War in South Asia: Britain, the United States and the Indian Subcontinent, 1945–1965* (Cambridge: Cambridge UP, 2013). On the other hand, some believe that the transatlantic partnership was a sham, as Britain lost its global position to a rapacious and/or uncaring America that always sought advantage over its partner: exemplary are J. Charmley, *Churchill's Grand Alliance: The Anglo-American Special Relationship, 1940–57* (London: Hodder & Stoughton, 1995); C.A. Pagedas, *Anglo-American Strategic Relations and the French Problem, 1960–1963: A Troubled Partnership* (London: Cass, 2000). Despite admitting the closeness of Anglo-American relations, others assert that they were perpetually fraught with difficulty and, in practice, often less than special: such views can be traced in R. Aldous, *Reagan and Thatcher: The Difficult Relationship* (London: Hutchinson, 2012); J. Colman, *A 'Special Relationship'? Harold Wilson, Lyndon B. Johnson and Anglo-American Relations 'at the Summit', 1964–68* (Manchester: Manchester UP, 2004). For a monumental and critical assessment of relations in the twentieth century, see D.C. Watt, *Succeeding John Bull: America in Britain's Place, 1900–1975: A Study of the Anglo-American Relationship and World Politics in the Context of British and American Foreign-policy-making in the Twentieth Century* (Cambridge: Cambridge UP, 1984). It needs comparison with D. Dimbleby and D. Reynolds, *An Ocean Apart: The Relationship between Britain and America in the Twentieth Century* (New York: Random House, 1988).

Perhaps the best overall study of the history of the two powers from the early seventeenth to the early twenty-first century is from an American-born British scholar who has lived all her professional life in Britain: K.M. Burk, *Old World, New World: Great Britain and America from the Beginning*

162   *Further reading*

(New York: Atlantic Monthly Press, 2008). The Relationship has a part in this masterful treatment, but only in its latter section.

An assortment of scholars have examined crucial aspects of the Relationship as it transformed from the bitter years after the American Revolution to the early twentieth century 'great rapprochement'. Chronologically, see T. Bickham, *The Weight of Vengeance: The United States, the British Empire, and the War of 1812* (Oxford: Oxford UP, 2012); K. Bourne, *Britain and the Balance of Power in North America, 1815–1908* (London: Longmans, 1967); A. Foreman, *A World On Fire: Britain's Crucial Role in the American Civil War* (New York: Random House); L.S. Kaplan, *Alexander Hamilton: Ambivalent Anglophile* (Wilmington, DE: SR Books, 2002); I. Adams, *Brothers across the Ocean: British Foreign Policy and the Origins of the Anglo-American 'Special Relationship' 1900–1905* (London: Tauris, 2005); B. Perkins, *The Great Rapprochement: England and the United States, 1895–1914* (New York: Atheneum, 1968); W. Tilchin, *Theodore Roosevelt and the British Empire: A Study in Presidential Statecraft* (New York: St. Martin's, 1997). Also important is D. Cooper, *Informal Ambassadors: American Women, Transatlantic Marriages, and Anglo-American Relations, 1865–1945* (Kent, OH: Kent State UP, 2014).

The course of Anglo-American relations for the First World War and the peace conferences has aroused detailed study. For instance, in chronological order, K.M. Burk, *Britain, America and the Sinews of War, 1914–1918* (Boston and London: Allen & Unwin, 1985); J.W. Coogan, *End of Neutrality: The United States, Britain, and Maritime Rights, 1899–1915* (Ithaca, NY: Cornell UP, 1981); E.W. Osborne, *Britain's Economic Blockade of Germany, 1914–1919* (London: Cass, 2004); T. Boghardt, *The Zimmermann Telegram: Intelligence, Diplomacy, and America's Entry into World War I* (Annapolis, MD: Naval Institute Press, 2012); S.P. Tillman, *Anglo-American Relations at the Paris Peace Conference of 1919* (Princeton, NJ: Princeton UP, 1961); G.W. Egerton, *Great Britain and the Creation of the League of Nations: Strategy, Politics, and International Organization, 1914–1919* (Chapel Hill, NC: North Carolina UP); L.C. Gardner, *Safe for Democracy: Anglo-American Response to Revolution, 1913–1923* (New York: Oxford UP); R.A. Kennedy, *The Will to Believe: Woodrow Wilson, World War I, and America's Strategy for Peace and Security* (Kent, OH: Kent State UP, 2009); G.R. Conyne, *Woodrow Wilson: British Perspectives, 1912–21* (New York: St. Martin's, 1992). Especially important for an overview of the peace settlement is G.D. Feldman and E. Glaser, eds., *The Treaty of Versailles: A Reassessment after 75 Years* (Cambridge: Cambridge UP, 1998).

The interwar period divides neatly into the 1920s and 1930s, the 'hinge years' between the two decades being the onset of the Great Depression. In this sense, 1920–1929 was not simply a prologue to the difficult 1930s. For the 1920s, which were marked by rivalry, compare P.O. Cohrs, *The Unfinished Peace after World War I: America, Britain and the Stabilisation of Europe, 1919–1932* (Cambridge: Cambridge UP, 2006); E. Goldstein and

Further reading 163

J. Maurer, eds., *The Washington Conference, 1921–22: Naval Rivalry, East Asian Stability and the Road to Pearl Harbor* (London: Cass, 1994); B. Kent, *The Spoils of War: The Politics, Economics, and Diplomacy of Reparations, 1918–1932* (Oxford: Clarendon, 1989); B.J.C. McKercher, ed., *Anglo-American Relations in the 1920s: The Struggle for Supremacy* (Houndmills: Macmillan and Edmonton: Alberta UP, 1991). Of recent importance is J.A. Tooze, *The Deluge: The Great War and the Remaking of Global Order 1916–1931* (London: Allen Lane, 2014).

For the 1930s, which became more cooperative, representative works are J.D. Doenecke and J.E. Wilz, *From Isolation to War, 1931–1941*, 4th edition (Chichester and Malden, MA: John Wiley & Sons, 2015); P. Haggie, *Britannia at Bay: The Defence of the British Empire against Japan, 1931–1941* (Oxford: Clarendon, 1981); R.E. Herzstein, *Roosevelt and Hitler: Prelude to War* (New York: Paragon House, 1989); R.E. Jenner, *FDR's Republicans: Domestic Political Realignment and American Foreign Policy* (Lanham, MD: Lexington, 2010); C.J. Kitching, *Britain and the Geneva Disarmament Conference* (Houndmills: Palgrave Macmillan, 2003); J.H. Maurer and C.M. Bell, *At the Crossroads between Peace and War: The London Naval Conference of 1930* (Annapolis, MD: Naval Institute Press, 2014); F. McDonough, *Neville Chamberlain, Appeasement, and the British Road to War* (Manchester: Manchester UP, 1998); B.J.C. McKercher, *Transition of Power: Britain's Loss of Global Pre-eminence to the United States, 1930–1945* (Cambridge: Cambridge UP, 1999). For the crucial period before America entered the war in 1941, see M.G. Carew, *The Impact of the First World War on U.S. Policymakers: American Strategic and Foreign Policy Formulation, 1938–1942* (Lanham, MD: Lexington, 2014); G. Prange, D.M. Goldstein, and K.V. Dillon, *At Dawn We Slept: The Untold Story of Pearl Harbor* (New York: McGraw-Hill, 1981); N. Wapshot, *The Sphinx: Franklin Roosevelt, the Isolationists, and the Road to World War II* (New York: W.W. Norton, 2015). Nonetheless, the best analysis remains D. Reynolds, *The Creation of the Anglo-American Alliance, 1937–41: A Study in Competitive Co-operation* (London: Europa, 1981).

Assessments of the advent of the Relationship and its place in the military and diplomatic history of the Second World War are legion. For a taste of this vast, rich, and especially disputatious historiography, see P. Clarke, *The Last Thousand Days of the British Empire: Churchill, Roosevelt, and the Birth of the Pax Americana* (New York: Bloomsbury Press, 2008); M. Dobbs, *Six Months in 1945: FDR, Stalin, Churchill, and Truman: From World War to Cold War* (New York: Alfred A. Knopf, 2012); R. Overy, *Why the Allies Won* (New York: W.W. Norton, 1996); T. Parrish, *To Keep the British Isles Afloat: FDR's Men in Churchill's London, 1941* (New York: Smithsonian Books/Collins, 2009); D. Reynolds, *From World War to Cold War: Churchill, Roosevelt, and the International History of the 1940s* (Oxford, NY: Oxford UP, 2006); D. Stafford, *Roosevelt and Churchill: Men of Secrets* (London and Boston: Little, Brown, 1999); M.A. Stoler, *Allies in War: Britain and America against the Axis Powers, 1940–1945* (London: Hodder Arnold, 2005); idem.,

164 *Further reading*

Allies and Adversaries: The Joint Chiefs of Staff, the Grand Alliance, and U.S. Strategy in World War II (Chapel Hill, NC: North Carolina UP, 2000); C.L. Symonds, *Neptune: The Allied Invasion of Europe and the D-Day Landings* (Oxford: Oxford UP, 2014). For a taste of the wartime conferences in chronological order, see B.P. Farrell, 'Symbol of Paradox: The Casablanca Conference, 1943', *Canadian Journal of History*, 28/1(1993), pp. 21–40; P.D. Mayle, *Eureka Summit: Agreement in Principle & the Big Three at Tehran, 1943* (Newark, DE: Delaware UP, 1987); S.M. Plokhy, *Yalta: The Price of Peace* (New York: Viking, 2010).

The Cold War provided the contours of the post-Second World War relationship. In this context consider S. Belletto and D. Grausam, eds., *American Literature and Culture in an Age of Cold War: A Critical Reassessment* (Iowa City, IA: Iowa UP, 2012); J. Bilsland, *The President, the State and the Cold War: Comparing the Foreign Policies of Truman and Reagan* (Abingdon: Routledge, 2015); J. Black, *The Cold War: A Military History* (London, NY: Bloomsbury Academic, 2015); C. Fink, *Cold War: An International History* (Boulder, CO: Westview Press, 2014): J.L. Gaddis, *The Cold War: A New History* (New York: Penguin, 2005); M. Gilbert, *Cold War Europe: The Politics of a Contested Continent* (Lanham, MD: Rowman & Littlefield, 2015); R. Hewison, *In Anger: British Culture in the Cold War, 1945–60* (New York: Oxford UP, 1981); C.G. Kodat, *Don't Act, Just Dance: The Metapolitics of Cold War Culture* (New Brunswick, NJ: Rutgers UP, 2015). And fundamental is J.L. Gaddis, *Strategies of Containment: A Critical Appraisal of American National Security Policy during the Cold War*, revised edition (New York: Oxford UP, 2005).

The course of the decade from the 1945 Potsdam Conference to the Suez crisis of 1956 was crucial for the Relationship. The following are helpful for Europe. See R.L. Beisner, *Dean Acheson: A Life in the Cold War* (Oxford, NY: Oxford UP, 2006); D.M. Bostdorff, *Proclaiming the Truman Doctrine: The Cold War Call to Arms* (College Station, TX: Texas A&M UP, 2008); A. Bullock, *The Life and Times of Ernest Bevin*, Volume III: *Foreign Secretary, 1945–1951* (London: Heinemann, 1983); S. Dockrill, *Britain's Policy for West German Rearmament, 1950–1955* (Cambridge: Cambridge UP, 1991); R.H. Immerman, *John Foster Dulles: Piety, Pragmatism, and Power in U.S. Foreign Policy* (Wilmington, DE: Scholarly Resources, 1999); L.S. Kaplan, *A Community of Interests: NATO and the Military Assistance Program, 1948–1951* (Washington, DC: GPO, 1980); K. Larres, *Churchill's Cold War: The Politics of Personal Diplomacy* (New Haven, CT: Yale UP, 2002); M. Neiberg, *Potsdam: The End of World War II and the Remaking of Europe* (New York: Basic Books, 2015); N. Mills, *Winning the Peace: The Marshall Plan and America's Coming of Age as a Superpower* (Hoboken, NJ: John Wiley & Sons, 2008). J. Savile, The *Politics of Continuity: British Foreign Policy and the Labour Government, 1945–46* (London, NY: Verso, 1993); D.C. Williamson, *Separate Agendas: Churchill, Eisenhower, and Anglo-American Relations, 1953–1955* (Lanham, MD: Lexington Books, 2006).

Further reading 165

For decolonisation in South and East Asia and the Middle East, see R.C. Barrett, *Greater Middle East and the Cold War: US Foreign Policy under Eisenhower and Kennedy* (London: Tauris, 2009); J. Cable, *Geneva Conference of 1954 on Indochina* (Houndmills: Macmillan, 1986); Y. Chaitani, *Dissension among Allies: Ernest Bevin's Palestine Policy between Whitehall and the White House, 1945–47* (London: Saqi, 2000); C.S. Dasgupta, *War and Diplomacy in Kashmir 1947–48* (Delhi: Sage, 2002); D. Fenton, *To Cage the Red Dragon: SEATO and the Defence of Southeast Asia, 1955–1965* (Singapore: NUS Press, 2012); J.B. Judis, *Genesis: Truman, American Jews, and the Origins of the Arab/Israeli Conflict* (New York: Farrar, Straus and Giroux, 2014); R.J. Moore, *Escape from Empire: The Attlee Government and the Indian Problem* (Oxford: Clarendon, 1983); J.T. McNay, *Acheson and Empire: The British Accent in American Foreign Policy* (Columbia, MO: Missouri UP, 2001); V.D. No^ng, *Churchill, Eden and Indo-China, 1951–1955* (London, NY: Anthem Press, 2010); S.C. Smith, *Ending Empire in the Middle East: Britain, the United States and Post-War Decolonization, 1945–1973* (New York and Abingdon: Routledge, 2012); D.M. Watry, *Diplomacy at the Brink: Eisenhower, Churchill, and Eden in the Cold War* (Baton Rouge, LA: Louisiana State UP, 2014); B.K. Yesilbursa, *The Baghdad Pact: Anglo-American Defence Policies in the Middle East, 1950–1959* (London, NY: Cass, 2005).

The historiography of the Suez crisis – the watershed for Britain's position as a Great Power and which also nearly ruptured the Relationship – has depth and breadth: for example, A. Gorst and L. Johnman, *The Suez Crisis* (London, NY: Routledge, 1997); J. Graham, *Eden's Empire* (London: Methuen Drama, 2006); Y. Henkin, *The 1956 Suez War and the New World Order in the Middle East: Exodus in Reverse* (Lanham, MD: Lexington, 2015); K. Kyle, *Suez: Britain's End of Empire in the Middle East* (London: I.B. Tauris, 2003); S. Lucas, *Britain and Suez: The Lion's Last Roar* (Manchester: Manchester UP, 1996); D.A. Nichols, *Eisenhower 1956: The President's Year of Crisis: Suez and the Brink of War* (New York: Simon & Schuster, 2011); J. Pearson, *Sir Anthony Eden and the Suez Crisis: Reluctant Gamble* (New York: Palgrave, 2002); L. Richardson, *When Allies Differ: Anglo-American Relations during the Suez and Falklands Crises* (New York: St. Martin's, 1996); S.C. Smith, ed., *Reassessing Suez 1956: New Perspectives on the Crisis and Its Aftermath* (Aldershot and Burlington, VT: Ashgate, 2008).

In the almost two decades from after Suez until the early 1970s, the strategic basis of the Relationship continued and revived. After Suez, Harold Macmillan, Eden's successor as prime minister, moved quickly to repair the Relationship, which had dimensions in Europe and the Middle East. For the Macmillan period, which lasted until 1963 and coincided with Eisenhower's final years in office and the presidency of John F. Kennedy, see R. Aldous, *Macmillan, Eisenhower and the Cold War* (Dublin and Portland, OR: Four Courts Press, 2005); R. Aldous and S. Lee, eds., *Harold Macmillan and*

166 *Further reading*

Britain's World Role (Houndmills: Macmillan, 1996); N.J. Ashton, *Eisenhower, Macmillan, and the Problem of Nasser: Anglo-American Relations and Arab Nationalism, 1955–59* (London: Macmillan, 1996); G. Bischof, S. Karner, and B. Stelz-Marx, eds., *The Vienna Summit and Its Importance in International History* (Lanham, MD: Lexington, 2014); S. Blackwell, *British Military Intervention and the Struggle for Jordan: King Hussein, Nasser and the Middle East Crisis, 1955–1958* (New York: Routledge, 2009); L.J. Butler and S. Stockwell, eds., *The Wind of Change: Harold Macmillan and British Decolonization* (Houndmills: Palgrave Macmillan, 2013); S. Dockrill, *Eisenhower's New-look National Security Policy, 1953–61* (London: Macmillan, 1996); E.B. Geelhoed and A.O. Edmonds, *Eisenhower, Macmillan, and Allied Unity, 1957–1961* (New York: Palgrave Macmillan, 2003); K. Newman, *Macmillan, Khrushchev and the Berlin Crisis, 1958–1960* (New York: Routledge, 2007); C. Sandford, *Harold and Jack: The Remarkable Friendship of Prime Minister Macmillan and President Kennedy* (Amherst, NY: Prometheus, 2014); R.D. Williamson, *First Steps toward Détente: American Diplomacy in the Berlin Crisis, 1958–1963* (Lanham, MD: Lexington, 2012); S. Yaqub, *Containing Arab Nationalism: The Eisenhower Doctrine and the Middle East* (Chapel Hill, NC: North Carolina UP, 2004). Particularly useful is N.J. Ashton, *Kennedy, Macmillan, and the Cold War: The Irony of Interdependence* (Basingstoke, NY: Palgrave, 2002). The foreign policy of the government of Alexander Douglas-Home, in power for only a year after Macmillan resigned, has one significant study: A. Holt, *Foreign Policy of the Douglas-Home Government: Britain, the United States and the End of Empire* (Basingstoke: Palgrave Macmillan, 2014).

From 1964 to 1974, two British governments – Labour (1964–1970) under Harold Wilson and Conservative (1970–1974) under Edward Heath – dealt with two American administrations (Democratic (1963–1969) under Lyndon Johnson and Republican (1969–1974) under Richard Nixon. The greatest international problem concerned Vietnam and Southeast Asia. Good over-views of the general crisis are: F. Logevall, *Embers of War: The Fall of an Empire and the Making of America's Vietnam* (New York: Random House, 2012); G.C. Herring, *America's Longest War: The United States and Vietnam, 1950–1975*, 5th edition (New York: McGraw-Hill, 2014); J.S. Olson and R.B. Roberts, *Where the Domino Fell: America and Vietnam, 1945–2010* (Hoboken, NJ: Wiley-Blackwell, 2014); C. Schwenkel, *The American War in Contemporary Vietnam: Transnational Remembrance and Representation* (Bloomington, IN: Indiana UP, 2009).

For the Wilson period with Johnson and Nixon, see P. Busch, *All the Way with JFK?: Britain, the US, and the Vietnam War* (Oxford, NY: Oxford UP, 2003); J. Colman, *A 'Special Relationship'? Harold Wilson, Lyndon B. Johnson and Anglo-American Relations 'at the Summit', 1964–68* (Manchester: Manchester UP, 2004); idem., *Kennedy, Johnson, and the Nonaligned World* (Cambridge: Cambridge UP, 2012); S. Dockrill, *Britain's Retreat from East of Suez: The Choice between Europe and the World, 1945–1968* (New

Further reading 167

York: Palgrave, 2002); O.J. Daddow, ed., *Harold Wilson and European Integration: Britain's Second Application to Join the EEC* (London and Portland, OR: Cass, 2003); S. Ellis, *Britain, America, and the Vietnam War* (Westport, CT: Praeger, 2004); D.J. Gill, *Britain and the Bomb: Nuclear Diplomacy, 1964–1970* (Stanford, CA: Stanford UP, 2014); G. Hughes, *Harold Wilson's Cold War: The Labour Government and East-West Politics, 1964–1970* (Woodbridge and Rochester, NY: Boydell Press, 2009); S.R. Ashton and W.R. Louis, eds., *East of Suez and the Commonwealth 1964–1971* (London: HMSO, 2004); T.T. Petersen, *The Decline of the Anglo-American Middle East, 1961–1969: A Willing Retreat* (Brighton: Sussex Academic Press, 2006); P.I. Pham, *Ending 'East of Suez': The British Decision to withdraw from Malaysia and Singapore 1964–1968* (Oxford, New York: Oxford UP, 2010); A. Priest, *Kennedy, Johnson and NATO: Britain, America and the Dynamics of Alliance, 1962–68* (London, NY: Routledge, 2006).

For the Heath-Nixon period, see C. Daigle, *Limits of Détente: The United States, the Soviet Union, and the Arab-Israeli Conflict, 1969–1973* (New Haven, CT: Yale UP, 2012); J. Hanhimäki, *The Flawed Architect: Henry Kissinger and American Foreign Policy* (Oxford, NY: Oxford UP, 2004); A. Horne, *Kissinger: 1973, The Crucial Year* (New York: Simon & Schuster, 2009); Baron Home of the Hirsel, *Britain's Changing Role in World Affairs* (London: David Davies Memorial Institute of International Studies, 1974); C. Hynes, *The Year that Never Was: Heath, the Nixon Administration and the Year of Europe* (Dublin: University College Dublin Press, 2009); F. Logevall and A. Preston, eds., *Nixon in the World: American Foreign Relations, 1969–1977* (Oxford, NY: Oxford UP, 2008); N.H. Rossbach, *Heath, Nixon and the Rebirth of the Special Relationship: Britain, the US and the EC, 1969–74* (Houndmills, NY: Palgrave Macmillan, 2009); A. Scott, *Allies Apart: Heath, Nixon and the Anglo-American Relationship* (Houndmills, NY: Palgrave Macmillan, 2011); R.C. Thornton, *Nixon-Kissinger Years: Reshaping America's Foreign Policy* (St. Paul, MN: Paragon House, 2001).

Anglo-American relations went into suspended animation from 1975 until 1980. Nonetheless, the following are helpful: K.M. Burk and A. Cairncross, *Goodbye, Great Britain: The 1976 IMF Crisis* (New Haven, CT: Yale UP, 1992); D. Caldwell, *The Dynamics of Domestic Politics and Arms Control: The SALT II Treaty Ratification Debate* (Columbia, SC: South Carolina UP, 1991); A.D. Crain, *The Ford Presidency: A History* (Jefferson, NC: McFarland, 2009); R. Fieldhouse, *Anti-Apartheid: A History of the Movement in Britain* (London: Merlin, 2005): H. Jordan, *Crisis: The Last Year of the Carter Presidency* (New York: Putnam, 1982); S. Kaufman, *Plans Unraveled: The Foreign Policy of the Carter Administration* (DeKalb, IL: Northern Illinois UP, 2008); J. Medhurst, *That Option No Longer Exists: Britain 1974–76* (Alresford: Zero Books, 2014); A. Seldon and K. Hickson, eds., *New Labour, Old Labour: The Wilson and Callaghan Governments, 1974–79* (London, NY: Routledge, 2004); J. Shepherd, *Crisis? What Crisis?: The Callaghan Government and the British 'Winter of Discontent'*

168 *Further reading*

(Manchester: Manchester UP, 2013); D. Strieff, *Jimmy Carter and the Middle East: The Politics of Presidential Diplomacy* (New York: Palgrave Macmillan, 2015); A. Thomson, *U.S. Foreign Policy towards Apartheid South Africa, 1948–1994: Conflict of Interests* (New York: Palgrave Macmillan, 2008); B. Zanchetta, *The Transformation of American International Power in the 1970s* (New York: Cambridge UP, 2014).

The Relationship achieved new heights in the 1980s in confronting Russian power through the joint efforts of Margaret Thatcher and Ronald Reagan. From a large literature, compare A. Adonis and T. Hames, eds., *A Conservative Revolution?: The Thatcher-Reagan Decade in Perspective* (Manchester: Manchester UP, 1994); K. Booth and J. Baylis, *Britain, NATO and Nuclear Weapons: Alternative Defence versus Alliance Reform* (Basingstoke: Macmillan, 1989); D.G. Boyce, *The Falklands War* (Basingstoke, NY: Palgrave Macmillan, 2005) J. Cooper, *Margaret Thatcher and Ronald Reagan: A Very Political Special Relationship* (Houndmills, NY: Palgrave Macmillan, 2012); G.K. Fry, *The Politics of the Thatcher Revolution: An Interpretation of British Politics, 1979–1990* (Basingstoke, NY: Palgrave Macmillan, 2008); K. Gottstein, ed., *SDI and Stability: The Role of Assumptions and Perceptions* (Baden-Baden: Nomos, 1988): B. Harrison, *Finding a Role?: The United Kingdom, 1970–1990* (Oxford: Clarendon, 2011); C. Hutchinson, *Reaganism, Thatcherism and the Social Novel* (Basingstoke, NY: Palgrave Macmillan, 2008); P.V. Lettow, *Ronald Reagan and His Quest to Abolish Nuclear Weapons* (New York: Random House, 2005); J. Mackby and P. Cornish, eds., *U.S.-UK Nuclear Cooperation after 50 Years* (Washington, DC: Center for Strategic and International Studies, 2008); R.H. Paterson, *Britain's Strategic Nuclear Deterrent: From before the V-Bomber to Beyond Trident* (London and Portland, OR: Cass, 1997); S. Wall, *A Stranger in Europe: Britain and the EU from Thatcher to Blair* (Oxford, NY: Oxford UP, 2008); J.G. Wilson, *The Triumph of Improvisation: Gorbachev's Adaptability, Reagan's Engagement, and the End of the Cold War* (Ithaca, NY: Cornell UP, 2014); G. Yoshitani, *Reagan on War: A Reappraisal of the Weinberger Doctrine, 1980–1984* (College Station, TX: Texas A&M UP, 2012).

Beginning in 1989 as the Cold War ended and Soviet Russia collapsed, the Relationship began to fray and, by the first decade of the twenty-first century, disappeared along with its strategic imperative. Illustrative histories are P. Baker, *Days of Fire: Bush and Cheney in the White House* (New York: Doubleday, 2013); F. Beckett and D. Hencke, *Survivor: Tony Blair in Peace and War* (London: Aurum, 2005); S.A. Bonn, *Mass Deception: Moral Panic and the U.S. War on Iraq* (New Brunswick, NJ: Rutgers UP, 2010); J.D. Boys, *Clinton's Grand Strategy: US Foreign Policy in a post-Cold War World* (London, NY: Bloomsbury Academic, 2015); B. Brivati, *End of Decline: Blair and Brown in Power* (London: Politico, 2007); D. Brown, *Development of British Defence Policy: Blair, Brown, and Beyond* (Farnham: Ashgate, 2010); H. Campbell, *NATO's Failure in Libya: Lessons for Africa* (Baltimore, MD: Project MUSE, 2013); D. Chollet, *The Road to the*

Dayton Accords: A Study of American Statecraft (New York: Palgrave Macmillan, 2005); P. Dorey, ed., *The Major Premiership: Politics and Policies under John Major, 1990–97* (Houndmills: Macmillan, 1999); C. Dueck, *The Obama Doctrine: American Grand Strategy Today* (New York: Oxford UP, 2015); J. Dumbrell, *Clinton's Foreign Policy: Between the Bushes, 1992–2000* (London, NY: Routledge, 2009); T. Englehart, *American Way of War: How Bush's Wars Became Obama's* (Chicago, IL: Haymarket Books, 2010); M. Foley, *John Major, Tony Blair and a Conflict of Leadership: Collision Course* (Manchester: Manchester UP, 2002); A. Edwards, *'Dual Containment' Policy in the Persian Gulf: The USA, Iran, and Iraq, 1991–2000* (New York: Palgrave Macmillan, 2014); T.H. Henrikson, *Clinton's Foreign Policy in Somalia, Bosnia, Haiti, and North Korea* (Stanford, CA: Hoover Institution on War, Revolution, and Peace, 1996); A.R. Hybel and J.M. Kaufman, *The Bush Administrations and Saddam Hussein: Deciding on Conflict* (New York: Palgrave Macmillan, 2006); S.F. Knott, *Rush to Judgment: George W. Bush, the War on Terror, and His Critics* (Lawrence, KS: Kansas UP, 2012); T. Lansford, R.P. Watson, and J. Covarrubias, eds., *America's War on Terror*, 2nd edition (Farnham and Burlington, VT: Ashgate, 2009); P. Lee, *Blair's Just War: Iraq and the Illusion of Morality* (Basingstoke, NY: Palgrave Macmillan, 2012); G.A. MacLean, *Clinton's Foreign Policy in Russia: From Deterrence and Isolation to Democratization and Engagement* (Aldershot and Burlington, VT: Ashgate, 2006); C. Maynard, *Out of the Shadow: George H.W. Bush and the End of the Cold War* (College Station, TX: Texas A&M UP, 2008): E.E. Otenyi and N.S. Lind, *The First World Presidency: George H.W. Bush, 1989–1993* (Youngstown, NY: Teneo Press, 2009); I. Parmar, L.B. Miller, and M. Ledwidge, eds., *Obama and the World: New Directions In US Foreign Policy* (Abingdon, NY: Routledge, 2014); N. Ritchie and P. Rogers, *Political Road to War with Iraq: Bush, 9/11 and the Drive to Overthrow Saddam* (London, NY: Routledge, 2007); G. Roberts, *US Foreign Policy and China: Bush's First Term* (Abingdon, NY: Routledge, 2015); M.A. Smith, *Power in the Changing Global Order: The US, Russia and China* (Cambridge and Malden, MA: Polity, 2012); C. Wang, *Obama's Challenge to China: The Pivot to Asia* (Farnham and Burlington, VT: Ashgate, 2015); J. Velasco Nevado, *Neoconservatives in U.S. Foreign Policy under Ronald Reagan and George W. Bush: Voices behind the Throne* (Baltimore, MD: Johns Hopkins UP, 2010).

References

Aburish, S.K. (2000) *Saddam Hussein: The Politics of Revenge*. New York: Bloomsbury.

Acheson, D. (1969) *Present at the Creation: My Years in the State Department*. New York: Norton, pp. 378–9.

Adams, I. (2005) *Brothers across the Ocean: British Foreign Policy and the Origins of the Anglo-American 'Special Relationship' 1900–1905*. London and New York: Tauris.

Addison, P. (2010) *No Turning Back: The Peacetime Revolutions of Post-war Britain*. Oxford: Oxford UP.

Aldous, R. (2012) *Reagan and Thatcher: The Difficult Relationship*. London: Hutchinson, p. 133.

Allison, W.T. (2012) *Gulf War, 1990–91*. Basingstoke, NY: Palgrave Macmillan.

Alperovitz, G. (1965) *Atomic Diplomacy: Hiroshima and Potsdam; The Use of the Atomic Bomb and the American Confrontation with Soviet Power*. New York: Simon and Schuster.

Ambrosius, L.W. (1991) *Wilsonian Statecraft: Theory and Practice of Liberal Internationalism during World War I*. Wilmington, DE: SR Books.

'. . . An attempt to understand The Falklands War', *Perspectives* (3 October 2014).

'Anatoly Chernyaev's notes (excerpts) from the Politburo Session, 8 May 1987 "On the Doctrine of the Warsaw Treaty Organization"': http://nsarchive.gwu.edu/NSAEBB/NSAEBB422/docs/Doc%203%2005.08.1987%20Politburo.pdf.

Andrew, C.M. and Mitrokhin, V. (1999) *The Mitrokhin Archive: The KGB in Europe and the West*. London: Penguin, pp. 150–5.

Annexes in CCS. 'Octagon Conference, September 1944. Papers and Minutes of Meetings, Octagon Conference and Minutes of Combined Chiefs of Staff Meetings in London, June 1944', Microfilm edition. Washington, DC: National Archives.

Anonymous. (1890) *Titled Americans: A List of American Ladies Who Have Married Foreigners of Rank*. New York: Smith and Smith.

Anonymous. (1896) 'Episodes of the Month', *National Review*, 156 (February, 1896), 739, pp. 717–740.

Anonymous. (1993) 'Report puts Iraqi dead at 1500', *Jane's Defence Weekly*, 19/11.

Anslover, N.L. (2014) *Harry S. Truman: The Coming of the Cold War*. New York: Routledge.

Argote-Freya, F. (2006) *Fulgencio Batista*. Brunswick, NJ: Rutgers UP, pp. 230–49.

Ashton, N. (2006) 'Harold Macmillan and the "Golden Days" of Anglo-American relations revisited, 1957–63', *DH*, 29/4, pp. 691–723.

Ashton, N. (2014) 'Anglo-American relations from World War to Cold War', *JCH*, 39/1, pp. 117–25.

References 171

Atkinson, R. (2002) *Army at Dawn: The War in North Africa, 1942–1943*. New York: Henry Holt.

Auerswald, D.P. and Saideman, S.M. (2014) *NATO in Afghanistan: Fighting Together, Fighting Alone*. Princeton, NJ: Princeton UP.

Avon, Earl of. (1960) *Full Circle; The Memoirs of Anthony Eden*. Boston: Houghton Mifflin, p. 484.

Baetzhold, H.G. (1970) *Mark Twain and John Bull: The British Connection*. Bloomington, IN: Indiana UP.

Bailey, G.J. (2013) *The Arsenal of Democracy: Aircraft Supply and the Evolution of the Anglo-American Alliance, 1938–1942*. Edinburgh: Edinburgh UP.

Baker, A. (2011) *Constructing a Post-War Order: The Rise of US Hegemony and the Origins of the Cold War*. London: Tauris.

Baldwin, R.E. (1995) 'The eastern enlargement of the European Union', *European Economic Review*, 39/3–4, pp. 474–81.

Ball, G.W. (1979) 'The "Special Relationship" in today's world', in W.E. Leuchtenberg et al. (eds.) *Britain and the United States*. London, Exeter, NH: Heinemann, pp. 47–59.

Bange, O. (2008) '*Ostpolitik* as a source of intrabloc tensions', in M.A. Heiss and S.V. Papacosma (eds.) *NATO and the Warsaw Pact: Intrabloc Conflicts*. Kent, OH: Kent State UP, pp. 106–21.

Barnes, J. and Nicholson, D. (eds.) (1988) *The Leo Amery Diaries 1929–1945*. London: Hutchinson, pp. 709–10 (Amery diary, 9, 11 August 1941).

Barnet, C. (1986) *The Audit of War: The Illusion and Reality of Britain as a Great Nation*. London and New York: Macmillan.

Bar-Noi, U. (2007) 'The Soviet Union and The Six-Day War: Revelations from the Polish Archives', *CWIHP e-Dossier*, 8: www.wilsoncenter.org/publication/the-soviet-union-and-the-six-day-war-revelations-the-polish-archives.

Bayandor, D. (2010) *Iran and the CIA: The Fall of Mosaddeq Revisited*. Houndmills: Palgrave Macmillan.

Baylis, J. (1992) *The Diplomacy of Pragmatism: Britain and the Formation of NATO, 1942–1949*. Basingstoke: Macmillan, pp. 107–30.

Baylis, J. (1995) *Ambiguity and Deterrence: British Nuclear Strategy, 1945–1964*. New York: Clarendon, pp. 34–66.

Baylis, J. and Stoddart, K. (2015) *The British Nuclear Experience: The Roles of Beliefs, Culture, and Identity*. Oxford: Oxford UP, pp. 174–5.

Beloff, N. (1985) *Tito's Flawed Legacy: Yugoslavia and the West 1939–84*. London: Victor Gollancz.

Ben-Dror, E. (2016) *Ralph Bunche and the Arab-Israeli Conflict: Mediation and the UN, 1947–1949*. London and New York: Routledge.

Bennett, M.T. (2012) 'Kissing Cousins: How Anglo-American relations became "Special"', in idem. (ed) *One World, Big Screen: Hollywood, the Allies, and World War II*. Chapel Hill, NC: North Carolina UP, pp. 136–68.

'The Berlin (Potsdam) Conference, July 17-August 2, 1945': Avalon Project: http://avalon.law.yale.edu/20th_century/decade17.asp.

Bernstein, R. (2014) *China 1945: Mao's Revolution and America's Fateful Choice*. New York: Knopf.

Bertsch, G.K. and Elliott, S. (1988) 'Controlling East-West trade in Britain: Power, politics, and policy', in G.K. Bertsch (ed.) *Controlling East-West Trade and Technology Transfer: Power, Politics, and Policies*. Duke, NC: Duke UP, pp. 207–8.

Besch, M.D. (2002) *A Navy Second to None: The History of U.S. Naval Training in World War I*. Westport, CT: Greenwood.

172 References

Bieber, F., Galijaš, A. and Archer, R. (eds.) (2014) *Debating the End of Yugoslavia.* Farnham: Ashgate.

Bischof, G. (2000) *Cold War Respite: The Geneva Summit of 1955.* Baton Rouge, LA: Louisiana State UP.

Bischof, G., Karner, S. and Ruggenthaler, P. (eds.) (2009) *The Prague Spring and the Warsaw Pact Invasion of Czechoslovakia in 1968.* Lanham, MD: Lexington.

Black, J. (2008) *Crisis of Empire: Britain and America in the Eighteenth Century.* London and New York: Continuum.

'Blair statement in full', *BBC News* (7 October 2001): http://news.bbc.co.uk/2/hi/uk_news/politics/1585238.stm.

Blang, E.M. (2011) *Allies at Odds: America, Europe, and Vietnam, 1961–1968.* Lanham, MD: Rowman & Littlefield, pp. 176–8.

Blau, G.E. (1997) *Invasion Balkans!: The German Campaign in the Balkans, Spring 1941.* Shippensburg, PA: Burd Street Press.

Bloed, A. and Wessel, R.A. (eds.) (1995) *The Changing Functions of the Western European Union (WEU): Introduction and Basic Documents.* Dordrecht: Brill, pp. 65–7. ('Communiqué', 30 April 1986).

Blower, B.L. (2014) 'From isolationism to neutrality: A new framework for understanding American political culture, 1919–1941', *DH*, 38/2, pp. 345–76.

Boemeke, M.F., Feldman, G.D. and Glaser, E. (eds.) (2006) *The Treaty of Versailles: A Reassessment after 75 Years.* Washington, DC: German Historical Institute.

Boghardt, T. (2012) *The Zimmermann Telegram: Intelligence, Diplomacy, and America's Entry into World War I.* Annapolis, MD: Naval Institute Press.

Boot, M. 'The U.S. strategy against the Islamic State must be retooled', *Washington Post* (14 November 2014): www.washingtonpost.com/opinions/the-us-strategy-against-the-islamic-state-must-be-retooled-heres-how/2014/11/14/7972e50c-6b8a-11e4-a31c-77759fc1eacc_story.html.

Bourne, K. (1967) *Britain and the Balance of Power in North America, 1815–1908.* London: Longmans.

Bowden, M. (1985) *Guests of the Ayatollah: The First Battle in America's War with Militant Islam.* New York: Atlantic Monthly Press, Part 2.

Bowers, B. 'Dick Cheney disputes Margaret Thatcher's famous "no time to go wobbly" quote', *Tampa Bay Times* (10 April 2013): www.politifact.com/truth-o-meter/statements/2013/apr/10/dick-cheney/dick-cheney-margaret-thatcher-go-wobbly/.

Bozek, F.J.G. (2013) 'Britain, European security and freer movement: The development of Britain's CSCE policy 1969–1972', *CWH*, 13/4, p. 446.

Bragg, M. (1997) *Richard Burton: A Life.* Boston: Little, Brown.

Braithwaite, R. (2011) *Afgantsy: The Russians in Afghanistan, 1979–1989.* Oxford: Oxford UP, Part 1.

Brands, Jr., H.W. (1986) 'What Eisenhower and Dulles saw in Nasser: Personalities and interests in U.S.-Egyptian relations', *Middle East Policy Council*, 4/2: www.mepc.org/journal/middle-east-policy-archives/what-eisenhower-and-dulles-saw-nasser?print.

Brands, H.W. (1989) *The Specter of Neutralism: The United States and the Emergence of the Third World, 1947–1960.* New York: Columbia UP.

Brands, H.W. (1999) 'The idea of the national interest', in M.J. Hogan (ed.) *The Ambiguous Legacy: U.S. Foreign Relations in the 'American Century'.* Cambridge: Cambridge UP.

Brands, H.W. (2008) *From Berlin to Baghdad: America's Search for Purpose in the Post-Cold War World.* Lexington, KY: Kentucky UP, pp. 12–22.

References   173

Brecher, F.W. (2013) *American Diplomacy and the Israeli War of Independence.* Jefferson, NC: McFarland, pp. 77–148.

Brenchley, F. (2005) *Britain, the Six-Day War and Its Aftermath.* London: Tauris, pp. 143–51.

'The Brezhnev doctrine' (2008): http://modernhistorian.blogspot.ca/2008/11/on-this-day-in-history-brezhnev.html.

Brinkley, D. (1990) 'Dean Acheson and the "Special Relationship": The West Point Speech of December 1962', *HJ*, 33/3, pp. 599–608.

'Britain eyes business opportunities in wake of Iran nuclear deal', *Reuters* (21 July 2015): www.reuters.com/article/2015/07/21/us-iran-nuclear-britainidUSKCN0PV21U 20150721.

British Berlin Airlift Association. 'Dates and statistics': www.bbaa-airlift.org.uk/statistics.html.

Broad, W.J. and Peçanha, S. 'The Iran Nuclear Deal – A simple guide', *NY Times* (14 July 2015): www.nytimes.com/interactive/2015/03/31/world/middleeast/simple-guide-nuclear-talks-iran-us.html?_r=0.

Brown, A. (2009) *The Rise and Fall of Communism.* London: Bodley Head.

Brown, A. (2010) 'Margaret Thatcher and perceptions of change in the Soviet Union', *Journal of European Integration History*, 16/1.

Bryce, J. (1888) *The American Commonwealth*, 2 volumes. London, NY: Macmillan.

Brzezinski, Z. (1983) *Power and Principle, Memoirs of the National Security Adviser, 1977–1981.* New York: Farrar, Straus, Giroux.

Bullock, A. (1983) *The Life and Times of Ernest Bevin*, Volume III. London: Heinemann.

Bulmer-Thomas, V. (2013) 'Margaret Thatcher's foreign policy legacy': www.chathamhouse.org/media/comment/view/190635#.

Burg, S.L. and Shoup, P.S. (1999) *The War in Bosnia-Herzegovina: Ethnic Conflict and International Intervention.* Armonk, NY, London: M.E. Sharp.

Burk, K.M. (2008) *Old World, New World: Great Britain and America from the Beginning.* New York: Atlantic Monthly Press, pp. 380–437.

Burk, K.M. and Cairncross, A. (1992) *Goodbye, Great Britain: The 1976 IMF Crisis.* New Haven, CT: Yale UP.

Burt, R. 'The deployment of missiles in Europe', *Washington Post* (27 November 1983): www.washingtonpost.com/archive/opinions/1983/11/27/the-deployment-of-missiles-in-europe/3b1846e2–70f4–4c1f-8dc2-afbe144d38e6/.

Busch, P. (2002) 'Killing the "Vietcong": The British advisory mission and the strategic Hamlet programme', *JSS*, 25/1, pp. 135–62.

G.H.W. Bush speech (31 May 1989) A 'Europe whole and free': http://usa.usembassy.de/etexts/ga6–890531.htm.

Bush, G.H.W. (1992) *Public Papers of the Presidents of the United States: Administration of George Bush, 1991.* Washington, DC: National Archives and Records Service, pp. 225–6.

Bush, G.H.W. and Scowcroft, B. 'Why we didn't remove Saddam', *Time* (2 March 1998).

Bush, G.H.W. and Scowcroft, B. (1998) *A World Transformed.* New York: Knopf, pp. 160, 173.

Butler, D. and Kavanaugh, D. (1984) *The British General Election of 1983.* London: Macmillan.

Butler, J.R.M. (1957) *Grand Strategy*, Volume II. London: HMSO.

Byrne, M. (2014) *Iran-Contra: Reagan's Scandal and the Unchecked Abuse of Presidential Power.* Lawrence, KS: Kansas UP.

174　*References*

Cable, J. (1986) *The Geneva Conference of 1954 on Indochina*. Basingstoke: Macmillan.

Cairncross, A. (1996) 'The Heath government and the British economy', in S. Ball and A. Seldon (eds.) *The Heath Government 1970–1974*. London and New York: Longman, pp. 107–38.

Cairo, M.F. (2004) 'The "Operational Code" of the Bush Administration: Leadership perceptions and foreign policy making', in W. Levantrosser and R. Perotti (eds.) *A Noble Calling: Character and the George H.W. Bush Presidency*. Westport, CT: Praeger, pp. 263–4.

Callahan, R. (2002) 'Churchill and Singapore', in B. Farrell and B. Hunter (eds.) *Sixty Years On: The Fall of Singapore Revisited*. Singapore: Eastern Universities Press, pp. 156–72.

Campbell, J. (2003) *Margaret Thatcher*, Volume II: *The Iron Lady*. London: Jonathan Cape, pp. 58–9.

Carothers, T. (1991) *In the Name of Democracy: U.S. Policy toward Latin America in the Reagan Years*. Berkeley, CA: California UP.

Casey, S. (2001) *Cautious Crusade: Franklin D. Roosevelt, American Public Opinion, and the War against Nazi Germany*. Oxford: Oxford UP.

Castle, M. (2003) *Triggering Communism's Collapse: Perceptions and Power in Poland's Transition*. Lanham, MD: Rowman & Littlefield.

Chaitani, Y. (2000) *Dissension among Allies: Ernest Bevin's Palestine Policy between Whitehall and the White House, 1945–47*. London: Saqi.

Cheng, S. (2012) *The U.S. Financial Crisis: Analysis and Interpretation*. San Francisco, CA: Long River.

Childs, D. (2001) *The Fall of the GDR*. Harlow: Longman, pp. 66–7.

Churchill to Roosevelt, 18 March 1944, reply, 20 March 1944, both Department of State (on-going) *FRUS, The Conference at Quebec 1944*. Washington, DC: Department of State, pp. 3–4.

Churchill, W.S. (1949a) *The Second World War*, Volume II. Boston: Houghton Mifflin.

Churchill, W.S. (1949b) *The Second World War*, Volume VI. Boston: Houghton Mifflin.

Clifford, J.G. and Spencer, Jr., S.R. (1986) *First Peacetime Draft*. Lawrence, KS: Kansas UP.

Cmd. 6808. 'Report of the Anglo-American committee of enquiry regarding the problems of European Jewry and Palestine, Lausanne' (20 April 1946).

Coffey, J.W. (2009) 'New thinking or new tactics in Soviet foreign policy', in E.P. Hoffmann, R.F. Laird, and F.J. Fleron (eds.) *Soviet Foreign Policy 1970–1991*. New Brunswick, NJ: Transaction, pp. 373–4.

Cohen, E.A. (2015) 'Ronald Reagan and American defense', in J.L. Chidester and P. Kengor (eds.) *Reagan's Legacy in a World Transformed*. Cambridge, MA: Harvard UP, pp. 124–37.

Cohrs, P.O. (2006) *The Unfinished Peace after World War I: America, Britain and the Stabilisation of Europe, 1919–1932*. Cambridge: Cambridge UP.

Cole, A. (1994) *François Mitterrand: A Study in Political Leadership*. Abingdon: Routledge.

Colman, J. (2004) *A 'Special Relationship'? Harold Wilson, Lyndon B. Johnson and Anglo-American Relations 'at the Summit', 1964–68*. Manchester: Manchester UP.

Colman, J. (2010) *The Foreign Policy of Lyndon B. Johnson: The United States and the World, 1963–1969*. Edinburgh: Edinburgh UP.

References 175

Colucci, I. (2012) *The National Security Doctrines of the American Presidency: How They Shape Our Present and Future*. Santa Barbara, CA: Praeger, pp. 38–41.

Connelly, M. (2001) *Reaching for the Stars: A New History of Bomber Command in World War II*. London: Tauris.

Coogan, J.W. (1981) *End of Neutrality: The United States, Britain, and Maritime Rights, 1899–1915*. Ithaca, NY: Cornell UP.

Cooper, J. (2012) *Margaret Thatcher and Ronald Reagan: A Very Political Special Relationship*. Houndmills and New York: Palgrave Macmillan.

Costigliola, F.C. (1977) 'Anglo-American financial rivalry in the 1920s', *JEH*, 37/4, pp. 911–34.

Council on Foreign Relations, 'Weapons of mass destruction and Iraq' (May 2005): www.cfr.org/weapons-of-mass-destruction/weapons-mass-destruction-iraq/ p8157.

Cox, M. and Hurst, S. (2002) '"His Finest Hour?": George Bush and the diplomacy of German unification', *DS*, 13/4, pp. 123–50.

Craddock, P. (1997) *In Pursuit of British Interests: Reflections on Foreign Policy under Margaret Thatcher and John Major*. London: John Murray.

Crain, A.D. (2009) *The Ford Presidency: A History*. Jefferson, NC: McFarland.

Daalder, I.H. (2003) 'The end of Atlanticism', *Survival*, 45/2, pp. 58.

D'Amato, P. (December 2000–January 2001) 'U.S. Intervention in the Middle East: Blood for oil', *International Socialist Review*: www.isreview.org/issues/15/blood_ for_oil.shtml.

Daalder, I.H. and Lindsay, J.M. (2003) *America Unbound: The Bush Revolution in Foreign Policy*. Washington, DC: Brookings.

Daalder, I.H. and O'Hanlon, M.E. (2000) *Winning Ugly: NATO's War to Save Kosovo*. Washington, DC: Brookings, p. 137.

Daalder, I.H. and Stavridis, J.G. (2012) 'NATO's victory in Libya. The right way to run an intervention', *FA*, 91/2, pp. 2–7.

Dallek, R. (1995) *Franklin D. Roosevelt and American Foreign Policy, 1932–1945*. Oxford: Oxford UP, pp. 212, 253–5.

Datta, M.N. (2014) *Anti-Americanism and the Rise of World Opinion: Consequences for the US National Interest*. Cambridge: Cambridge UP.

Daum, A.W. (2008) *Kennedy in Berlin*. Cambridge: Cambridge UP.

Davis, R. (2015) 'The Falkland Islands and the special relationship', in C. Berbéri and M.O'B. Castro (eds.) *30 Years After: Issues and Representations of the Falklands War*. Farnham: Ashgate, pp. 71–94.

Davis, R.G. (2006) *Bombing the European Axis Powers: A Historical Digest of the Combined Bomber Offensive 1939–1945*. Maxwell, AL: AUP, pp. 14–90.

Dayer, R.A. (1981) *Bankers and Diplomats in China, 1917–1925: The Anglo-American Relationship*. London and Totowa, NJ: Cass, pp. 109–230.

'Declaration on European identity', Copenhagen (14 December 1973): www.cvce. eu/content/publication/1999/1/1/02798dc9-9c69-4b7d-b2c9-f03a8db7da32/ publishable_en.pdf.

Desch, M.C. (2008) *Power and Military Effectiveness: The Fallacy of Democratic Triumphalism*. Baltimore, MD: Johns Hopkins UP.

Dockrill, S. (1991) *Britain's Policy for West German Rearmament, 1950–1955*. Cambridge: Cambridge UP, pp. 133–50.

Dockrill, S. (2002) *Britain's Retreat from East of Suez: The Choice between Europe and the World?*. New York: Palgrave, pp. 225–6.

176   *References*

Doenecke, J.D. (2000) *Storm on the Horizon: The Challenge to American Intervention, 1939–1941*. Latham, MD: Rowman & Littlefield.

Domber, G.F. (2014) *Empowering Revolution: America, Poland, and the End of the Cold War*. Chapel Hill, NC: North Carolina UP, pp. 217, 279.

Dorman, A. (2001) 'John Nott and the Royal Navy: The 1981 defence review revisited', *Contemporary British History*, 15/2, pp. 98–120.

Dorman, A.M. (2009) *Blair's Successful War: British Military Intervention in Sierra Leone*. Farnham: Ashgate.

Doyle, T. (2013) *Man on the Run: Paul McCartney in the 1970s*. Edinburgh: Polygon.

Duiker, W.J. (1976) *The Rise of Nationalism in Vietnam, 1900–1941*. Ithaca, NY: Cornell UP.

Dumbrell, J. (2006) *A Special Relationship: Anglo-American Relations from the Cold War to Iraq*, 2nd edition. Basingstoke: Palgrave Macmillan, pp. 49–74.

Dumbrell, J. (2013) 'Personal diplomacy: Relations between prime ministers and presidents', in A.P. Dobson and S. Marsh (eds.) *Anglo-American Relations: Contemporary Perspectives*. Abingdon: Routledge, pp. 93–4.

Dumbrell, J. and Ellis, S. (2003) 'British involvement in Vietnam peace initiatives, 1966–1967: Marigolds, Sunflowers, and "Kosygin Week"', *DH*, 27/1, pp. 113–49.

Dunlop, C.G.H. (2009) 'Ebb and flow: The British War with the Japanese', in N. Kosuge and H. Dobson (eds.) *Japan and Britain at War and Peace*. New York: Routledge, pp. 11–24.

Dunn, S. (2013) *1940: FDR, Willkie, Lindbergh, Hitler – The Election and the Storm*. New Haven, CT: Yale UP.

Dyson, S.B. (2012) 'The United Kingdom', in R. Sobel, P. Furia, and B. Barratt (eds.) *Public Opinion and International Intervention: Lessons from the Iraq War*. Washington, DC: Potomac, pp. 37–42.

'East-West German immigration statistics (1961–1990)': http://germanhistorydocs. ghi-dc.org/sub_document.cfm?document_id=925.

Eden to Baldwin [former prime minister], 19 December 1938, Baldwin 124.

'Editorial Note about the Bermuda Conference', *FRUS, 1955–1957, Western Europe and Canada*, Volume XXVII, Document 284: http://history.state.gov/historical documents/frus1955–57v27/d284.

'Eisenhower Doctrine, 1957': http://coursesa.matrix.msu.edu/~hst306/documents/ eisen.html.

Eisenhower, D. (1986) *Eisenhower at War 1943–1945*. London: Collins, pp. 464–5.

'Elizabeth II to Ford, 19 June 1975': www.fordlibrarymuseum.gov/library/document/ 0351/1555868.pdf.

Elliot, M. (1996) *'Independent Iraq': The Monarchy & British Influence, 1941–1958*. London: Tauris, pp. 138–62.

Ellis, S.E. (2004) *Britain, America, and the Vietnam War*. Westport, CT: Praeger.

'Episodes of the Month', *National Review*, 156 (February 1896), pp. 717–740.

Esposito, C. (1994) *America's Feeble Weapon: Funding the Marshall Plan in France and Italy, 1948–1950*. Westport, CT: Greenwood.

European Commission. (2011) *EU-Russia Energy Dialogue: The First Ten Years: 2000–2010*. Brussels: European Commission.

Farrell, B.P. (1993) 'Symbol of paradox: The Casablanca conference, 1943', *CJH*, 28/1, pp. 21–40.

Faucher-King, F. and Le Galès, P. (2010) *The New Labour Experiment: Change and Reform under Blair and Brown*. Stanford, CA: Stanford UP.

References 177

Fauser, A. (2013) *Sounds of War: Music in the United States during World War II*. Oxford: Oxford UP.

Fawcett, L.L.'E. (1992) *Iran and the Cold War: The Azerbaijan Crisis of 1946*. Cambridge: Cambridge UP.

Feis, H. (1967) *Churchill, Roosevelt, Stalin: The War They Waged and the Peace They Sought*, 2nd edition. Princeton, NJ: Princeton UP, pp. 623–6.

Fenton, D. (2012) *To Cage the Red Dragon: SEATO and the Defence of Southeast Asia, 1955–1965*. Singapore: NUS Press.

Ferrell, R.H. (ed.) (1980) *Off the Record: The Private Papers of Harry S. Truman*. New York: Harper & Row, pp. 79–80.

Ferris, J.R. (1989) *Men, Money, and Diplomacy: The Evolution of British Strategic Policy, 1919–26*. Ithaca, NY: Cornell UP.

Ferris, J.R. (2013) *Nasser's Gamble: How Intervention in Yemen Caused the Six-Day War and the Decline of Egyptian Power*. Princeton, NJ: Princeton UP, pp. 24–69.

Fink, C. and Schaefer, B. (eds.) (2009) *Ostpolitik, 1969–1974: European and Global Responses*. Cambridge and New York: Cambridge UP.

Fischer, C. (2003) *Ruhr Crisis, 1923–1924*. Oxford, NY: Oxford UP.

Flavell, J. and Conway, S. (eds.) (2004) *Britain and America Go to War: The Impact of War and Warfare in Anglo-America, 1754–1815*. Gainesville, FL: UP Florida.

Ford, D. (2012) *The Pacific War: Clash of Empires in World War II*. London and New York: Continuum, pp. 36–50.

Foreman, A. (2012) *A World on Fire: Britain's Crucial Role in the American Civil War*. New York: Random House.

Fraudet, X. (2006) *France's Security Independence: Originality and Constraints in Europe, 1981–1995*. Bern: Peter Lang.

Freedman, L. (2005) *The Official History of the Falklands Campaign*, Volume 2: *War and Diplomacy*. Routledge, pp. 3–32.

Freedman, L. and Gearson, J. (1999) 'Interdependence and independence: Nassau and the British nuclear deterrent', in K.M. Burk and M. Stokes (eds.) *The United States and the European Alliance since 1945*: Oxford, NY: Berg, pp. 179–203.

Frontline, 'Interview: William Kristol' (n.d.): www.pbs.org/wgbh/pages/frontline/shows/iraq/interviews/kristol.html.

Fuller, A.L. (2012) *Taking the Fight to the Enemy: Neoconservatism and the Age of Ideology*. Lanham, MD: Lexington.

Gaddis, J.L. (2005) *The Cold War: A New History*. New York: Penguin.

Gaddis, J.L. (2011) *George F. Kennan: An American Life*. New York: Penguin, Chapters 10–11.

Garthoff, R.L. (1985) 'European theater nuclear forces, 1977–1980', in idem. (ed.) *Detente and Confrontation: American-Soviet Relations from Nixon to Reagan*. Washington, DC: Brookings, pp. 849–86.

Gassend, J.L. (2014) *Le débarquement de Provence: opération Dragoon: août-septembre 1944*. Bayeux: Heimdal.

Gat, M. (2006) 'Britain and the occupied territories after the 1967 war', *Middle East Review of International Affairs*, 10/4.

Gati, C. (2006) *Failed Illusions: Moscow, Washington, Budapest, and the 1956 Hungarian Revolt*. Stanford, CA: Stanford UP.

Gavrilov, V. (2012) 'Soviet Union military planning, 1948–1968', in J. Hoffenaar and D. Krüger (eds.) *Blueprints for Battle: Planning for War in Central Europe, 1948–1968*. Lexington, KY: Kentucky UP, pp. 121–6.

178   References

Gedmin, J. (1992) *The Hidden Hand: Gorbachev and the Collapse of East Germany*. Lanham, MD: UPA, pp. 55–6.

Gendercide Watch, 'Case study: The Srebrenica Massacre, July 1995': www.gendercide.org/case_srebrenica.html.

Gibb, P. (2005) 'Unmasterly inactivity? Sir Julian Pauncefote, Lord Salisbury, and the Venezuela Boundary Dispute', *DS*, 16/1, pp. 23–55.

Gibbs, N.H. (1976) *Grand Strategy*, Volume I: *Rearmament Policy*. London: HMSO, pp. 681–4.

Gilbert, M. (1986) *Winston S. Churchill*, Volume VII. London: Heinemann, pp. 23–44.

Glaurdić, J. (2011) *The Hour of Europe: Western Powers and the Breakup of Yugoslavia*. New Haven, CT: Yale UP, pp. 1–11.

Gleijeses, P. (2013) *Visions of Freedom: Havana, Washington, and Pretoria and the Struggle for Southern Africa, 1976–1991*. Chapel Hill, NC: North Carolina UP, pp. 17–97.

'Globalization' (n.d.): www.worldbank.org/economicpolicy/globalization/.

Goldstein, E. and Maurer, J. (eds.) (1994) *The Washington Conference, 1921–22: Naval Rivalry, East Asian Stability and the Road to Pearl Harbor*. London: Cass.

Goldstein, G.M. (2008) *Lessons in Disaster: McGeorge Bundy and the Path to War in Vietnam*. New York: Times Books/Holt.

Graham, Jr., T. and LaVera, D.J. (2003) *Cornerstones of Security: Arms Control Treaties in the Nuclear Era*. Seattle, WA: Washington UP, pp. 514–15.

Granieri, R.J. (2003) *The Ambivalent Alliance: Konrad Adenauer, the CDU/CSU, and the West, 1949–1966*. New York: Oxford: Berghahn Books, pp. 110–49.

Grayson, R.S. (1997) *Austen Chamberlain and the Commitment to Europe: British Foreign Policy, 1924–29*. London and Portland, OR: Cass, pp. 170–211.

Gregg, H.S., Rothstein, H.S. and Arquilla, J. (eds.) (2010) *The Three Circles of War: Understanding the Dynamics of Conflict in Iraq*. Washington, DC: Potomac.

'Grenada: No.10 record of telephone conversation' (26 October 1983): www.margaretthatcher.org/document/128153.

'Gulf War Coalition Forces: Countries compared': www.nationmaster.com/country-nfo/stats/Military/Gulf-War-Coalition-Forces.

Gurman, H. (2012) *Dissent Papers: The Voices of Diplomats in the Cold War and Beyond*. New York: Columbia UP.

Gustafson, L.S. (1998) *The Sovereignty Dispute over the Falkland (Malvinas) Islands*. New York: Oxford UP, pp. 190–2.

Haglund, D.G. (1980) 'George C. Marshall and the question of military aid to England, May-June 1940', *JCH*, 15/4, pp. 745–60.

Hahn, P.I. (2006) 'Securing the Middle East: The Eisenhower Doctrine of 1957', *PSQ*, 36/1, pp. 38–47.

Hakkarainen, P. (2011) *A State of Peace in Europe: West Germany and the CSCE, 1966–1975*. New York: Berghahn.

Halberstam, D. (1965) *The Making of a Quagmire: America and Vietnam during the Kennedy Era*. New York: Random House.

Hamilton, K. (1998) *The Last Cold War Warriors: Britain, Détente, and the CSCE 1972*. Oxford: European Inter-dependence Unit.

Hancock, W.K. and Gowing, M.M. (1975) *British War Economy*. London: HMSO.

Hanhimäki, J.M. (2013) *Rise and Fall of Détente: American Foreign Policy and the Transformation of the Cold War*. Washington, DC: Potomac, pp. 21–4.

References   179

Harbutt, F.J. (2010) *Yalta 1945: Europe and America at the Crossroads*. New York: Cambridge UP.

Harry, B. (2004) *The British Invasion: How the Beatles and other UK Bands Conquered America*. New Malden: Chrome Dreams.

Hartmann, C. (2013) *Operation Barbarossa: Nazi Germany's War in the East, 1941–1945*. Oxford: Oxford UP.

Haruki, W. (2014) *The Korean War: An International History*. Lanham, MD: Rowman & Littlefield.

Harvey, J. (ed.) (1978) *The War Diaries of Oliver Hardy*. Collins, p. 348 (Hardy [Eden's private secretary] diary, 15 July 1944).

Hasegawa, T. (2005) *Racing the Enemy: Stalin, Truman, and the Surrender of Japan*. Cambridge, MA: Belknap Press, 2005.

Haslop, D. (2013) *Britain, Germany and the Battle of the Atlantic*. London: Bloomsbury.

Haug, H.K. (2012) *Creating a Socialist Yugoslavia: Tito, Communist leadership and the National Question*. London: Tauris.

Head, W. and Tilford, E.H. (eds.) (1996) *The Eagle in the Desert: Looking Back on U.S. Involvement in the Persian Gulf War*. Westport, CT: Praeger, Parts III–V.

Hebel, K. and Lenz, T. (2009) 'The EU as a "Civilian Model": The CSCE origins', International Studies Association Conference: http://citation.allacademic.com/meta/p_mla_apa_research_citation/3/1/3/8/4/pages313841/p313841-1.php.

Henderson [British ambassador, Washington] diary, 'Talks in London about the visit' (18 February 1981): www.margaretthatcher.org/archive/displaydocument.asp?docid=110521.

Henderson, M. (1997) *Star Wars: The Magic of Myth*. New York: Spectra.

Hendrickson, Jr., K.E. (2003) *The Spanish-American War*. Westport, CT: Greenwood.

Hendrix, H.J. (2009) *Theodore Roosevelt's Naval Diplomacy: The U.S. Navy and the Birth of the American Century*. Annapolis, MD: Naval Institute Press.

Henry, C. (2003) *The Battle of the Coral Sea*. Annapolis, MD: Naval Institute Press.

Henry, D.H. (1984) 'The War Powers Resolution: A tool for balancing power through negotiation', *Virginia Law Review*, 70/5, pp. 1037–58.

Herszenhorn, D. 'A year after seizing Crimea, Putin celebrates as Ukraine seethes', *NY Times* (18 March 2015).

Hill, C. and Lord, C. (1996) 'The foreign policy of the Heath government', in S. Ball and A. Seldon (eds.) *The Heath Government 1970–1974*. London and New York: Longman, pp. 285–314.

Hilpert, H.G. and Kecker, K.-J. (2008) 'Interregional trade and investment between Asia and Europe: An empirical investigation', in J. Ruland et al. (eds.) *Asian-European Relations: Building Blocks for Global Governance?* London and New York: Routledge, pp. 88–9.

'HMG recognizes Tibet as an integral part of the PRC', *Telegraph* (29 October 2008): www.telegraph.co.uk/news/worldnews/asia/tibet/3385803/UK-recognises-Chinas-direct-rule-over-Tibet.html.

Hobeck, M. (1999) *Der Rest ist Österreich!: zum Vertrag von Saint-Germain-en-Laye 1919*. Wien: Österreichische Landsmannschaft.

Hodge, C.C. (2002) 'The vocation of peace, the hypothesis of war', in idem. (ed.) *NATO for a New Century: Atlanticism and European Security*. Westport, CT: Praeger.

Hogan, M.J. (1977) *Informal Entente: The Private Structure of Cooperation in Anglo-American Economic Diplomacy, 1918–1928*. Columbia: Missouri UP.

180   References

Hogan, M.J. (1987) *The Marshall Plan: America, Britain, and the Reconstruction of Western Europe, 1947–1952*. Cambridge: Cambridge, UP.

Hogan, M.J. (1998) *A Cross of Iron: Harry S. Truman and the Origins of the National Security State, 1945–1954*. Cambridge: Cambridge UP, pp. 291–314.

Holdich, P.G.H. (1987) 'A policy of percentages? British policy and the Balkans after the Moscow conference of October 1944', *IHR*, 9/1, pp. 28–47.

Holloway, D. (1994) *Stalin and the Bomb: The Soviet Union and Atomic Energy, 1939–1956*. New Haven, CT: Yale UP, pp. 134–71.

Holmes, A.R. and Rofe, J.S. (2012) *The Embassy in Grosvenor Square: American Ambassadors to the United Kingdom, 1938–2008*. Houndsmills: Palgrave Macmillan, pp. 223–4.

Hopf, T. (2012) *Reconstructing the Cold War: The Early Years, 1945–1958*. New York: Oxford UP, pp. 140–1.

Hopkins, M.F. (2014) 'The United States and Eastern Europe, 1943–1948', in M. Kramer and V. Smetana (eds.) *Imposing, Maintaining, and Tearing Open the Iron Curtain: The Cold War and East-Central Europe, 1945–1989*. Lanham, MD: Lexington, pp. 8–26.

Horlemann, R. (2003) *Hong Kong's Transition to Chinese Rule*. London: Routledge Curzon.

Horn, M. (2002) *Britain, France, and the Financing of the First World War*. Montreal: McGill-Queen's UP.

Horne, A. (1989) *Macmillan, 1957–1986*. London: Macmillan.

House of Commons Library, 'UK Trade Statistics' (8 October 2012), Table 9.

Hughes, R.C. (1990) *SDI: A View from Europe*. Washington, DC: NDU Press, pp. 140–1.

Hughes, R.C. (2009) *Harold Wilson's Cold War: The Labour Government and East-West Politics, 1964–1970*. Woodbridge: Boydell.

Hughes, R.G. (2014) *The Postwar Legacy of Appeasement: British Foreign Policy since 1945*. London: Bloomsbury Academic, pp. 71–84.

Hughes, R.G. and Robb, T. (2013) 'Kissinger and the diplomacy of coercive linkage in the "Special Relationship" between the United States and Great Britain, 1969–1977', *DH*, 37/4, pp. 861–905.

Hunt, K. 'Obama: Russia cannot be allowed to redraw borders "at the barrel of a gun"', *MSNBC* (2 February 2015): www.msnbc.com/msnbc/obama-west-cannot-allow-russia-redraw-borders-the-barrel-gun.

Hutner, G. (2009) *What America Read: Taste, Class, and the Novel, 1920–1960*. Chapel Hill, NC: North Carolina UP, Chapters 1–2.

Hynes, C. (2009) *The Year that Never Was: Heath, the Nixon Administration and the Year of Europe*. Dublin: University College Dublin Press.

Iatrides, J.O and Wrigley, L. (eds.) (1995) *Greece at the Crossroads: The Civil War and Its Legacy*. University Park, PA: Pennsylvania UP.

Imlay, T. (2004) '"We have to act quickly or lose the war": A reassessment of Anglo-French strategy during the Phony War, 1939–1940', *EHR*, 119/481, pp. 333–72.

Indyk, M. (1992) 'Watershed in the Middle East', *FA*, 71/1, pp. 70–93.

Insall, T. and Salmon, P. (eds.) (2014) *The Brussels and North Atlantic Treaties, 1947–1949: Documents on British Policy Overseas*, Series I, Volume X. London and New York: Routledge.

IPSOS MORI, 'Iraq, the last pre-war polls' (21 March 2003): www.ipsos-mori.com/newsevents/ca/287/Iraq-The-Last-PreWar-Polls.aspx.

Jackson, D.R. (2007) *Jimmy Carter and the Horn of Africa: Cold War Policy in Ethiopia and Somalia*. Jefferson, NC: McFarland, Chapters 2–3.

References   181

Jackson, J. (2003) *The Fall of France: The Nazi Invasion of 1940*. Oxford: Oxford UP, 2003.

Jacobson, P. 'Gulf war ended too soon, says Thatcher', *Telegraph* (21 February 2001).

James, H. (2013) *International Cooperation and Central Banks*. Waterloo: CIGI, pp. 5–9.

Jankowski, J. (2002) *Nasser's Egypt, Arab Nationalism, and the United Arab Republic*. Boulder, CO: Lynn Reinner, pp. 69–73.

Jeffreys-Jones, R. (1999) *Peace Now!: American Society and the Ending of the Vietnam War*. New Haven, CT: Yale UP.

Johns, A.L. (ed.) (2015) *A Companion to Ronald Reagan*. Malden, MA and Chichester: Wiley Blackwell, Part 1.

Jones, C. (2004) *Britain and the Yemen Civil War, 1962–1965: Ministers, Mercenaries and Mandarins: Foreign Policy and the Limits of Covert Action*. Brighton: Sussex Academic Press.

Jones, M. (2003) 'Anglo-American relations after Suez, the rise and decline of the working group experiment, and the French challenge to NATO, 1957–59', *DS*, 14/1, pp. 49–79.

Jones, P. (1997) *America and the British Labour Party: The Special Relationship at Work*. London: Tauris.

Jones, P. (2005) 'From the Secret Speech to the burial of Stalin: Real and ideal responses to de-Stalinisation', in idem. (ed.) *The Dilemmas of De-Stalinisation: A Social and Cultural History of Reform in the Khrushchev Era*. London and New York: Routledge, pp. 41–63.

Joshi, S. 'British options in Iraq: Capabilities, strategies, and risks', *RUSI* (13 August 2014): www.rusi.org/analysis/commentary/ref: C53EB5BC49555 B/#.VbFjzfnMJWA.

Kacowicz, A.M. (1994) *Peaceful Territorial Change*. Columbia, SC: South Carolina UP, pp. 172–4.

Kalman, L. (2010) *Right Star Rising: A New Politics, 1974–1980*. New York: Norton.

Kaplan, L.S. (2013) *NATO before the Korean War: April 1949-June 1950*. Kent, OH: Kent State UP, Chapters 1–3.

Kaufman, B.I. (2006) *The Carter Years*. New York: Facts on File, pp. 105–6.

Kaufman, J.P. (2002) *NATO and the Former Yugoslavia: Crisis, Conflict, and the Atlantic Alliance*. Lanham, MD: Rowman & Littlefield, pp. 91–136.

Kaufman, V.S. (2001) *Confronting Communism: U.S. and British Policies toward China*. Columbia, MO: Missouri UP, pp. 74–7.

Keller, E.J. (1991) *Revolutionary Ethiopia: From Empire to People's Republic*. Bloomington, IN: Indiana UP.

Kemp-Welch, T. (1996) 'Khrushchev's "Secret Speech" and Polish politics: The Spring of 1956', *Europe-Asia Studies*, 48/2, pp. 181–206.

Kennedy, G.C. (2002) 'Neville Chamberlain and strategic relations with the US during his chancellorship', *DS*, 13/1, pp. 95–120.

Kennedy, P.M. (1987) *The Rise and Fall of the Great Powers: Economic Change and Military Conflict from 1500 to 2000*. New York: Vintage Books, pp. 275–91.

Kennedy-Pipe, C. (1995) *Stalin's Cold War: Soviet Strategies in Europe, 1943 to 1956*. Manchester: Manchester UP, pp. 89–94.

Kent, B. (1989) *The Spoils of War: The Politics, Economics, and Diplomacy of Reparations, 1918–1932*. Oxford: Clarendon Press.

Kettenacker, L. (2009) *Germany 1989: In the Aftermath of the Cold War*. Harlow: Pearson Longman.

182   References

'Khamenei: Opposition to US persists after nuclear deal', *Aljazeera* (18 July 2015): www.aljazeera.com/news/2015/07/iran-nuclear-deal-150718051925210.html.

Kimball, W.F. (ed.) (1984) *Churchill & Roosevelt: The Complete Correspondence*, Volume I. Princeton, NJ: Princeton UP.

Kimball, W.F. (2003) 'The Anglo-American relationship: Still special after all these years', in A. Capet and A. Sy-Wonyu (eds.) *The 'Special Relationship'/La «relations spéciale» entre le Royaume-Uni et les États-Unis*. Rouen: C.É.L.C.L. Rouen, pp. 207–24.

Kipping, M. (1990) *Zwischen Kartellen und Konkurrenz: der Schuman-Plan und die Ursprünge der europäischen Einigung 1944–1952*. Berlin: Duncker & Humbolt.

Kissinger, H. (1979) *White House Years*. Boston: Little, Brown.

Kissinger, H. (1994) *Diplomacy*. New York: Simon & Schuster.

Kitchen, M. (2009) *Rommel's Desert War: Waging World War II in North Africa, 1941–1943*. Cambridge: Cambridge, UP.

Kramer, M. (2010) 'The Soviet Union, the Warsaw Pact, and the Polish Crisis of 1980–1981', in L. Trepanier, S. Domaradzki, and J. Stanke (eds.) *The Solidarity Movement and Perspectives on the Last Decade of the Cold War*. Krakow: Krakow Society for Education, pp. 27–66.

Kramer, M. (2012) 'The demise of the Soviet bloc', in T. Cox (ed.) *Reflections on 1989 in Eastern Europe*. Abingdon: Routledge, pp. 23–4.

Kukutz, I. (2009) *Chronik der Bürgerbewegung Neues Forum 1989–1990*. Berlin: BasisDruck.

Kutler, S.I. (ed.) (1996) *Watergate: The Fall of Richard M. Nixon*. St. James, NY: Brandywine.

Lahey, D.J. (2013) 'The Thatcher government's response to the Soviet invasion of Afghanistan, 1979–1980', *CWH*, 13/1, pp. 21–42.

Laurendeau, L. (1988) *The Politics of NATO Defense Policy: Lessons of the EDC Debate, 1950–1954*. Cambridge, MA: Kennedy School of Government.

Lawrence, M.A. (2005) *Assuming the Burden: Europe and the American Commitment to War in Vietnam*. Berkeley, CA: California UP.

Lawrence, M.A. and Logevall, F. (eds.) (2007) *The First Vietnam War: Colonial Conflict and Cold War Crisis*. Cambridge, MA: Harvard UP.

Lellouche, P. (1983–1984) 'France and the Euromissiles', *FA*, 62/2, pp. 318–34.

Lewkowicz, N. (2010) *The German Question and the International Order, 1943–48*. Basingstoke: Palgrave Macmillan, pp. 82–103.

Library of Congress. (2007) *PEPFAR: From Emergency to Sustainability*. Washington, DC: USGPO.

Lieb, P. (2014) *Unternehmen Overlord: Die Invasion in der Normandie und die befreiung Westeuropas*. München: C.H. Beck.

Liedtke, G. (2016) *Enduring the Whirlwind: The German Army and the Russo-German War, 1941–1943*. Solihull: Helion.

Logevall, F. (2012) *Embers of War: The Fall of an Empire and the Making of America's Vietnam*. New York: Random House, Part 6.

Lothian despatch to Halifax, 29 April 1940, FO 800/324.

Lothian to Halifax, 5, 15 September 1939, Halifax to Lothian, 27 September 1939, FO 800/324.

Louis, W.R. (1977) *Imperialism at Bay, 1941–1945: The United States and the Decolonization of the British Empire*. Oxford: Oxford UP.

References   183

Louis, W.R. (1989) 'The tragedy of the Anglo-Egyptian settlement of 1954', in W.R. Louis and R. Owen (eds.) *Suez 1956: The Crisis and Its Consequences*. Oxford: Clarendon, pp. 43–72.

Louis, W.R. (1990) 'Dulles, Suez, and the British', in R.H. Immerman (ed.) *John Foster Dulles and the Diplomacy of the Cold War*. Princeton, NJ: Princeton UP, pp. 133–58.

Low, M. (1909–1911) *The American People: A Study in National Psychology*, 2 volumes. Boston and New York: Houghton Mifflin.

Lowe, P. (2009) *Contending with Nationalism and Communism: British Policy towards Southeast Asia, 1945–65*. Basingstoke: Palgrave Macmillan.

Lucas, W.S. (1996) *Britain and Suez: The Lion's Last Roar*. Manchester: Manchester UP.

Lundestad, G. (2012) *The Rise and Decline of the American "Empire": Power and Its Limits in Comparative Perspective*. Oxford: Oxford UP.

McCourt, D. (2011) 'The New Labour governments and Britain's role in the world', in O. Daddow and J. Gaskarth (eds.) *British Foreign Policy: The New Labour Years*. Houndmills: Palgrave Macmillan, pp. 31–47.

McDonald, I.S. (1974) *Anglo-American Relations since the Second World War*. London: St. Martin's Press, pp. 181–2.

MacDonald to Borah [American senator], 26 August 1929, MacDonald PRO 30/69/673/1.

McGarr, P.M. (2013) *The Cold War in South Asia: Britain, the United States and the Indian Subcontinent, 1945–1965*. Cambridge: Cambridge UP.

McKay, D. (2007) *The Domino that Stood: The Malayan Emergency, 1948–1960*. Singapore: Cultured Lotus.

McKercher, B.J.C. (1984) *The Second Baldwin Government and the United States, 1924–1929: Attitudes and Diplomacy*. Cambridge: Cambridge UP, pp. 55–76.

McKercher, B.J.C. (1988) 'Wealth, power, and the new international order: Britain and the American challenge in the 1920s', *DH*, 12/4, p. 433 and the relevant notes.

McKercher, B.J.C. (1989) *Esme Howard. A Diplomatic Biography*. Cambridge: Cambridge UP.

McKercher, B.J.C. (1998) 'Towards the post-war settlement: Winston Churchill and the Second Quebec Conference', in D.B. Woolner (ed.) *The Second Quebec Conference Revisited: Waging War, Formulating Peace: Canada, Great Britain, and the United States in 1944–1945*. New York: St. Martin's Press, pp. 17–48.

McKercher, B.J.C. (1999) *Transition of Power: Britain's Loss of Global Pre-eminence to the United States, 1930–1945*. Cambridge: Cambridge UP.

McKercher, B.J.C. (2008) 'The continental commitment and British foreign policy: The field force and the strategy of the national government, 1933–1938', *EHR*, 123/500, pp. 98–131.

McKercher, B.J.C. (2015) 'Prologue: The international order and the new century', in idem. (ed.) *The Handbook of Diplomacy and Statecraft*. London and New York: Routledge, pp. ix–xxviii.

McNamara, R. (2003) *Britain, Nasser and the Balance of Power in the Middle East, 1952–1967*. London: Cass, pp. 238–61.

McNamara, R.S. (1995) *In Retrospect: The Tragedy and Lessons of Vietnam*. New York: Times Books.

Mahan, A.T. (1894) *The Influence of Sea Power upon History, 1660–1783*, 7th edition. Boston: Little, Brown.

184 *References*

Mahan, E.R. (2002) *Kennedy, de Gaulle, and Western Europe*. New York: Palgrave Macmillan.

Mainwaring, S. and Scully, T.R. (eds.) (2010) *Democratic Governance in Latin America*. Stanford, CA: Stanford UP.

Major, J. (2011) *America, Britain and Europe: An Evolving Relationship*. London: RIIA.

Mangold, P. (2006) *The Almost Impossible Ally: Harold Macmillan and Charles de Gaulle*. London: Tauris, pp. 141–212.

Mardell, M. 'Obama's thick red line on Syria', *BBC* (22 August 2013).

Mark, E. (1997) 'The war scare of 1946 and its consequences', *DH*, 21/3, pp. 383–415.

Martin, G. (1995) *Britain and the Origins of Canadian Confederation, 1837–67*. Vancouver: UBC Press.

Matthews, J.P.C. (2006) 'John Foster Dulles and the Suez crisis of 1956', *American Diplomacy*: www.unc.edu/depts/diplomat/item/2006/0709/matt/matthews_suez. html#note11.

May, E.R. (ed.) (1993) *American Cold War Strategy: Interpreting NSC 68*. Boston: Bedford Books, pp. 21–82 (A Report to the National Security Council, 14 April 1950).

Mayle, P.D. (1987) *Eureka Summit: Agreement in Principle and the Big Three at Tehran, 1943*. Newark, DE: Delaware UP.

Maynard, C. (2008) *Out of the Shadow: George H. W. Bush and the End of the Cold War*. College Station, TX: Texas A&M UP.

Meacham, J. 'Bush, Yalta and the blur of hindsight', *NY Times* (15 May 2005).

Medlicott, W.N. (1952) *The Economic Blockade*. London: HMSO, pp. 43–62.

Melady, J. (2006) *Pearson's Prize: Canada and the Suez Crisis*. Toronto: Dundurn.

Memorandum, 'Call by the foreign minister of Pakistan', 17 June 1980, PREM 19/320: http://09b37156ee7ea2a93a5e-6db7349bced3b64202e14ff100a12173. r35.cf1.rackcdn.com/ PREM19/1980/PREM19–0320.pdf.

'Memorandum of conversation', 20 March 1959, *FRUS, 1958–1960, Western Europe*, Volume VII, Part 2, Document 357: http://history.state.gov/historicaldocuments/ frus1958–0v07p2/d35.

'Memorandum of a telephone conversation', 15 August 1958, *FRUS, 1958–60, Lebanon and Jordan*, Volume XI, Document 273: http://history.state.gov/historical documents/frus1958–60v11/d273.

Middlebrook, M. (2009) *Argentine Fight for the Falklands*. Barnsley: Pen & Sword, pp. 1–3.

Miller, E. (2013) *Misalliance: Ngo Dinh Diem, the United States, and the Fate of South Vietnam*. Cambridge, MA: Harvard UP, Chapters 1–2.

Miller, J.R. (1974) *George C. Marshall, Mission to China, 1945–1947*. Athens, GA: Georgia UP.

'Million march against Iraq war', *BBC* (16 February 2003): http://news.bbc.co.uk/2/ hi/uk_news/2765041.stm.

Mingjiang, L. and Kemburi, K.M. (eds.) (2014) *New Dynamics in US-China Relations: Contending for the Asia Pacific*. Abingdon: Routledge.

Miscamble, W.D. (2007) *From Roosevelt to Truman: Potsdam, Hiroshima, and the Cold War*. Cambridge: Cambridge UP.

Mitchell, B.R. (1990) *British Historical Statistics*. Cambridge: Cambridge UP, pp. 284, 368.

References   185

Mitter, R. (2013) *Forgotten Ally: China's World War II, 1937–1945*. Boston: Houghton Mifflin Harcourt.

Moore, C. (2013) *Margaret Thatcher: The Authorized Biography: From Grantham to the Falklands*. New York: Knopf, Parts 1–2.

Moore, R.J. (1983) *Escape from Empire: The Attlee Government and the Indian Problem*. Oxford: Clarendon.

Morison, E.E. and Blum, J.M. (eds.) (1952) *The Letters of Theodore Roosevelt*, Volume 6. Cambridge, MA: Harvard UP, p. 1159 (Roosevelt to Lee, 7 August 1908).

Muldoon, A. (2009) *Empire, Politics, and the Creation of the 1935 India Act: Last Act of the Raj*. Farnham: Ashgate.

'National Security Directive 45' (20 August 1990): http://nsarchive.gwu.edu/NSAEBB/NSAEBB39/document2.pdf.

NATO, 'Peace support operations in Bosnia and Herzegovina' (11 November 2014): www.nato.int/cps/en/natolive/topics_52122.htm.

Nau, H.R. (2008) 'Iraq and previous transatlantic crises: Divided by threat, not institutions or values', in J. Anderson, G.J. Ikenberry, and T. Riise (eds.) *The End of the West?: Crisis and Change in the Atlantic Order*. Ithaca, NY: Cornell UP, pp. 82–111.

Neustadt, R.F. (1999) *Report to JFK: The Skybolt Crisis in Perspective*. Ithaca, NY: Cornell UP.

Neville, P. (2006) *Hitler and Appeasement: The British Attempt to Prevent the Second World War*. New York: Continuum, pp. 192–7.

Newhouse, J. (1989) *Cold Dawn: The Story of SALT*. Washington, DC: Pergamon-Brassey's.

Newhouse, J. (1999) 'De Gaulle and the Anglo-Saxons', in D. Brinkley and R.T. Griffith (eds.) *John F. Kennedy and Europe*. Baton Rouge, LA: Louisiana State UP.

Newman, K. (2007) *Macmillan, Khrushchev and the Berlin Crisis, 1958-1960*. London and New York: Routledge.

Newton, S. (2012) 'The Sterling devaluation of 1967, the International economy and post-war social democracy', *EHR*, CXXV/515, pp. 912–45.

Nichols, D.A. (2011) *Eisenhower 1956: The President's Year of Crisis: Suez and the Brink of War*. New York: Simon and Schuster.

Nixon, R.M. (1967) 'Asia after Vietnam', *FA*, 46/1, pp. 111–25.

Nong, N.D. (2010) *Churchill, Eden and Indo-China, 1951–1955*. New York: Anthem.

NSA, 'Iraq and weapons of mass destruction' (February 2004): http://nsarchive.gwu.edu/ NSAEBB/NSAEBB80/.

NSA, 'May 4, 1982 – Argentines sink the British HMS Sheffield. 20 British men die': http://nsarchive.gwu.edu/NSAEBB/NSAEBB374/.

NSA, 'Shaking hands with Saddam Hussein: The U.S. tilts toward Iraq, 1980–1984' (25 February 2003): http://nsarchive.gwu.edu/NSAEBB/NSAEBB82/.

O'Connor, R.G. (1971) *Diplomacy for Victory: FDR and Unconditional Surrender*. New York: Norton.

O'Hara, V.P. (2015) *Torch: North Africa and the Allied Path to Victory*. Annapolis, MD: Naval Institute Press.

O'Sullivan, J. (2006) *The President, the Pope, and the Prime Minister: Three Who Changed the World*. Lanham, MD: Regnery.

Obama, Barack and Cameron, David, 'Not just special, but an essential relationship', *The Times* (24 May 2011): www.thetimes.co.uk/tto/opinion/columnists/article3033133.ece.

186 References

Osborne, E.W. (2004) *Britain's Economic Blockade of Germany, 1914–1919*. London and New York: Cass.

Ottolenghi, M. (2004) 'Harry Truman's recognition of Israel', *HJ*, 47/4, pp. 963–88.

Owen, D. (1995) *Balkan Odyssey*. New York: Harcourt Brace, pp. 15–16.

Owen, D. (2013) *Bosnia-Herzegovina: The Vance/Owen Peace Plan*. Liverpool: Liverpool UP.

Pagedas, C.A. (2000) *Anglo-American Strategic Relations and the French Problem, 1960–1963: A Troubled Partnership*. London: Cass, Chapters 5–6.

Painter, D. (2012) 'Oil and the American century', *JAH*, 99/1, pp. 28–30.

Panofsky, W.K.H. (1979) *Arms Control and SALT II*. Seattle, WA: Washington UP.

Papp, D.S. (1996) 'The Gulf War coalition: The politics and economics of a most unusual alliance', in W. Head and E.H. Tilford (eds.) *The Eagle in the Desert: Looking Back on U.S. Involvement in the Persian Gulf War*. Westport, CT: Praeger.

Parker, G. 'David Cameron urges NATO to deter Russian aggression', *Financial Times* (1 August 2014).

Parsons, M. (2012) 'New directions in British foreign policy?', in M. McNaught (ed.) *Reflections on Conservative Politics in the United Kingdom and the United States: Still Soul Mates?* Lanham, MD: Lexington. pp. 57–8.

Patman, R.G. (1993) 'Soviet-Ethiopian relations: The horn of dilemma', in Margot Light (ed.) *Troubled Friendships: Moscow's Third World Ventures*. London: Tauris, pp. 110–12.

Perkins, B. (1968) *The Great Rapprochement: England and the United States, 1895–1914*. New York: Atheneum.

Persson, M. (1998) *Great Britain, the United States, and the Security of the Middle East: The Formation of the Baghdad Pact*. Lund: Lund UP.

Petersen, T.T. (2008) 'Post-Suez consequences: Anglo-American relations in the Middle East from Eisenhower to Nixon', in S.C. Smith (ed.) *Reassessing Suez 1956: New Perspectives on the Crisis and Its Aftermath*. Aldershot and Burlington, VT: Ashgate, pp. 215–26.

Petersen, T.T. (2015) *Anglo-American Policy toward the Persian Gulf, 1978–1985: Power, Influence and Restraint*. Brighton: Sussex Academic Press.

Pfiffner, J.P. (2011) 'Decision making in the Obama White House', *PSQ*, 41/2, pp. 257–60.

Phelps, S. (2010) *The Tizard Mission: The Top-Secret Operation that Changed the Course of World War II*. Yardley, PA: Westholme.

Phillips, D.L. (2012) *Liberating Kosovo: Coercive Diplomacy and U.S. Intervention*. Cambridge, MA: MIT Press.

Phythian, M. (2008) 'The British road to war: Decisionmaking, intelligence, and the case for war in Iraq', in J.P. Pfiffner and M. Phythian (eds.) *Intelligence and National Security Policymaking on Iraq: British and American Perspectives*. College Station, TX: Texas A&M UP, pp. 93–4.

Plokhy, S. (2014) *The Last Empire: The Final Days of the Soviet Union*. New York: Basic Books.

Poggiolini, L. (2012) 'Thatcher's double-track road to the end of the Cold War: The irreconcilability of liberalization and preservation', in F. Bozo, Marie-Pierre Rey, N. Piers Ludlow and Bernd Rother (eds.) *Visions of the End of the Cold War in Europe, 1945–1990*. New York, Oxford: Berghahn, pp. 271–3.

Prados, J. (2011) *How the Cold War Ended: Debating and Doing History*. Washington, DC: Potomac, pp. 163–4.

References   187

Prange, G.W., Goldstein, D.M. and Dillon, K.V. (1982) *Miracle at Midway*. New York: McGraw-Hill.

'President Kennedy's news conference, April 24, 1963': www.mtholyoke.edu/ acad/ intrel/pentagon2/ps31.htm.

'The President's meetings with President Gorbachev' (2–3 December 1989): http:// nsarchive.gwu.edu/NSAEBB/NSAEBB298/ Document%209.pdf.

'The President's news conference of April 7, 1954': http://coursesa.matrix.msu. edu/~hst 306/documents/domino.html.

'Press briefing by National Security Advisor Sandy Berger' (23 October 1997): http:// www.presidency.ucsb.edu/ws/?pid=48615.

'Press conference after Camp David talks' (15 November 1986): www.margaret thatcher. org/document/106514.

Price, J. (2001) 'A just peace: The 1951 San Francisco Peace Treaty in historical perspective', Working Paper No. 78. La Jolla, CA: JPRI.

'Proclamation defining terms for Japanese surrender', *State Department Bulletin*, 33/318 (29 July 1945).

Quandt, W.B. (1986) *Camp David: Peacemaking and Politics*. Washington, DC: Brookings.

Quandt, W.P. (2001) *Peace Process: American Diplomacy and the Arab-Israeli Conflict Since 1967*, revised edition. Washington, DC: Brookings; Berkeley, CA: California UP, pp. 98–173.

Queshi, L.Z. (2009) *Nixon, Kissinger, and Allende: U.S. Involvement in the 1973 Coup in Chile*. Lanham, MD: Lexington.

Rahman, Z.A., A.S. Ghazali, R. Fauzi and N.H. Yaacob (2013) 'Britain, the United Nations and the Iranian crisis of 1946', *Middle-East Journal of Scientific Research*, 18/11, pp. 1544–56.

Ramos, J.M. (2013) *Changing Norms through Actions: The Evolution of Sovereignty*. New York: Oxford UP.

Rawnsley, G. (2009) '"The great movement to resist America and assist Korea": How Beijing sold the Korean war', *Media, War and Conflict*, 2/3, pp. 285–315.

'Reagan telegram to Thatcher, 24 October 1983': www.margaretthatcher.org/docu ment/ 131574.

Reagan, R. (1990) *An American Life*. New York: Simon and Schuster.

'Record of a meeting between the Prime Minister and Chairman Deng Xiaoping' (19 December 1984): www.slideshare.net/HKDF/841219–1600-mt-deng-memcon-prem19–1502-f41–3108199?related=2.

'Record of conversation between Gorbachev and Thatcher' (6 April 1989): http:// nsarchive. gwu.edu/NSAEBB/NSAEBB422/docs/Doc%205%201989–04–06%20 Gorbahcev-Thatcher%20mem con.pdf.

'Record of conversation between Mikhail Gorbachev and Margaret Thatcher' (23 September 1989): http://nsarchive.gwu.edu/NSAEBB/NSAEBB422/docs/Doc%207% 201989–09–23%20Gorbachev% 20Thatcher.pdf.

Rees, W. (1989) 'The 1957 Sandys White Paper: New priorities in British defence policy?', *JSS*, 12/2, pp. 215–29.

Reitan, E.A. (2003) *The Thatcher Revolution: Margaret Thatcher, John Major, Tony Blair, and the Transformation of Modern Britain, 1979–2001*. Lanham, MD and Oxford: Rowman & Littlefield, pp. 42–3. (On the 'evil empire', see Document 21).

188 References

'Remarks by the President at the Democratic National Convention' (6 September 2012): www.whitehouse.gov/the-press-office/2012/09/07/remarks-president-democratic-national-convention.

'Remarks on accepting a bust of Winston Churchill and an exchange with reporters' (16 July 1991): www.presidency.ucsb.edu/ws/?pid=73620.

Reyn, S. (2010) *Atlantis Lost: The American Experience with De Gaulle, 1958–1969*. Amsterdam: Amsterdam UP.

Reynolds, D. (1981) *The Creation of the Anglo-American Alliance, 1937–41: A Study in Competitive Co-operation*. London: Europa, pp. 85–7, especially n134.

Reynolds, D. (1993) 'Churchill in 1940: The worst and finest hour', in R.B. Blake and W.R. Louis (eds.) *Churchill*. Oxford: Clarendon Press, pp. 250–1.

Reynolds, D. (1995) *Rich Relations: The American Occupation of Britain, 1942–1945*. New York: Random House.

Reynolds, D. (2003) 'Churchill's war memoirs and the invention of the "Special Relationship"', in A. Capet and A. Sy-Wonyu (eds.) *The 'Special Relationship'/ La «relations spéciale» entre le Royaume-Uni et les États-Unis*. Rouen: C.É.L.C.L Rouen.

Reynolds, D. (2013) 'A British perspective on Cold War origins', in M.R. Fitzgerald and A. Packwoods (eds.) *Out of the Cold: The Cold War and Its Legacy*. New York: Bloomsbury.

Ricks, T.E. "Rumsfeld signals shift to Pacific in overhaul of defense thinking," *Guardian Weekly* (19 March–4 April 2001).

Riedel, B.O. (2010) 'The Clinton Administration': http://iranprimer.usip.org/resource /clinton-administration.

Rigby, R. (2012) *Allied Master Strategists: The Combined Chiefs of Staff in World War II*. Annapolis, MD: Naval Institute Press.

Robb, T. (2010) 'Henry Kissinger, Great Britain and the "Year of Europe": The "Tangled Skein"', *Contemporary British History*, 24/3, pp. 297–318.

Roberts, G. (1999) 'Ideology, calculation, and improvisation: Spheres of influence and Soviet foreign policy 1939–1945', *Review of International Studies*, 25/4, pp. 671–3.

Roll, D. (2013) *The Hopkins Touch: Harry Hopkins and the Forging of the Alliance to Defeat Hitler*. New York: Oxford UP, pp. 172–5.

Roosevelt, E. (1954) *India and the Awakening East*. London: Hutchinson.

Ruane, K. (2002) 'Agonizing reappraisals: Anthony Eden, John Foster Dulles and the crisis of European defence, 1953–54', *DS*, 13/4, pp. 151–85.

Rust, W.J. (2014) *So Much to Lose: John F. Kennedy and American Policy in Laos*. Lexington, KY: Kentucky UP.

Saltoun-Ebin, J. (ed.) (2010) *The Reagan Files: The Untold Story of Reagan's Top-Secret Efforts to Win the Cold War*. Seattle, WA: CreateSpace (NSC Meeting, 22 December 1981).

Sarotte, M.E. (2014) *The Collapse: The Accidental Opening of the Berlin Wall*. New York: Basic Books.

Saxonberg, S. (2001) *The Fall: A Comparative Study of the End of Communism in Czechoslovakia, East Germany, Hungary, and Poland*. Amsterdam: Harwood.

Schaeffer, H.B. (2009) *The Limits of Influence: America's Role in Kashmir*. Washington, DC: Brookings, pp. 9–35.

Schake, K.N. (2004) 'NATO strategy and the German-American relationship', in D. Junker, P. Gassert, W. Mausbach and D.B. Morris (eds.) *The United States and Germany in the Era of the Cold War, 1945–1990*, Volume II. New York: Cambridge UP, pp. 134–5.

References   189

Schneer, J. (2010) *The Balfour Declaration: The Origins of the Arab-Israeli Conflict.* New York: Bloomsbury.

Schoen, D.E. and Kaylan, M. (2014) *The Russia-China Axis: The New Cold War and America's Crisis of Leadership.* New York: Encounter.

Schwartz, D.N. (1993) *NATO's Nuclear Dilemmas.* Washington, DC: Brookings, pp. 96–103.

Self, R. (2006) *Neville Chamberlain: A Biography.* Aldershot: Ashgate, pp. 418–39.

Seng, T.S. (2014) 'Engaging China and the United States: Perils and prospects for ASEAN diplomacy in the age of rebalancing', in L. Mingjiang and K.M. Kemburi (eds.) *New Dynamics in US-China Relations: Contending for the Asia Pacific.* Abingdon: Routledge, pp. 67–84.

Sharp, P. (1997) *Thatcher's Diplomacy: The Revival of British Foreign Policy.* Houndmills: Macmillan, Chapters 1–2.

Shih, C.-Y. and Huang, C.-C. (2016) 'The identity and international role of China: Relational grand strategy', in S. Harnisch, S. Bersick and J.-C. Gottwald (eds.) *China's International Roles: Challenging or Supporting International Order?* New York and Abingdon: Routledge.

Shlaim, A. (1997) 'The protocol of Sèvres, 1956: Anatomy of a war plot', *IA*, 73/3, pp. 509–30.

Siniver, A. (2015) 'Abba Eban and Development of American-Israeli relations, 1950–1959', *DS*, 26/1, pp. 65–83.

'Sir Esme Howard's retirement', *Times* (21 February 1930).

Sloan, J.W. (2004) 'The burden of the Reagan legacy on the Bush presidency', in R. Himelfarb and R. Perotti (eds.) *Principle Over Politics? The Domestic Policy of the George H.W. Bush Presidency.* Westport, CT: Greenwood, pp. 105–18.

Smith, G. (1989) *Battles of the Falklands War.* London: Allan.

Smith, R., Salmon, P. and Twigge, S. (eds.) (2012) *The Brussels and North Atlantic Treaties, 1947–1949: Documents on British Policy Overseas, Series III, Volume 8: The Invasion of Afghanistan and UK-Soviet Relations, 1979–1982.* Abingdon: Routledge (Appendix: JIC(80)(N)4, 'Soviet Intervention in Afghanistan – An Interim Assessment', 10 January 1980).

Smith, R., Salmon, P. and Twigge, S. (eds.) (2014) *The Brussels and North Atlantic Treaties, 1947–1949: Documents on British Policy Overseas, Series III, Volume II.* Abingdon: Routledge.

Søndergaard, R.S. (2015) 'Bill Clinton's "Democratic Enlargement" and the securitisation of democracy promotion', *DS*, 26/3, pp. 534–51.

'Soviet transcript of the Malta Summit' (2–3 December 1989): http://nsarchive.gwu.edu/NSAEBB/NSAEBB298/Document%2010.pdf.

Spence, J. (1990) 'The superpowers in Southern Africa: From competition to condominium?', in M. Cox (ed.) *Beyond the Cold War: Superpowers at the Crossroads.* Lanham, MD: UP America, pp. 225–8.

Spohr, K. (2015) 'NATO's nuclear politics and the Schmidt-Carter rift', in L. Nuti, F. Bozo, M.-P. Rey and B. Rother (eds.) *The Euromissile Crisis and the End of the Cold War.* Washington, DC: Woodrow Wilson Center.

Stacey, C.P. (1970) *Arms, Men and Governments: The War Policies of Canada, 1939–1945.* Ottawa: Queen's Printer, pp. 310–14.

Steiner, Z.S. (2005) *The Lights that Failed: European International History 1919–1933.* Oxford, NY: Oxford UP, Part II.

Steiner, Z.S. (2011) *The Triumph of the Dark: European International History, 1933–1939.* Oxford, NY: Oxford UP, pp. 765–866.

190   References

Stimson diary, 17 January 1930, with Stimson memorandum, 'Conference with the Prime Minister of Great Britain', 17 January 1930, both Stimson 12.

Stivers, W. (1982) *Supremacy and Oil: Iraq, Turkey, and the Anglo-American World Order, 1918–1930*. Ithaca, NY: Cornell UP.

Stoddart, K. (2012) *Losing an Empire and Finding a Role: Britain, the USA, NATO and Nuclear Weapons, 1964–70*. Basingstoke: Palgrave Macmillan, Chapters 5–8.

Stoddart, K. (2015) 'Creating the "Seamless Robe of Deterrence": Great Britain's role in NATO's INF debate', in L. Nuti, F. Bozo, M.-P. Rey and B. Rother (eds.) *The Euromissile Crisis and the End of the Cold War*. Washington, DC: Woodrow Wilson Center, pp. 203–25.

Stoler, M.A. (2000) *Allies and Adversaries: The Joint Chiefs of Staff, the Grand Alliance, and U.S. Strategy in World War II*. Chapel Hill, NC: North Carolina UP, pp. 115–21.

Strachan, H. (2001) *The First World War*, Volume I. Oxford, NY: Oxford UP.

Sudworth, J. 'Osborne China visit: Business deal cuts both ways', *BBC* (15 October 2013): www.bbc.com/news/business-24535722.

Summ, G.H. and Kelly, T. (eds.) (1988) *The Good Neighbors: America, Panama, and the 1977 Canal Treaties*. Athens, OH: Ohio University Center for International Studies.

'Syria crisis: Cameron loses Commons vote on Syria action', *BBC* (30 August 2013).

Takemae, E. (2002) *Inside GHQ: The Allied Occupation of Japan and Its Legacy*. New York: Continuum.

Talbot, I. (2013) *The Independence of India and Pakistan: New Approaches and Reflections*. Karachi: Oxford UP.

Taw, J.M. (1996) *Operation Just Cause: Lessons for Operations other than War*. Santa Monica, CA: Rand.

Taylor, R. (2004) 'The rise and fall of the social contract', in A. Seldon and K. Hickson (eds.) *New Labour, Old Labour: The Blair, Wilson, and Callaghan Governments*. London and New York: Routledge, pp. 55–104.

Thatcher, 'Speech at banquet given by Pakistan President' (8 October 1981): www.margaretthatcher.org/document/104716.

Thatcher, 'Speech at dinner given by Polish Government' (3 November 1988): www.margaretthatcher.org/document/107368.

Thatcher, 'Speech at Gdansk Town Hall' (4 November 1988): www.margaretthatcher.org/document/107370.

Thatcher Foundation, 'The Polish crisis of 1981–82': www.margaretthatcher.org/archive/us-reagan%20%28Poland%29.asp.

Thatcher, M. (1993) *The Downing Street Years*. New York and London: Harper Collins, p. 331.

Thomas, I.Q.R. (1997) *The Promise of Alliance: NATO and the Political Imagination*. Lanham, MD: Rowman & Littlefield.

Thomas, M. (2014) *Fight or Flight: Britain, France, and their Roads from Empire*. Oxford: Oxford UP, pp. 164–89.

Thompson, L.M. (2001) *A History of South Africa*. New Haven, CT: Yale UP, pp. 232–3.

Thorne, C. (1978) *Allies of a Kind: The United States, Britain and the War against Japan, 1941–1945*. London: Hamish Hamilton.

Tilchin, W.N. and Neu, C.E. (eds.) (2006) *Artists of Power: Theodore Roosevelt, Woodrow Wilson, and Their Enduring Impact on U.S. Foreign Policy*. Westport, CT: Praeger.

References 191

Tohmatsu, H. and Willmott, H.P. (2004) *A Gathering Darkness: The Coming of War to the Far East and the Pacific, 1921–1942*. Lanham, MD: SR Books, Chapters 3–4.

Tomlinson, J. (2004) 'Economic policy', in A. Seldon and K. Hickson (eds.) *New Labour, Old Labour: The Blair, Wilson, and Callaghan Governments*. London and New York: Routledge, pp. 55–69.

Tooze, A. (2014) *The Deluge: The Great War and the Remaking of Global Order 1916–1931*. London: Allen Lane.

'Transcript of meeting between Iraqi President, Saddam Hussein and U.S. Ambassador to Iraq, April Glaspie – July 25, 1990': www.globalresearch.ca/gulf-war-docu ments-meeting-between-saddam-hussein-and-ambassador-to-iraq-april-glaspie/ 31145.

Trask, D.F. (1993) *The AEF and Coalition Warmaking, 1917–1918*. Lawrence, KS: Kansas UP.

Troen, S.I. (1990) 'The Sinai campaign as a "War of No Alternative": Ben-Gurion's view of the Israel-Egyptian conflict', in S.I. Troen and M. Schemesh (eds.) *The Suez-Sinai Crisis, 1956: Retrospective and Reappraisal*. New York: Columbia UP, pp. 148–64.

Truman, H.S. (1955) *Year of Decisions*. Garden City, NJ: Doubleday, pp. 416.

Tucker, N.B. (1983) *Patterns in the Dust: Chinese-American Relations and the Recognition Controversy, 1949–1950*. New York: Columbia UP.

Tucker, N.B. (1990) 'Afterword: Vietnam, the never-ending war', in E.J. Errington and B.J.C. McKercher (eds.) *The Vietnam War as History*. New York: Praeger, pp. 177–90.

Tudda, C. (2012) *A Cold War Turning Point: Nixon and China, 1969–1972*. Baton Rouge, LA: Louisiana State UP.

'TV interview for BBC' (17 December 1984): www.margaretthatcher.org/document/ 105592.

'TV interview for Soviet television' (31 March 1988): www.margaretthatcher.org/ document/106604.

'UN Security Council. (1982) 'Resolutions concerning the Falkland Islands (Islas Malvinas), *International Legal Materials*, 21/3, pp. 679–81.

Vaïsse, M. (1998) *La grandeur: Politique étrangère du général de Gaulle, 1958–1969*. Paris: Fayard.

Vaitiolingam, R. (2009) *Recession Britain*. London: Economic and Social Council.

Verbeek, B. (2003) *Decision Making in Great Britain during the Suez Crisis*. Aldershot and Burlington, VT: Ashgate.

Vinen, R. (2009) *Thatcher's Britain: The Politics and Social Upheaval of the 1980s*. New York: Simon & Schuster.

Virden, J. (1996) *Good-Bye Piccadilly: British War Brides in America*. Urbana, IL: Illinois UP.

Walker, T.W. and Wade, C.J. (2011) *Nicaragua: Living in the Shadow of the Eagle*. Boulder, CO: Westview, pp. 25–62.

Wall, S. (2013) *The Official History of Britain and the European Community*, Volume II. Routledge, pp. 492–4.

Wappshot, N. (2007) *Ronald Reagan and Margaret Thatcher: A Political Marriage*. New York: Sentinel, pp. 160–85.

Warner, G. (1996) 'From ally to enemy: Britain's relations with the Soviet Union, 1941–1948', in M.L. Dockrill and B.J.C. McKercher (eds.) *Diplomacy and World Power: Studies in British Foreign Policy, 1890–1950*. Cambridge: Cambridge UP, pp. 237–8.

192 References

Watababe, S. (2015) 'The 1950 Commonwealth foreign ministers' meeting and the international aid programme for Asia', in S. Akita, G. Krozewski, and S. Watanabe (eds.) *The Transformation of the International Order of Asia: Decolonization, the Cold War, and the Colombo Plan*. Milton Park: Routledge, pp. 15–33.

Waters, B. (1995) *The Empire Fractures: Anglo-Australian Conflict in the 1940's*. Melbourne: Australian Scholarly Publications.

Watry, D.M. (2014) *Diplomacy at the Brink: Eisenhower, Churchill, and Eden in the Cold War*. Baton Rouge, LA: Louisiana State UP, pp. 111–37.

Watson, D. (2002) 'Molotov, the making of the Grand Alliance and the Second Front 1939–1942', *Europe-Asia Studies*, 54/1, pp. 51–85.

Watson, W. (2011) 'Trust but verify: Reagan, Gorbachev, and the INF Treaty', *Hilltop Review*, 5/1: http://scholarworks.wmich.edu/cgi/viewcontent.cgi?article=104 5&context=hilltop review.

Watt, D.C. (1989) *How War Came: The Immediate Origins of the Second World War, 1938–1939*. London: Heinemann.

Watt, D.C. (2003) 'Commentary', in G. Staerck and M.D. Kandiah (eds.) *Anglo-German Relations and German Unification*. London: Institute of Contemporary British History, pp. 59–60.

Wedgwood, R. (2006) 'The multinational action in Iraq and international law', in R. Thakur and W.P.S. Sidhu (eds.) *The Iraq Crisis and World Order: Structural, Institutional and Normative Challenges*. Tokyo, NY: UNUP, p. 416.

Weigold, A. (2008) *Churchill, Roosevelt, and India: Propaganda during World War II*. New York: Routledge.

Weisman, J. and Hirschfeld, J. 'Republican lawmakers vow fight to derail nuclear deal', *NY Times* (14 July 2015): www.nytimes.com/2015/07/15/world/middleeast/congress-iran-nuclear-deal.html.

Whisler, T.R. (1999) *The British Motor Industry, 1945–94: A Case Study in Industrial Decline*. Oxford: Oxford UP, pp. 127–9.

White House memorandum, 'Meeting with Eduard Shevardnadze, foreign minister of the Soviet Union' (21 September 1989): http://nsarchive.gwu.edu/NSAEBB/NSAEBB481/docs/Document %208.pdf.

White, L. (2015) *Unpopular Sovereignty: Rhodesian Independence and African Decolonization*. Chicago, IL: Chicago UP, Chapters 10–11.

White, N. (1999) 'Macmillan, Kennedy and the Key West meeting: Its significance for the Laotian Civil War and Anglo-American relations', *Civil War*, 2/2, pp. 35–55.

Wilde, O. (1956) 'Impressions of America', in C. Neider (ed.) *Essays of the Masters*. New York: Rinehart, pp. 421–7.

Williamson, R.D. (2012) *First Steps toward Détente: American Diplomacy in the Berlin Crisis, 1958–1963*. Lanham, MD: Lexington, pp. 73–108.

Wilson, T.A. (1991) *First Summit: Roosevelt and Churchill at Placentia Bay, 1941*. Lawrence, KS: Kansas UP.

Wilson, W. (1885) *Congressional Government: A Study in American Politics*. Boston: Houghton Mifflin.

Woodward, D.R. (1971) 'The origins and intent of David Lloyd George's January 5 war aims speech', *Historian*, 34/1, pp. 22–39.

Woolner, D.B. (ed.) (1998) *The Second Quebec Conference Revisited: Waging War, Formulating Peace: Canada, Great Britain, and the United States in 1944–1945*. New York: St. Martin's Press.

References 193

Woolner, D.B. (2013) 'An American perspective on Cold War origins', in M.R. Fitzgerald and A. Packwoods (eds.) *Out of the Cold: The Cold War and Its Legacy*. New York: Bloomsbury, pp. 24–30.

'World proven crude oil reserves by country, 1980–2004': www.opec.org/library/Annual%20Statistical%20Bulletin/interactive/2004/FileZ/XL/T33.HTM.

Wyatt, D. (2014) *When America Turned: Reckoning with 1968*. Amherst, MA: Massachusetts UP.

Wynia, G.W. (1986) *Argentina: Illusions and Realities*. New York: Holmes & Meier (Transcript of a conversation between General Galtieri and President Reagan (1 April 1982)).

'X' (1947) 'The sources of Soviet conduct', *FA*, 25/4, pp. 566–82.

Xiang, X. (1995) *Recasting the Imperial Far East: Britain and America in China, 1945–1950*. Armonk, NY: M.E. Sharpe.

Xuefeng, S. (2006) 'The efficiency of China's policy towards the United States', *Chinese Journal of International Politics*, 1/1, p. 68.

Yetiv, S.A. (1995) *America and the Persian Gulf: The Third Party Dimension in World Politics*. Westport, CT: Praeger.

Young, J.W. (1996) 'The Heath government and British entry into the European community', in S. Ball and A. Seldon (eds.) *The Heath Government 1970–1974*. Reading, MA: Longman, pp. 259–84.

Young, J.W. (2011) 'Ambassador David Bruce and LBJ's War: Vietnam viewed from London', *DS*, 22/1, pp. 81–100.

Young, J.W. and Kent, J. (2004) *International Relations since 1945: A Global History*. Oxford: Oxford UP.

Zanchetta, B. (2014) *The Transformation of American International Power in the 1970s*. New York: Cambridge UP.

Zubok, V.M. (1993) 'Khrushchev and the Berlin Crisis (1958–1962)', CWIHP Working Paper, pp. 6–8: www.wilsoncenter.org/ sites/default/files/ACFB7D.pdf.

Zubok, V.M. (2007) *A Failed Empire: The Soviet Union in the Cold War from Stalin to Gorbachev*. Chapel Hill, NC: North Carolina UP, pp. 62–75.

Zuehlke, M. (2012) *Tragedy at Dieppe: Operation Jubilee, August 19, 1942*. Vancouver: Douglas & McIntyre.

Index

Abyssinia/Ethiopia 90, 105
Acheson, Dean 47, 51, 53, 67, 75, 131
Adenauer, Konrad 50, 72, 73–4
Afghanistan 8, 89–90, 98, 109, 133, 134; allied invasion 119, 121; American policy 119–20, 121; *mujahidin* 94, 101, 106, 120, 121, 134; NATO 119, 123; Russian invasion 90–1, 93–4, 100, 101, 104, 119, 133, 134, 135; Taliban 119; Thatcher policy 93–4; and withdrawal 123
Africa 7, 8, 15, 88, 89–90, 93, 100, 101, 105, 121, 122, 131, 133, 135
Al Qaeda 119
al-Said, Nuri 61, 63, 66
Anaya, Admiral Jorge 97
anti-Americanism 80–1, 83, 90, 107, 108, 124, 133
ANZUS Pact (August 1951) 52
appeasement, British 22, 23, 106; the Falklands War 99; Suez Crisis (1956) 62, 131
Argentina 14, 25; the Falklands War 97–100; Reagan-Thatcher relationship 99–100
Armas, Carlo Castillo 68
ASEAN 121, 124
Atlantic Charter: August 1941 30–1, 130; proposed transformation (1973) 85
atomic bomb 33, 36, 42, 130, 131; Anglo-American co-operation 35, 76; Iran-Azerbaijan crisis (1946) 45, 130; successful American test (July 1945) 42; successful Russian test (August 1949) 57, 59; use against Japan (August) 1945 44
Attlee, Clement 42, 43–4, 45, 55, 65; decolonisation 55, 57–8, 65, 131; Truman 44, 45, 46, 49, 131

Australia 52, 60, 80, 124; Britain 52; United States 52, 8–81, 82, 124
Austria 17, 42, 110
'axis of evil' 120

Baghdad Pact 61, 62, 66
Baker, James 110, 111, 112
Baldwin, Stanley 21, 22, 57
Balkans 8, 17, 27–8, 46, 108; crisis (1992–1998) 115–18
Baltic States 33, 110, 125
Baruch, Bernard 41
Benelux powers 49, 50, 70; Belgium 20, 24, 70
Berlin 42, 45, 50, 72–3, 75, 78; Allied Control Council 42; Berlin Wall 72–3, 109, 132; blockade and airlift (1948–1949) 49–51, 131
Bevin, Ernest 43–4, 48, 49, 55, 65, 131; Brussels Treaty (March 1948) 50–1, 131; NATO 50–1, 131; Truman 44, 49, 131; Western European defence 50–1
bin Laden, Osama 119, 120, 129
Blair, Tony 8, 118, 120, 121, 123, 134–5; Afghanistan 118–21, 134–5; American policy 119–20, 121; 'Doctrine of the International Community' 118, 119; 'war on terror' 119–21; WMD 120, 121
Brandt, Willi 84, 85
Brezhnev, Leonid 84, 89–90, 100, 133; Angola 89–90, 100, 133; SALT II 89, 133; SS-20 MIRVs 94, 96
Brezhnev Doctrine (1968) 84, 90, 109
British Empire 14, 15, 25, 31, 36, 130; Cold War 46, 57; decolonisation 7, 31, 36, 43, 52, 57–8, 77, 122, 130, 131; Imperial defence 14, 15, 27; North America 13–14, 15

Index 195

Brown, Gordon 9, 123; Bush, G.W. 123; Iraq 123; missile collaboration 123; Obama 123–4

Brussels Treaty (March 1948) 50–1, 71, 131

Brzezinski, Zbigniew 90, 91

Bundy, McGeorge 79–80, 81

Burma 29, 52, 57, 60, 78, 129

Bush, George H.W. 8, 106, 108, 109, 110–11, 112–13, 115, 119, 134; balance 109, 110, 114, 115, 120, 125; Central and Eastern Europe 109, 110, 134; Germany 109, 111, 134; Gorbachev 108, 109, 110, 111–12, 134; Gulf War (1990–1991) 112–15, 134; neoconservatives 114–15; new world order (January 1991) 115, 134; Panama 112; Reagan 108, 109; Russia 109, 110–11, 135; Thatcher 108–9, 110–11

Bush, George W. 8, 119; Afghanistan 118–19, 134; 'axis of evil' 120; Blair 119, 120, 121, 134–5; East Asia 119; Europe 119; Iraq 120, 121; President's Emergency Plan for AIDS Relief 121; unilateralism 108, 119, 134, 135; 'war on terror' 119–21, 120; WMD 120, 121

Byrnes, James 43–4

Callaghan, James 87, 88, 90, 92, 93; Carter 89, 90

Cambodia 54, 55, 78, 80, 131

Cameron, David 9, 123; Afghanistan 123, 134; Iraq 24; Libya 124–15; 'Not just special, but an essential relationship' 123; Obama 123–4, 124–5

Canada 13, 14, 19, 33, 42, 46, 48, 60, 63; CSCE 81; NATO 51; United States 15, 26, 48, 51, 80–1

Carter, Jimmy 88, 92, 107, 113, 133; Afghanistan 90–1, 93; Callaghan 89, 90; Camp David Accords (September 1978) 89; Iran 90; moral foreign policy 88–9, 90, 112; SALT II 89, 90, 94, 133; South Africa 90, 93; Thatcher 93–4

Carter Doctrine (January 1980) 91

Castro, Fidel 89–90

Central America 13, 14, 89, 98, 101, 102

Central Europe 7, 17, 36, 42, 44, 45–6, 49, 130, 134

Central Intelligence Agency (CIA) 61, 94, 109

Central Treaty Organisation (CENTO) 61, 65, 66

Chamberlain, Neville 5, 22, 23–4

Cheney, Dick 119; Iraq 120; no anglophile 119; Thatcher 119; WMD 120, 121

Chernenko, Konstantin 100, 103

Chile 14, 88, 99

China 7, 34, 51; Chinese Communist Party 28, 29, 52, 53, 54; Civil War 52, 53; Cold War 131; Japan 21–2, 28–9, 52; Korean War 53–4, 55, 131; Kuomintang 28, 29, 32, 43, 52, 53, 54; Nationalist China 19, 20, 21–2, 28, 52, 53, 122; Peoples' Republic of China 8, 53, 68, 75, 78, 108, 121; post-Cold War 121, 124, 125 (Britain 122, 123; Hong Kong 122, 124; United States 122); Russia 52, 53, 75, 81; UN 54; United States 55–6, 67, 80, 89, 125, 131; Vietnam 54

Churchill, Winston 5, 6, 23–4, 27, 42, 44, 76, 119; Atlantic Charter (August 1941) 30–1, 130; atomic bomb 33, 35, 36, 76, 131; Baghdad Pact (1955) 61; CENTO 61, 65; Combined Chiefs of Staff 32, 130; cross-Channel invasion 31, 32, 34, 130; Egypt 62; family 3–4; France 24, 25, 30, 31, 36; Germany 71, 130, 131; India 57; Iron Curtain speech (March 1946) 45–6; Japan 26, 27–8, 29, 30, 31, 32, 35, 130, 135; Malayan Emergency (1947–1957) 55, 131; Mediterranean theatre 27, 28, 30, 31, 32, 34–5; Nazi Germany 29–30, 31; Normandy campaign 29, 30, 34, 130; peripheral strategy 31, 32, 130; prime minister 1940–1945 130; prime minister 1951–1955 55, 130; *realpolitik* 27, 36; Roosevelt 6, 8, 23–4, 25–6, 27, 29–30, 30–2, 33–4, 34–5, 36–7, 130; Russia 31, 32–3, 34, 35, 36–7; SEATO 60–1, 65, 131; Stalin 31, 32–3, 34, 35, 36; UN 31, 34; unconditional surrender 32–3; war aims 23, 29–30, 33–4, 35, 36

Cinema 2,000 Women 30; Adventures of Robin Hood 6; Big Fella 6; Casablanca 30; Charge of the Light Brigade 6; Deer Hunter 87; Four Just Men 6; Gone with the Wind

196   Index

6; Invitation to the Waltz 6; Private
Lives of Elizabeth and Essex 6;
Rocky 87; Star Wars 87; Thin Man
series 6
Clifford-Elsey Report (September 1946)
47, 48
Clinton, Bill 8, 115, 116, 117, 118;
Balkan crisis (1992–1998) 115,
116, 117, 118–19, 134; 'Democratic
Enlargement' 117; disparages the
'Special relationship' 117, 118; Major
117, 118; PRC 122; unilateralism and
unipolar world view 108, 117, 121,
134, 135
Cold War 41, 46, 48–51, 55–6, 57,
62–5, 66–7, 73, 77, 134; Afghanistan
90–1, 93–4, 100, 101, 104, 109, 134;
arms limitation conventional 104–5;
arms limitation nuclear 81, 84, 94,
103, 112; Baghdad Pact (1955) 61,
62; Brezhnev Doctrine (1968) 84, 85,
109; CENTO 61, 65, 66; China 52,
53; containment 48, 50, 52, 60, 61,
70, 71, 74, 75, 76, 115, 131; CSCE
81, 84–5, 88, 109, 133; *détente* 75,
83, 91, 94, 133; East Asia 52–3, 55–6,
82; Eastern Europe 45–6, 54, 71, 100,
105, 107, 108, 109, 130, 134; EPC
84–5; France 55–6, 71–2, 75, 77,
83, 85–6, 131; Greece 46, 65, 130;
India 57–8, 131; Iran 33–4, 44–5, 60,
61, 90–1, 130; Jordan (1958) 66–7;
Korean War 54, 55, 60, 65, 70, 131;
Malaya 55, 65, 131; Middle East
44–5, 57–8, 60, 61, 66–7, 70, 131,
82–2, 87; NATO 49–51, 65, 70–1, 74,
83, 84–5, 97, 112, 119, 131; Pakistan
57–8, 60, 61; Palestine 58–9, 6, 131;
perceptions of Soviet threat 37, 41,
44, 45–6, 130, 135; Poland 100,
105–6, 132; SEATO 60–1, 65, 131;
Southeast Asia 52, 53, 55–6, 60, 131;
Yemen 68, 82, 105, 131
Colombo Plan (1950) 60, 131
Combined Chiefs of Staff 32, 34, 130;
Anglo-American leadership 32
Commonwealth 46, 52, 54, 57, 60,
63, 75, 82, 98, 131; Grenada crisis
(1983) 101–2
Conference on Security and Co-operation
in Europe (CSCE) (July 1976) 81,
84–5, 87, 109
conferences: Arcadia (December 1941–
January 1942) 31–2, 130; Atlantic

(August 1941) 30; Casablanca
(January 1943) 32–3; Geneva (May
1961–July 1962) 78; Geneva (May–
July 1954) 54, 55–6, 57, 60, 77, 79,
82, 131; Paris (1919–1922) 17–18;
Potsdam (July–August 1945) 42–4,
51; Quebec (first – August 1943)
33; (second – September 1944) 35;
San Francisco (April–June 1945) 36;
Tehran (November 1943) 33–4, 35,
36; Yalta (February 1945) 36, 42, 44,
51, 56
containment 47–8, 50, 51, 52, 53, 61,
68, 71, 76, 78–9, 91, 115, 131; 'X'
article 47–8
Coolidge, Calvin 18, 21
Council of Foreign Ministers (CFM) 42,
44–5, 52
Croatia 115–18
Cuba 15, 68, 75, 78, 98, 105, 115;
Abyssinia 90; Angola 89–90, 93; 'axis
of evil' 120; Grenada 101–2; missile
crisis 73; Nicaragua 89, 98
Czechoslovakia 17, 22, 42, 62, 84,
109, 110, 134; Warsaw Pact invasion
(1968) 83–4, 134

'Declaration on Atlantic Relations'
(June 1974) 86–7
'Declaration on European Identity'
(December 1973) 85–6
decolonisation 7, 31, 36, 43, 52, 57–8,
61, 65, 67–8, 70, 78, 122, 130, 131
De Gaulle, Charles 71, 73, 76, 83;
Britain 73, 77; nuclear weapons 77,
84; United States 77
destroyers for bases agreement (1940)
25, 26, 130
détente 75, 81, 83, 89, 91, 94, 133
'Doctrine of the International
Community' 118, 119
domino theory 78, 79
Douglas-Home, Alexander 85, 132;
Anglo-American bureaucratic
connexions 76, 81–2, 132
Dulles, John Foster 59, 66, 67; Eden 65,
71, 131; Macmillan 73; 'rolling back'
communism 56, 59, 72; Russia 63;
Suez Crisis (1956) 62–5, 131

Eagleburger, Lawrence 100
East Asia 7, 15, 20, 25, 26, 28–9, 30,
54, 119, 123–4, 125, 133; Cold War
51–6; nationalism 53; post-Cold War

Index 197

121, 122, 123, 124; Second World War 35

Eastern Europe 7, 8, 17, 34, 36, 42, 45–6, 48, 54, 71, 100, 105, 106–7, 108, 115, 130, 134; Brezhnev Doctrine (1968) 84, 109; EU 121

Eden, Anthony 5, 23; Dulles 65; EEC 77; Eisenhower 62, 131; foreign secretary 1940–1945 33, 34, 35, 44; foreign secretary 1951–1955 71, 131; prime minister (1955–1957) 65; Russia 63, 135; SEATO 60; Suez Crisis (1956) 62–5, 131; UN 63; West German rearmament 71

Egypt 14, 59, 61, 63, 66, 68, 69, 82, 89, 113, 114, 131; Suez Crisis (1956) 62–5, 131

Eisenhower, Dwight 54, 67; Baghdad Pact 61; CENTO 61, 66; Churchill 72; domino theory 78, 79; Eden 62, 65, 72, 131; Hungary 72; India 58; Macmillan 65, 66–7, 73, 76, 132; Pakistan 58; president (1953–1961) 56, 60, 73; Russia 65–6, 135; SEATO 60–1, 131; Second World War 34; Suez Crisis (1956) 62–5, 67, 131; Vietnam 79

Eisenhower Doctrine (1957) 65–6, 69; Jordan (1957) 66; Lebanon (1958) 66–7

Elizabeth II 87

European Coal and Steel Community (ECSC) 70, 75

European Defence Community (EDC) 70–1

European Economic Community (EEC) 8, 75, 82–3, 98, 108; British membership 83; CSCE 84; 'Declaration on European Identity' (December 1973) 85–6; Eastern Europe 105–6; EPC 84–5; Poland 105; Rome Treaty (1957) 75; Russia 106; Thatcher 92, 94, 105–7; United States 75, 82–3, 85, 108

European Political Co-operation (EPC) 84–5

European Union (EU) 108, 121, 124–5

Falklands War 97–100, 101, 133; diplomacy 98–100; military operations 97–8; Reagan-Thatcher relationship 99–100

Ford, Gerald 81, 87, 88

France 13, 15–16, 17, 20, 21, 36, 44, 61, 70, 76; Britain 55, 71–2, 76, 77, 83, 85, 94, 96; Cold War 53, 74, 75, 79, 134; containment 50, 75, 76, 131; decolonisation 54, 55–6, 131; ECSC 70, 75; EDC 70–1; EEC 75, 77, 82–3, 94, 96; Germany 49, 70–4, 75, 84, 96, 105, 111, 134; Gulf War 113, 114, 134; Indo-China 53, 54, 78, 131; INF 96, 104; Iran 124; NATO 50–1, 84, 94, 96, 101, 103, 104–5; nuclear weapons 77, 84, 96, 104, 105, 112, 130; post-Cold War 108; SEATO 60; Second World War 24, 25, 28, 30, 31; Suez Crisis (1956) 62–3, 131; Thatcher 92, 94, 96; United States 49, 54, 55–6, 71–2, 75, 78, 85–7, 105, 131

freedom of the seas 13, 16, 17, 31

Galtieri, General Leopoldo 97, 98, 99

Geneva Accords 55–6, 60; Indo-China 55–6, 131; Korean War 55, 131

Geneva Summit (1955) 72

Germany 72, 76; 1920s–1930s 5, 20, 22; Atlantic, Battle of 29, 33; Britain, Battle of 27; Danzig 42; decartelisation 42, 50; decentralisation 42; demilitarisation 35, 42, 130; democratisation 42, 49, 50; de-Nazification 42, 49, 50; disarmament/rearmament 17, 22; East Germany (Democratic Republic) 71, 81, 84, 90, 109–10, 132, 13 (Berlin 72–3, 109; Berlin Wall 73, 109, 110, 111, 132, 134; collapse 110, 111; CSCE 81, 84–5); First World War 5, 15–17; North African campaign 28, 29, 31, 32, 130; Occupied Germany 7, 48–51, 130, 131; pre-1914 4, 15; reparations 17, 20, 42, 49; Russian policy 48–9, 135; Russo-German theatre 29, 30, 31, 32, 33, 34, 36; Second World War 23, 24, 25, 28, 31–2, 35, 36, 135; submarine campaign 16, 24, 27, 28, 33; surrender 37; West Germany 72–3, 84, 132; West Germany (Federal Republic) 48–9, 50, 70–4, 76, 78, 85–7, 96, 130, 132 (Berlin 72–3, 109–10, 111, 132, 134; containment 50, 71, 131; CSCE 81, 84–5; détente 94; East Germany 72–3, 84, 132; ECSC 70, 75; EDC 70–1; EEC 82–3, 93–4, 96; euromissiles 94, 96, 97, 101, 103, 104, 105, 133; Gorbachev

198   *Index*

105; INF 96, 104, 134; Marshall Plan 50, 131; MLF 77; NATO 50–1, 70–1, 77, 94, 96, 97, 101, 103, 104–5, 133, 134; *Ostpolitik* 84, 96, 105; peace advocates 96; public opinion and unification 50; rearmament 70–1, 84; Russia 115; Thatcher 92, 94, 96, 134; unification 72, 73–4, 78, 111, 125, 134; unified Germany (1990–present) 110, 124, 134; United States 48–9, 50, 70–4, 75, 85–7, 109, 134; zonal division 33, 35, 36, 42, 49, 50, 51)

globalisation 121, 122

Gorbachev, Mikhail 100–1, 101–7, 109–10, 134, 135; Afghanistan 100, 101, 104, 109, 134; Bush, G.H.W. 108, 109, 110, 111–12; domestic reforms 101, 109, 110, 111, 133; Eastern Europe 108, 109, 110, 134; East Germany 109–10; euromissiles 101, 103, 104, 133; nuclear arms negotiations 101, 112, 134 (Geneva – November 1985 103; Malta – December 1989 111–12; Reykjavik – October 1986 104; START 103, 104; Washington, DC 104); Poland 105–6, 109, 110; Reagan 101, 103–7, 134; Thatcher 101, 102–3, 104–7, 108, 109, 110, 133–4; United States sanctions 105–6; Warsaw Pact 109; West Germany 105, 111

Great Britain 14–15, 19–20, 34, 42, 46, 81–2, 92, 101, 115, 118, 120; Anglo-American bureaucratic connexions 76, 81–2, 132; anti-Americanism 81, 120, 121, 133; blockade 13, 16, 21, 24, 25; Cabinet 21, 23, 57, 60, 65, 71, 79, 81–2, 83, 95, 97, 132; Conservative-Liberal coalition 123; Conservative Party 5, 21, 42, 81, 87, 88, 92, 93, 96, 97, 101, 115; decolonisation 7, 31, 36, 43, 52, 55, 57, 58, 61, 65, 77, 88, 89, 93, 122–3, 124, 131; *détente* 75, 83, 91, 94, 133; 'Doctrine of the International Community' 118, 119; economic situation 7, 14, 18–19, 20, 27, 34, 46, 58, 65, 83, 87–8, 94, 122, 123, 133 (IMF loan – 1976 88, 133; post-Cold War trade 123; sterling-gold crisis – 1967–1968 83; Thatcher reforms 92; trade 113, 123); EEC 8, 75, 77, 82–3, 84–5, 106–7, 108; Egypt 62–3, 68; EU 124–5; the Falklands War 97–100, 101; France 5, 15–16, 17,

20, 24, 25, 28, 30, 31, 35, 49, 70–1, 76, 77, 83, 85, 103–6, 112; Gulf War (1990–1991) 112–15, 122, 134; Iran 44–5, 60, 130; Israel 58–9, 62–3, 65, 69–70, 120, 124, 131; Italy 29, 30, 32, 33, 130, 135; Japan 19–20, 21–2, 27–8, 29, 30, 31, 32, 33, 35, 43, 52, 130, 135; Labour Party 5, 8, 21, 42, 58, 70, 81, 82, 86, 87, 88, 94, 96, 101, 118, 134 (economic failure – 1970s 83, 87–8); NATO 50–1, 65, 70–1, 72, 83, 84–5, 92, 94–5, 97, 102–3, 104–7, 111, 119, 123, 131, 133, 134; New Labour 118, 119, 120; nuclear weapons 76–7, 82, 83, 92, 94–6, 96, 97, 101, 102–3, 104–7, 119, 102–3, 104, 123, 130, 132, 133, 134; Pakistan 60, 61, 93–4, 131; public opinion 8, 58, 59, 99, 120, 121, 134–5; Russia 28, 31, 32–3, 34, 35, 41, 42–4, 45–6, 49–51, 57, 60, 61, 63, 65, 73, 74, 83–4, 85, 92, 93–4, 99, 100, 104–7, 109–12, 130, 132, 135 (Gorbachev era 100–1, 101–7, 108, 109–10, 111–12, 133, 134); Sierra Leone 121; Southeast Asia 28, 29, 35, 43, 55–6, 57–8, 131; SALT I 84; START 103, 104; Suez Crisis (1956) 62–5, 76, 131; Thatcher rearmament 92, 102–3, 104–7, 133; UN 31, 34, 35, 36, 50; Vietnam War 7, 76, 82, 85, 131–2; war debts (1919–1935) 19; war loans (1914–1918) 16, 19; 'war on terror' 120, 134–5; Western European defence 104–7, 133; withdrawal East of Suez 7–8, 82, 113, 122, 132; WMD 120, 121, 135; *see also* 'Cold War'; 'post-Cold War'; 'World War, First'; 'World War, Second'

Greece 28, 48, 65; Civil War (1944–1947) 46, 130

Grenada crisis (October 1983) 101–2

Gulf States 113, 114, 122

Gulf War (1990–1991) 112–15, 122, 134; Thatcher–G.H.W. Bush 113, 115

Haig, Alexander 98–9, 103

Halifax, Lord 24

Harding, Warren 18, 20

Healy, Denis 84

Heath, Edward 84–5, 87, 92, 132; European outlook 81, 82–3, 84–5;

Index 199

'natural', not 'special', Anglo-American Relationship 81, 92, 132; Vietnam War 81–2, 131–2

Hitler, Adolph 20, 22, 24, 25, 42, 48; Russo-German theatre (1941–1945) 28, 32–3, 36

Ho Chi Minh 54, 56, 78

Holland/Netherlands 24, 61, 70, 96

Honecker, Erich 110, 134

Hong Kong 52, 53, 122, 124

Hoover, Herbert 18, 21

Howe, Geoffrey 101

Hull, Cordell 24, 25, 33, 34

Hungary 17, 42, 109, 110; Gulf War 113; uprising (1956) 63, 72, 83, 134

Hurd, Douglas 117

Hussein, King 61, 66

Hussein, Saddam 112, 113–14, 119, 120, 135; WMD 113, 120, 135

India 7, 29, 52, 56, 60, 63, 121; Britain 57–8, 131; Pakistan 57–8, 131; United States 58

Indo-China 28, 43, 53, 78; International Control Commission (1954–1973) 56, 79; War (1946–1954) 54, 55–6, 131

Indonesia 60

intermediate-range nuclear forces (INF) 96, 104, 134

International Monetary Fund (IMF) 36, 88, 130, 133

Iran 7, 33–4, 45, 48, 49, 60, 124, 130; 'axis of evil' 120; Iran-Azerbaijan Crisis (1946) 44–5, 130; Iran-Contra (1987) 104, 112; Iran-Iraq war (1980–1988) 112; Iraq 120; Mossadegh crisis (1953) 61, 90; multinational oil consortium (1954) 61; nuclear weapons 121, 124; revolution (1979) 90; Russia 90, 135

Iraq 8, 59, 61, 62, 66, 115, 124, 131; American invasion (2003) 120; 'axis of evil' 120; CENTO 61; Gulf War (1990–1991) 112–15, 134; Iran-Iraq war (1980–1988) 112; ISIS 124; neoconservatives 114–15; Thatcher–G.H.W. Bush 113, 115

Islamic State of Iraq and al-Sham (ISIS) 124

Israel 58, 59, 65, 66, 68, 131; Gulf War 11, 114, 58–9; Six-day War (1957) 69–70; Suez Crisis (1956) 62–3, 131; Yom Kippur War (October 1973) 82, 87, 89

Italy 17, 20, 21; 1930s 5, 22; 1939–1945 24, 27–8, 29, 30, 32, 33, 130, 135; Cold War 51, 70

Japan 5, 42, 60; 1920s 19–20; 1939–1941 26, 27–8; 1941–1945 21–2, 27–8, 31, 32–3, 35, 36, 42, 43, 44, 130, 135; Gulf War 113, 114; occupied Japan (September 1945–September 1951) 52, 130

Jay, Peter 88

John Paul II, Pope 105

Johnson, Lyndon 69; Britain 82, 132; sterling-gold crisis (1967–1968) 83; Vietnam 79–80, 81, 82

Jordan 59, 62, 66, 68, 131; CENTO 61; Six-day War (1967) 69–70

Kennan, George 47–8, 59

Kennedy, John F. 73, 79, 101; Berlin Wall crisis 73, 132, 134; Cuba missile crisis 73; domino theory 78, 79; 'Golden Days' 76, 77, 125, 32; Khrushchev 73, 79; Laos 78–9; Macmillan 74, 75, 76, 79, 132; MAD 77, 101; nuclear collaboration 76–7, 12–03, 104, 130, 132, 133

Khomeini, Ayatollah Ruhollah 90

Khrushchev, Nikita 71, 72, 100; Berlin Wall crisis 72–3; Cuba missile crisis 73; de-Stalinisation speech 71; Kennedy 73, 79; Macmillan 73

Kirkpatrick, Jeanne 99

Kissinger, Henry 87, 133; national security advisor 81, 82–3, 85–6, 85–7, 88, 132, 133; secretary of state 81, 132

Kohl, Helmut 96, 105, 111, 112

Korea 7, 53, 60; DMZ 55; Korean War (1950–1954) 53–4, 55, 60, 65, 70, 131

Kosygin, Alexei 82

Kuwait 66; Gulf War (1990–1991) 112, 113, 114, 134

Laos 54, 55, 60, 78–9, 80, 131

Latin America 13, 15, 16, 68, 89, 98, 101, 115, 122, 133; Mercosur 121; PRC 122

Leach, Admiral Sir Henry 97

League of Nations 17, 19, 22, 30

Leahy, Admiral William 41

Lebanon 59, 62, 66–7, 124

Lend-Lease Act (1941) 27, 28, 30, 35

200 *Index*

Libya 44, 129; Arab Spring (2010–2012) 124
Lothian, Lord 23, 24, 25, 27

Macdonald, James Ramsay 5, 21, 22, 57
McFarlane, Robert 103
Macmillan, Harold 65, 70; Berlin diplomacy 73, 74, 131; EEC 76, 77; Eisenhower 65, 66–7, 74, 76, 77, 132; 'Golden Days' 76, 77, 125, 132; Jordan (1958) 66–7, 131; Kennedy 74, 75, 76, 79, 132; Laos 79; nuclear collaboration 76–7, 102–3, 104, 130, 132, 133; prime minister (1957–1963) 65, 66, 72, 77, 131, 132; repairing 'Relationship' 65–6, 76, 131; Russia 76; Yemen 68, 131
McNamara, Robert 77, 79, 101; MAD 77, 101
Major, John 8, 118; Balkan crisis 116–17, 118, 134; Clinton 116, 117, 118; Kosovo 116; NATO 117, 118; PRC 122; Srebrenica 117; Thatcher 122; UN 115, 117, 118; Vance-Owen peace plan 117
Malaya 29, 52, 55, 60, 65, 78; Malayan Emergency (1947–1957) 55, 82, 131
Marshall, General George 26, 32, 46, 48, 53, 59, 130, 131
Marshall Plan (June 1947) 48, 50, 51, 131
Middle East 8, 18, 32, 58–9, 61–3, 65, 108, 113, 121, 123, 131; Arab Spring (2010–2012) 124–2; Britain 59, 62–5, 70, 124–5; CENTO 61, 65, 66; Cold War 41, 47, 53, 60, 61; Eisenhower Doctrine (January 1957) 65–6; Gulf War (1990–1991) 112–15, 122, 134; Iran 124; Jordan (1957) 66; oil 7, 32, 33, 47, 59, 61, 112, 134; Palestine 58–9, 61; Persian Gulf 91, 113; PLO 69; post-Cold War 124–5; Russia 59, 63, 135; Six-day War (1967) 69; Suez Crisis (1956) 62–5, 131; Yom Kippur War 82, 89
Milosevic, Slobodan 115, 116, 118
missiles: ABMs 81, 101, 104; Blue Steel/Blue Streak 76; cruise 94, 96, 104–5; euromissiles 94, 96, 101, 103, 104, 133; MIRVs 89, 94, 96; Pershing 94, 96, 104; Polaris 76, 77, 82, 132, 133; Skybolt 76–7, 132; Trident 94–5, 102–3, 105, 133, 134
Mitterrand, Francois 96, 101, 111; West Germany 96, 111

Molotov, Vyacheslav 33, 42, 50
Monroe Doctrine 13, 15, 16
Mossadegh, Mohammed 61
Movimento Popular de Libertação de Angola (MPLA) 89–90
Mozambique 89–90, 100, 105, 133
mujahidin 94, 101, 106, 120, 121, 134
Mussolini, Benito 20, 33
mutual and balanced force reduction talks 104–5, 109
mutual assured destruction strategy (MAD) 77, 101

Nasser, Gamal Abdel 61, 65, 66, 68, 131; CENTO 61; Suez Crisis (1956) 62–5, 131
Nehru, Jawaharlal 58, 65, 68
new international orders: post-First World War 17; post-Second World War 42; post-Cold War, 'new world order' 115, 117, 121, 134
New Zealand 52, 60; Britain 52; United States 52, 80–1, 82
Nicaragua 89, 102, 104, 105, 115, 133; Cuba and 89, 98; Sandinista regime 89, 98, 102, 104
Nitze, Paul 59
Nixon, Richard 53, 80, 87, 133; 'Asia after Vietnam' 81; Britain 82–3, 132; Chile 88; PRC 80, 89, 125; president (1969–1974) 80, 88; Russia 85; SALT I 81; Watergate scandal 85, 88
Nixon Doctrine (July 1969) 81
North Atlantic Treaty Organisation (NATO) 8, 50–1, 60, 61, 63, 65, 71, 72, 83, 94, 97, 104–5, 109, 111, 115, 130, 131; Afghanistan 94, 119, 123; Balkan crisis (1992–1998) 115, 117, 134; Brezhnev Doctrine (1968) 84, 109; Brussels Treaty (March 1948) 50–1, 71, 131; cruise missiles 94, 96, 104–5; 'Declaration on Atlantic Relations' (June 1974) 86–7; 'dual-track' 94, 96; euromissiles 94, 96, 97, 101, 103, 104, 133; the Falklands War 99–100; French withdrawal (1966) 84; German membership 70–1, 111; INF 96, 104, 134; Iraq 124, 125; MLF 77; NATO Planning Group (1967, Schröder-Healey report) 84; Pershing missiles 94, 96, 104; Reagan 104–5; Warsaw Pact invasion of Czechoslovakia (August 1968) 83–4, 134; West German rearmament 70–1

Index 201

North Korea 53–4, 55, 67–8, 89, 124; 'axis of evil' 120; PRC 123
North Vietnam 54, 55–6, 67, 77–82, 131–2; Britain 82
Nott, John 95, 97
NSC-68, 59–60, 70, 98
nuclear weapons 112, 125; Anglo-American collaboration 66, 76–7, 82, 119, 123, 130, 132, 133; British independence 77, 102–3, 104, 132, 133, 134; dual-key system 77; limitations 72, 77; MAD 77, 101; MIRVs 87, 94, 96; MLF 77; SALT I 81, 89, 103; SALT II 89, 94, 103, 133; START 103, 104; successful American test 57; successful Russian test 57, 59; verification 89, 103

Obama, Barack 8, 9, 123, 129, 135; Afghanistan 123, 129, 134; Brown 123; Cameron 123–4; East Asia 123–4, 135; Iran 124; Iraq 123; ISIS 124; Libya 124–5; Middle East 129; 'Not just special, but an essential relationship' 123; Pacific Ocean 123, 135; PRC 123, 135; Russia 125; Syria 124; terrorism 129
Organisation for European Economic Co-operation (OEEC) 48, 51
Ostpolitik 84, 96, 105
Owen, David 116–17

Pacific Ocean 15, 20, 125, 130, 133; Cold War 82; Obama 123–4; Second World War 29, 32, 33, 35
Pahlavi, Shah Reza 61, 90, 131; United States 61
Pakistan 57–8, 60, 61, 131; Afghanistan 93–4; India 57–8, 131; SEATO 60; United States 58
Panama Canal 89, 90, 112
Paris Summit (May 1960) 73
Pearl Harbor 20, 26, 29, 31, 52, 130
Persian Gulf 91, 113; Carter Doctrine (January 1980) 91
Philippines 15, 25, 29, 52, 60, 68, 124, 130
Poland 17, 22, 24, 33, 34, 35, 42, 56, 81, 100, 105–6, 109, 110, 111, 125, 132, 134; 1956 crisis 71–2; 1981–1982 crisis 100, 105–6; 1987 crisis 105–6; Danzig/Gdansk 42, 106; East Germany 110; Oder-Neisse frontier 33, 42; Polish guarantee (1939) 22, 42; Solidarity 100, 105, 106

Pompidou, Georges 83, 85
Portugal 51; imperial collapse 89
post-Cold War 108; Hong Kong 122, 124; Iran 120, 121; Iraq 119, 120, 121; Middle East 119, 120, 121, 124–5; Russia 125; trade 123; 'war on terror' 119–21, 123, 134–5; WMD 120, 121, 135
Potsdam declaration 43
President's Emergency Plan for AIDS Relief 121
Putin, Vladimir, NATO 125; PRC 125

Reagan, Ronald 8, 104, 108, 113; Afghanistan 104, 106, 133, 134; Bush, G.H.W. 108, 109; euromissiles 101, 103, 104; Geneva (November 1985) 103; the Falklands War 97–100, 133; Gorbachev 100–1, 101–7, 134; Grenada 101–2; INF 96, 104, 134; Iran-Contra (1987) 104, 112; Nicaragua 98, 102, 104, 133; nuclear arms negotiations 101, 102–7, 112, 134; Poland 105–6; Reagan's military policies 101, 103–4; rearmament 92, 102–3, 104, 110; Reykjavik (October 1986) 104; Russia 92, 94, 96, 101, 102–3, 105–6, 110, 135; SALT 103; SDI 101, 102–3, 106; START 103, 104; supply side economics 92, 108; Thatcher 92–3, 94, 99–100, 101–2, 102–3, 104–5, 106, 107, 110–11, 133; Vietnam 102; Washington, DC 104; 'zero-zero' policy 96
Reagan Doctrine (February 1985) 94
Rhodesia 88, 89, 90; power-sharing agreement (1979) 93
Rome Treaty (1957) 75, 77
Romney, Mitt 129
Roosevelt, Eleanor 58
Roosevelt, Franklin 6, 19, 22, 23–4, 25, 26, 27, 28, 37, 42, 76; Atlantic Charter (August 1941) 30–1, 130; atomic bomb 33, 35, 36, 76; cash-and-carry bill (1939) 24–5; China 28, 34, 52, 53; Churchill 6, 8, 23–4, 25–6, 27, 30–2, 33–4, 34–5, 36, 37, 130; decolonisation 7, 31, 36, 130, 131; fourth term as president 35; France 24, 25, 30, 31; Germany (1941–1945) 31–2, 33–4, 35, 36, 135; Japan (1940–1945) 28, 29, 30, 31, 32, 35, 36, 130, 135; Mediterranean theatre 31, 32, 31,

202 Index

32, 34–5; Normandy campaign 29, 30, 34, 130; percentages agreement (October 1944) 35; peripheral strategy 31, 32, 130; *realpolitik* 27, 36; Stalin 32–3, 34, 35, 36; third term as president 26, 27; UN 31, 34, 35, 36; unconditional surrender 32–3; war aims 7, 23, 25, 26, 27, 29–30, 33–4, 35, 36

Roosevelt, Theodore 4, 15

Royal Navy 4, 13, 14, 15, 20, 21, 25, 26, 27, 35; blockade 13, 16, 24; co-operation with USN 27; the Falklands War 97–8

Rumsfeld, Donald 119; Iraq 120; no anglophile 119

Russia, tsarist 15–16; Abyssinia 90, 105; Afghanistan 90–1, 93–4, 98, 100, 104, 109, 134; Africa 89–90, 105, 131; Angola 89–90, 93, 100, 105, 133; atomic weapons 42, 44, 57, 59, 130, 131; Brezhnev Doctrine (1968) 84, 85, 109; Britain 42–4, 45–6, 49–51, 57, 60, 61, 63, 65, 73, 74, 83–4, 99; Central and Eastern Europe 33, 34, 35, 36; Central Europe 42, 44, 45–6, 49–51, 130; China 52, 53, 75, 81; Cold War 41, 57, 134, 135; CSCE 81, 109, 133; Cuba 68, 75, 78, 89–90, 93; *détente* 75, 81, 83, 91, 94, 133; East Asia 52, 53, 54; Eastern Europe 42, 44, 45–6, 54, 71, 105, 107, 108, 130; economy 100–1; the Falklands War 98, 99, 101; Germany 70–4; Gorbachev era 100, 101–7, 109–10, 108, 109, 110, 111–12, 133–4, 135; Hungary 72; Iran 7, 33, 34, 60, 61, 90, 124, 130; Iran-Azerbaijan Crisis (1946) 44–5, 130; Japan 28, 35, 43, 52; Korean War 53–4, 55, 60, 131; Laos 79; Libya 44; Middle East 59, 68, 69, 82, 131; Mozambique 89–90, 100, 105, 133; NATO 72, 125, 131; Nicaragua 105; Occupied Germany 42–4, 48–9, 130, 131 (East Germany 71, 72–3, 132, 134, 109–10, 134; West Germany 70–4, 132); *Ostpolitik* 84, 96, 105; perceptions of Anglo-American hostility 44; Poland 71–2, 100, 105–6, 132; post-Cold War Russia 8, 108, 110, 115, 121, 125; PRC 125; *realpolitik* 41; Russo-German theatre (1941–1945) 28,

29, 31, 32, 33, 34, 36; second front 31, 32, 34, 44; Second World War, Britain 28, 31, 32–3, 34, 35, 36; Soviet Russia 6, 7, 8, 17, 18, 22, 31, 34, 58, 79, 100–7, 108, 135; SS-20 MIRVs 94, 96; Thatcher 92, 93–6, 101, 102–3, 109; Turkey 44, 47, 49, 130; UN 35, 36, 42, 50, 54; United States 31, 32–3, 34, 35, 36, 41, 42–4, 48–51, 70–4, 78, 89–91, 93–6, 100; Vietnam 54, 82; Warsaw Pact (1955) 71, 72, 100, 109; Warsaw Pact invasion of Czechoslovakia (August 1968) 83–4, 134

Saudi Arabia 59, 62, 68, 113, 119, 131; Afghanistan 119, 120; Gulf War 113, 114

Schmidt, Helmut 96

Schultz, George 103

Scowcroft, Brent 110, 111; post-Gulf War balance 114

Selwyn Lloyd, John 67

Shevardnadze, Eduard 111, 112

Sierra Leone 121

Singapore 20, 28, 29, 52, 55, 60

South Africa 90; Carter 93; Thatcher 93

South America 13, 14, 18, 115, 133; Mercosur 121

South Asia 7, 8, 60, 108, 110, 133; nationalism 53; post-Cold War 121; Soviet Russian adventurism (post-1975) 88, 133, 135

Southeast Asia 7, 18, 33, 35, 52, 53, 55–6, 60, 73, 77–82, 83, 131; ASEAN 121, 124

Southeast Asia Treaty Organisation (SEATO) 60, 61, 66, 79, 131

South Korea 53–4, 55, 68

South Vietnam 54, 55–6; United States support 60, 68, 77–82, 131–2

the Special relationship 6, 7, 8, 9, 23, 34, 51, 57, 76, 81–2, 85–7, 91, 106–7, 108, 109–12, 115–18, 119, 121, 129–35; American criticism of Britain and UN Security Council seat 117; American Transatlantic Brides and Parents Association 30; Anglo-American bureaucratic connexions 76, 81–2, 132; Carter's morality-*realpolitik* dichotomy 90; Clinton disparages 117, 118; commonalities 3, 5, 23, 36, 41; cultural links 4, 6, 30, 36, 87, 108; *détente* 75, 83, 91,

94, 133; 'Golden Days' 76, 77, 125, 132; Heath and 'natural', not 'special' Relationship 81, 132; *realpolitik* 3, 9, 23, 27, 36, 41, 99–100; strategic basis 3, 6, 7, 8, 9, 23, 29–30, 36, 51, 73, 75–6, 108; trans-Atlantic marriages 3–4; transnationalism 4–6, 7, 8, 23, 30, 87, 108, 135

Stalin, Joseph 31, 32, 33, 71, 100; Berlin Blockade (June 1948–May 1949) 49–51; Britain 42–4, 44–5, 49–51, 55–6, 57; Central and Eastern Europe 42, 44, 45–6, 48, 49, 130; Churchill 31, 32–3, 34, 35, 36; Cold War, atomic weapons 42, 44, 49, 57, 59, 76, 130, 131; Germany (East Germany 50, 71, 132, 134; Occupied Germany 42–4, 48, 49, 130, 131; West Germany 50, 70–4, 132); Greece 46, 49, 130; Iran 44–5, 49, 60, 130; Japan 35, 36, 44; Korean War 53, 60, 131; Marshall Plan 48, 131; percentages agreement (October 1944) 35, 46; Poland 33, 34, 35; realism 43; Roosevelt 31, 32–3, 34, 35, 36; Second World War, Britain 31, 32–3, 34, 35, 36, 41; Truman 42–3, 45, 48, 131; UN 31, 35, 36, 50; United States 31, 32–3, 34, 35, 36, 42–4, 49–51, 57

Stimson, Henry 5, 6, 26, 41

Strategic Arms Limitation: SALT I (May 1972) 81, 84, 89, 103; SALT II 89, 94, 103, 133

Strategic Defence Initiative (SDI) 101, 102–3, 133

Suez Crisis (1956) 7, 62–5, 66, 67, 76, 77, 131

Syria 59, 62, 66, 76, 131; Gulf War 113, 114; Six-day War (1967) 69

terrorism 108, 129; *see also* 'war on terror'

Thatcher, Margaret 8, 88, 91, 94, 109, 115, 119, 134; Afghanistan 93–4, 101, 104, 106, 133, 134; arms limitation 81, 84, 94, 103, 104–5; British rearmament 92, 93–6, 102–3, 105, 133, 134; Bush, G.H.W. 108–9, 119; Carter 93–4, 107, 133; Eastern Europe 105–6, 107, 109, 134; economic policies 108–9, 118, 122; EEC 92, 94, 105–6, 106–7; euromissiles 94, 96, 99, 101, 103;

France 92, 94, 96, 105; Germany 109, 111, 125, 134; Gorbachev 100–1, 101–7, 109–10, 108, 109, 133–4; Grenada 101–2; Gulf War (1990–1991) 113, 114, 115, 119, 122, 134; Hong Kong 122; INF 96, 104, 134; Pakistan 93–4; Poland 106, 134; Reagan 92–3, 94, 96, 99–100, 101–2, 102–3, 104–5, 106, 107, 110–11, 133; realism 101; Rhodesia 93; Russia 92–3, 93–4, 95–6, 106–7, 109, 135; SDI 101, 103–4; South Africa 93; the Special Relationship 92, 106–7, 108; West Germany 92, 94, 96, 105, 109, 111; Western European defence 104–7, 109

Tito, Marshal Josip Broz 115

Truman, Harry 7, 41–2, 67, 79, 131; atomic bomb 42–3, 44, 57, 130; Attlee 44, 45, 46, 49; Berlin Blockade (June 1948–May 1949) 49–51; Bevin 44, 48, 49, 50–1, 131; China 53; Churchill 45–6; Germany 42–4, 48–51, 130, 131, 135; India 58, 131; Iran 45, 130; Israel 58–9, 131; Japan 42; Marshall Plan (June 1947) 48, 131; Middle East 47, 58–9, 131; NATO 50–1; NSC-68, 60, 70; Pakistan 58, 131; Palestine 58–9; perceptions of Soviet threat 41, 42–4, 45–6, 46–7, 130, 135; Stalin 42–3

Truman Doctrine (March 1947) 46–7, 48, 51, 131

Turkey 17, 44, 45, 47, 48, 49, 60, 61, 130

United Arab Republic (UAR) 66, 68

United Nations (UN) 34, 35, 36, 50, 51, 54, 58, 59, 62, 115, 130; American criticism of Britain and UN Security Council seat 117; Balkan crisis (1992–1998) 115, 117, 134; 'Declaration by the United Nations' (January 1942) 31; the Falklands War 97, 98, 99; 'four policemen' 34, 52; Iran 45, 124; Iraq 120, 121; Korean War 54, 55, 131; peace-keeping 63, 115; Six-day War (1967) 69; Suez Crisis (1956) 62–3, 131; Syria 123; WMD 120, 121

United States 7, 14, 16, 19–20, 21, 34, 60, 61; 9/11 attacks 8, 119, 120; ABMs 81, 101, 104; Allied war debts (1919–1935) 19; Allied war loans

204 Index

(1914–1918) 16; Anglo-American bureaucratic connexions 76, 81–2, 132; anti-British sentiment 16; Canada 15, 48, 56; Caribbean 7, 13, 14, 26, 68, 101–2; CSCE 81, 109, 133; Cuba 68, 73, 75, 89, 101–2, 105; decolonisation 7, 31, 36, 43, 52, 54, 57, 58, 61, 67–8, 70, 77, 78, 130, 131; Democratic Party 4, 5, 7, 26, 53, 80, 88, 108, 114, 125, 134; *détente* 75, 81, 83, 89, 91, 94, 133; EEC 75, 82–3, 85, 108; Egypt 62–5, 68, 69, 82, 87, 89, 113, 131, 131; EU 109; Europe-first strategy 31, 46, 61, 66, 119, 130, 131; exceptionalism 4, 8; the Falklands War 97–100; France 49, 54, 55–6, 71–2, 75, 78, 85–7, 94, 96, 97, 101, 103, 104, 105, 131; freedom of the seas 13, 16, 17, 25, 31; India 58, 68, 131; isolationism 5, 18, 19, 22, 26, 27, 36, 47; Israel 59, 62–3, 66, 69–70, 82, 87, 89, 113, 131; Italy 30, 32, 33, 120; Japan 19–20, 21–2, 27–8, 29, 31–2, 33, 35, 36, 42, 130, 135; Laos 78–9, 80, 131; Latin America 13, 15, 16, 68; Middle East 47, 59, 65–6, 82, 87–9, 113, 124–5, 129, 131; National Security Council 59–60, 106; NATO 49–51, 65, 70–1, 99–100, 109, 111, 112, 131; naval power 15, 16, 19–20, 20–1, 25; neoconservatism 8, 108, 114–15, 119, 120, 121, 122; neutrality 16, 24; neutrality laws (1935–1939) 22, 24; Palestine 58–9; Panama 112; Panama Canal 89, 90; Poland 100, 105–6; public opinion 26, 27, 30–1, 46, 62, 80, 88, 90, 108; Republican Party 4, 5, 7, 18, 24, 26, 51, 53, 54, 80, 88, 89, 92, 108, 114, 124, 125, 129, 134; Southeast Asia 7, 54, 55–6, 60, 73, 77–82, 83, 131; Third World 65, 67–8, 75; UN 50, 51, 58, 62, 117; unilateralism and unipolar world view 108, 117, 119, 121, 134, 135; Vietnam 54, 55–6, 60, 68, 76, 77–82, 83, 85, 92, 131, 132; *see also* 'Cold War'; 'post-Cold War'; 'World War, First'; 'World War, Second'

United States Department of State 19, 25, 25, 47, 59–60, 77, 80–1, 117, 132

United States Navy 15, 16, 20, 21, 27, 53, 122

Vance, Cyrus 89, 90, 116–17

Vance-Owen peace plan 117

Vandenburg Resolution 51

Versailles, Treaty of 17–18

Vienna 42, 45; Allied Control Commission 42

Vietnam 7, 54, 55–6, 76, 131–2; PRC 54; Soviet Russia 54; Tet offensive 80; unification 80; United States 7, 54, 55–6, 76, 77–82; United States bombing campaign 80, 82; Vietcong 78, 79–80; Viet Minh 54, 56; Vietnam War 132 (1946–1954 54; 1961–1973 7, 76, 77–82, 83, 85)

'war on terror' 119–21; 9/11 attack on United States 119, 120; Afghanistan 119, 121, 119–20, 123, 134; American policy 119–20; 'axis of evil' 120; Blair 119, 120, 121, 134–5; G.W. Bush policy 119–20, 121; Iran 120, 121; Iraq 119, 120, 121; WMD 120, 121

Warsaw Pact (1955) 71, 72, 85, 100, 105, 109; invasion of Czechoslovakia (August 1968) 83–4, 134

weapons of mass destruction (WMD) 8, 113, 120, 121

Weinberger, Caspar 100, 101

Western Europe 45–6, 50–1, 80, 83; defense of 50–1, 54, 76, 94, 96, 101, 103, 104, 104–5, 133; Marshall Plan 48, 50, 51, 131; peace movements 96; Siberian pipeline 106

Western European Union (WEU) 104, 131

Western Union Defence Organisation (WUDO) 51

Wilson, Harold 70, 86–7, 88, 92, 132; sterling-gold crisis (1967–1968) 83; Vietnam War 81–2, 132; withdrawal East of Suez 82, 132

Wilson, Woodrow 4–5, 16–17, 30, 88, 117; Fourteen Points 17, 30; Wilsonianism 17, 31, 88, 117

Wolfowitz, Paul 108, 114–15, 119, 121; no anglophile 119

World Bank 36, 62, 115, 130

World Trade Organisation 122

World War, First (1914–1918) 3, 5, 15–17, 23, 25; war aims, American 17; war aims, British 17

World War, Second 81, 3, 6, 9, 27–8; Allied bombing campaign 29, 31, 32, 33; Allied campaign against Germany

(August 1944–May 1945) 35, 135; Anglo-American combined strategy 31–2, 33; Atlantic, Battle of 29, 33; Atlantic Charter (August 1941) 30–1, 130; Balkans 28; Britain, Battle of 27; cross-Channel invasion 31, 32, 34, 130; Europe-first strategy 31, 130, 131; France 24, 25, 28, 29, 31, 34, 36; immediate origins 22; Iran 7, 33–4, 44–5, 130; Italy 29, 30, 32, 33, 130, 135; Japan 28–9, 30, 31, 33, 35, 36, 42, 44, 130; Mediterranean theatre 27, 28, 30, 31, 32, 34–5, 44; Normandy campaign 29, 30, 34, 130; North Africa 28, 29, 31, 32, 130; peripheral strategy 31, 32, 130; 'Phony War' 24, 25; Poland 22, 24, 33, 34, 35; Polish guarantee (1939) 22; Russia 31, 32, 33–4, 35, 36, 42–4; Russo-German theatre (1941–1945) 28, 29, 31, 32, 33, 34, 36; second front 31, 32, 34; Southeast Asia 28, 29, 35; unconditional surrender 32–3; war aims, American 7, 23, 25, 26, 27, 29–30, 33–4, 35, 36; war aims, British 23, 29–30, 33–4, 35, 36

Yeltsin, Boris 110
Yemen 62, 68, 69, 70, 82, 105, 131
Yugoslavia 30, 46; crisis (1992–1998) 115–18; Kosovo 118–19

Zedong, Mao 53
Zia-ul-Haq, Mohammed 94
Zimbabwe 93

Printed in the United States
by Baker & Taylor Publisher Services